Books by Richard Barrett:

What My Soul Told Me:
A Practical Guide to Soul Activation

The Values-Driven Organisation:
Unleashing Human Potential for Performance and Profit

The New Leadership Paradigm

Love, Fear and the Destiny of Nations:
The Impact of the Evolution of Consciousness on World Affairs

EVOLUTIONARY COACHING

A VALUES-BASED APPROACH TO UNLEASHING HUMAN POTENTIAL

RICHARD BARRETT

Cover design by Pete Beebe, Creative Principal at Forge.

For information on the purchase of books go to:
http://valuescentre.com/resources

ISBN: 978-1-4834-1178-1 (sc)
ISBN: 978-1-4834-1179-8 (e)

Lulu Publishing Services rev. date: 05/15/2014

CONTENTS

FIGURES AND TABLES

PREFACE

If you are like me, the first thing you want to know when you pick up a book is what it is about. So let's start there. This book is about is the practice of evolutionary coaching—what coaches and other caring professionals need to know in order to support the healthy psychological growth and development of the adults they are working with, particularly how their clients relate to their "work." This book is also about human emergence, sometimes referred to as self-realisation.

Part I explores the theory of human emergence, providing a detailed description of the seven stages of psychological development, the evolution of cultural world views, the evolving structure and operation of the human mind/brain and the six evolutionary stages in human decision-making.

Part II describes the exercises required to facilitate evolutionary coaching: determining your clients' primary and secondary motivations and determining the degree to which the cultures your clients are embedded in, support or hinder their human emergence.

Part III describes the skills and techniques used in evolutionary coaching: how to help your clients master their fears; how to support them in living a values- and purpose-driven life; how to guide them in making a difference in their world; and how to help them fulfil their potential by leading a life of selfless service for the good of humanity and the planet.

Before digging deeper, let's pause for a moment to reflect on the meaning of these four words, *growth, development, emergence* and *self-realisation* in a human context.

- *Growth* suggests progression: in particular, the continuing ability to demonstrate increasingly higher levels of maturity.

- *Development* suggests learning: in particular, staged learning where each new stage expands on, and adds value, to what has been learned in previous stages.
- *Emergence* suggests breakthroughs: in particular, the ability to access insights that lead to new ways of thinking which support growth and development.
- *Self-realisation* suggests fully expressing who you are at the deepest level of your being.

If I were to choose one word that encapsulates the meaning of these four words—growth, development, emergence and self-realisation—that word would be *evolution*. This is what the book is about—*human evolution*— not our species evolution or our collective human cultural evolution, although that has an integral part to play in evolutionary coaching, but *individual psychological evolution* which begins the moment we are born and continues until the moment we die.

It is important to point out from the beginning that I am using the word *psychology* and its derivatives not so much in its modern sense—the science of the mind—but in its original and literal sense—*the study of the soul.*

How far you advance with your psychological evolution (the emergence of your soul) before you die depends on many factors, the most important being the extent to which the parental programming and cultural conditioning you receive in your formative years supports or hinders your psychological growth.

> *Conditioning is an automatic survival and learning mechanism that starts almost as soon as we are born, long before we are able to speak. The purpose of this automatic response is to evaluate threats to our survival and trigger a response that keeps us alive.*[1]

Anyone who hires a coach who understands the process of human emergence—the development of the ego, the blending of the ego with the soul, and the emergence of the soul—has a significant advantage in life. Without access to this knowledge, we stumble through life doing the best we can to make decisions that enable us to meet whatever needs we think we have at any specific moment in time. We have no idea about the stages of human development or how to find fulfilment in our lives.

Our consciousness is focused on two things. First, what potential *threats* there are in our environment that could prevent us from meeting our needs or take away the things we have already acquired or accumulated, second, what potential *opportunities* there are in our environment for satisfying our unmet needs—getting more of what we want.

Motivation

At the core of the theory of human psychological evolution are two ideas: first, we grow and evolve in stages, and second, each stage has its own specific needs. What motivates us is the satisfaction of the needs of the stage of psychological development we have reached—our primary motivation, and the satisfaction of the needs of the stages of psychological development we have passed through where we still have unmet needs— our secondary motivations. For whatever reason and for whatever period of time our secondary needs predominate over our primary needs, we become arrested in our evolutionary development. Whilst our conscious awareness is focused on satisfying our secondary needs, we cannot focus on our primary needs.

When we are able to satisfy our needs we experience a sense of internal stability and external equilibrium. We feel aligned and comfortable in ourselves and we feel aligned and comfortable with those around us and with our environment. When we are unable to satisfy our needs we experience either internal instability or external disequilibrium. We feel misaligned and uncomfortable in ourselves or we feel misaligned and uncomfortable with those around us or with our environment.

Whatever needs we have that we have not been able to satisfy, or whatever needs we require to help us remain aligned and comfortable in ourselves and with those around us, is what we value. Thus our values are always a reflection of our needs. Our values are an expression of what is missing in our lives and what we require in our lives to remain in a state of internal stability and external equilibrium.

Roberto Assagioli, an Italian psychiatrist and pioneer in the fields of humanistic and transpersonal psychology, makes the following observation about the link between values and stages of development (levels of being):

The existence of different levels of being having different values is an evident and undeniable manifestation of the great law of evolution, as it progresses from simple and crude stages to more refined and highly organized ones.[2]

Most people have no concept of where their motivations come from, what stage of psychological development they are at, what stages they have passed through, or what stages they still need to master to find fulfilment in their lives. The only criteria they have for making choices are: what makes them feel happy in the moment, or what gives their life a sense of meaning and fulfilment.

Happiness, meaning and fulfilment are not synonymous. What makes us happy is the satisfaction of our ego's needs, and what gives our life meaning and fulfilment is the satisfaction of our soul's needs. Often people gain a sense of meaning from dealing with situations that are intrinsically sad, unjust or unfair, or physically or emotionally challenging. Alleviating poverty, rectifying injustice and caring for the sick, elderly or dying are not always "happy" experiences: what makes these experiences meaningful is our ability to make a difference. When we are able devote our lives to such pursuits, or whatever activities we invest our time in that make a difference, we find fulfilment.

At a certain point in life, and in certain circumstances, meaning can be just as important to our psychological survival as oxygen and water are to our physical survival. Finding meaning can also act as a source of resilience.

Viktor Frankl *noticed while he was a prisoner in a Nazi concentration camp that those who saw meaning in life, or who gave it meaning, demonstrated a surprising degree of strength and resistance. Finding this meaning proved to be of decisive survival value.*[3]

Finding happiness, meaning and fulfilment is not always easy. It sometimes involves making tough choices; choices you have never had to make before. Often the choices we are faced with are challenging: They involve choosing between competing needs—between our growth needs and our safety needs.

When you have as a resource someone you can trust who has an intimate understanding of the stages of psychological development because they have been through the process of human emergence themselves, then you are in a good position to make the right choices—the choices that increase your happiness, give your life meaning, and enable you to find a sense of fulfilment. In other words, when you have an *evolutionary coach* (someone who understands what you are going through) you are in a good position to make the choices that will help you to accelerate your evolution.

"That sounds good" I can hear you saying, "but why can't I rely on my parents or my priest or even the latest scientific findings to guide me on my journey through life?" Of course, you can try. The problem is that our parents, our priests, our scientists and even our psychologists and psychiatrists are so deeply embedded in their own cosmologies—cultural, religious, scientific, and psychological—that their answers will be for the most part incomplete. There is no culture, religion or scientific paradigm that embraces the whole. Each of these belief systems deals with different aspects of our reality and each has their own vocabulary. In this respect, the following words written by Peter D. Ouspensky in the early part of the twentieth century are as meaningful today as they were then:

> We fail to understand many things because we specialize too easily and too drastically, philosophy, religion, psychology, natural sciences, sociology, etc., each has their own special literature. There is nothing embracing the whole in its entirety.[4]

Here comes your next question: "Are you saying that this book embraces the whole?" "Isn't that just a little bit arrogant?" Well, yes, it might seem that way. (Although I would suggest that what you find among these pages is only an approximation to the whole.) All I would ask, dear reader, is to hold your judgement on this matter until you have dug into the material contained in these pages. As you uncover the evolutionary complexities that lie behind your existence you will come to understand and appreciate why few people and almost none of the scientific, social, religious or psychological disciplines have been able to grasp the whole.

Having said that, I would like to suggest that someone who I believe had a significant appreciation of the issues involved in human emergence was Abraham Maslow: he called it self-actualisation: Another was Clare Graves: he called it the Emergent Cyclical Levels of Existence Theory. Whereas, in my opinion Maslow focused on *personal* human development—the evolution of healthy individual consciousness, Graves focused more on the *cultural* aspect of human development—the evolution of our collective world views. I will show how these two approaches intersect later in this book. For the moment, let us focus on Maslow.

I find much wisdom in Maslow's writings. The particular wisdom I want to draw on at the start of this book is Maslow's conceptualisation of growth (psychological evolution), and, in particular, the answer he gives to the question: How does growth take place? He states:

> *The answer ... is a simple one, namely ... growth takes place when the next step forward is subjectively more delightful, more joyous, more intrinsically satisfying than the previous gratification with which we have become familiar and even bored; that the only way we can ever know what is right for us is that it feels better subjectively than any alternative. The new experience validates itself rather than by any outside criterion. It is self-justifying, self-validating. ... This is the way we discover the ... answer to the ultimate questions Who am I? and What am I?*[5]
>
> *Growth is not in the pure case a goal out ahead, nor is self-actualization, nor is the discovery of Self. In the child, it is not specifically purposed; rather it just happens. [A child] doesn't so much search as find.*[6]

What Maslow is positing in this statement is what I hinted at earlier: until we reach the higher stages of our psychological development, we are not aware that we are on an evolutionary journey. All we know is what is happening to us, what is changing outside us and what is changing within us, what needs we have that are currently satisfied, and what needs we have that are unmet.

You have no way of knowing that your primary needs are linked to the stage of development you are at, and that at some point in the future when you have mastered the satisfaction of these needs, you will enter the next stage of your development where you seek to satisfy a different set of needs. You have no idea that this shift will affect your values and your motivations.

What this means is simply for the average person, life is a continuing stream of choices, where during the first half of our lives we try to maximise our desire for happiness, and during the second half of our lives, if we continue to evolve, we try to maximise our desire for meaning and fulfilment.

What prevents growth?

Having established that growth is something that happens to us, at least in the first half of our lives, and only later is it something we actively seek, it is important to ask, "What prevents growth?"

Once more, I would like to draw on Maslow's wisdom:

> *Why is it so hard and painful for some to grow...? Here we must become fully aware of the fixative and regressive power of ungratified deficiency-needs, of the attraction of safety and security, of the functions of defence and protection against pain, fear, loss and threat, of the need for courage in order to grow...*
>
> *Every human being has both sets of forces within him. One set clings to safety and defensiveness out of fear, tending to regress backward, hanging on to the past, afraid to grow ... afraid to take chances, afraid to jeopardize what he already has, afraid of independence, freedom, separateness (ego). The other set of forces impels him forward toward wholeness of Self and uniqueness of Self, toward full functioning of all his capacities, toward confidence in the face of the external world at the same time that he can accept his deepest, real, unconscious Self (soul).*
>
> *This basic dilemma or conflict between the defensive forces and the growth trends I conceive to be existential, imbedded in the deepest nature of the human being, now and forever into the future. If it is diagrammed (as below) then we can very easily classify the various mechanisms of growth in an uncomplicated way.*[7]

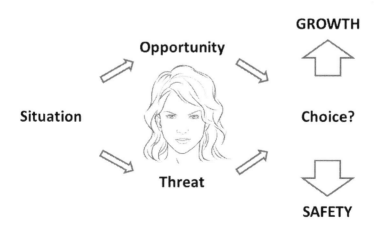

Figure P.1 The conflict between safety and growth

Whenever we encounter a new situation we must first decide if it presents a potential threat or a potential opportunity to meeting our needs.

If we see the situation as a potential threat, we must decide whether to advance and overcome the threat, or whether to do nothing, retreat and run to safety. We will only advance if we have confidence in our abilities to cope with the difficulties the situation may present and the courage to face the fear we are feeling: this constitutes growth. We retreat when the level of fear we feel is greater than our belief in our ability to cope: this constitutes safety.

If we see the situation as a potential opportunity, we seek to take advantage of it if we feel that we can be successful without expending too much energy, and we hold back when we judge the amount of energy we would have to expend would be greater than the potential value we believe the opportunity might present. In other words, when our minds enhance the attractiveness and minimise the dangers of a situation we will move towards it. When our minds enhance the dangers and minimise the attractiveness of a situation, we will retreat from it.

> *Therefore, we can consider the process of healthy growth to be a never ending series of free choice situations, confronting each individual at every point throughout his (or her) life, in which he (or she) must choose between safety and growth, dependence and independence, regression or progression, and immaturity and maturity.*[8]

We can conclude from this that growth is a choice: We grow when we are willing to embrace the changes that are happening around us, even if they bring up fear, and we regress when we resist the changes that are happening around us, and give in to our fear. The fear we are giving in to is either the fear of not being able to cope—not having the strength, skills, talents or resources that we feel would be necessary to guarantee a successful outcome—or the fear of uncertainty—not being willing to embrace the unknown.

Maslow states:

> *...if free choice is really free and if the chooser is not too sick or frightened to choose, he [she] will choose wisely, in a healthy and growthward direction, more often than not.*[9]

...growth forward is made possible by the feeling of being safe, of operating out into the unknown from a safe home port, of daring because retreat is possible. ... Assured safety permits higher needs and impulses to emerge and to grow towards mastery. To endanger safety, means regression backward to the more basic foundation. What this means is that in the choice between giving up safety or giving up growth, safety will ordinarily win out. Safety needs are prepotent over growth needs ... only a child that feels safe dares to grow forward healthily. ... The more safety needs are gratified, the less valence they have for the child...[10]

Maslow makes reference to the child because under normal circumstances the first three stages of psychological development—surviving, conforming and differentiating—begin to unfold before we reach our teenage years. As an adult, who we are at the ego level and how confident we are in meeting our needs, is significantly influenced by our experiences in our formative years.

The single holistic principle that binds together the multiplicity of human motives is the tendency for a new and higher need to emerge as a lower need fulfils itself by being sufficiently gratified. The child who is fortunate enough to grow normally and well get satiated and bored with the delights he has savoured sufficiently, and eagerly ... goes on to higher more complex, delights as they become available to him without danger or threat. ... He wants to go on, to move, to grow. Only if frustration, failure, disapproval, ridicule come at the next step does he [she] fixate or regress, and we are then faced with the intricacies of pathological dynamics of neurotic compromises in which the impulses remain alive but unfulfilled, or even of loss of impulse and capacity.[11]

Once we have become adults the game changes: the stages of development are no longer thrust upon us by the changing demands of our ego development and physical growth, but by the internal pull we feel towards exploring our higher nature and the willingness we have to examine who we might be beyond our parental programming and cultural conditioning.

This stage of development is individuation. We individuate when we feel confident enough to choose independence over dependence—when we are willing to risk separation from the safety and security of the parental and cultural milieu in which we were raised so we can delight in the exploration of our true nature and find answers to the question "Who am I?"

When we have established our independence and become fully responsible and accountable for our lives, we are pulled forward in our development, not by the need of the ego for happiness, but by the need of the soul for meaning and fulfilment.

First, we feel the pull towards self-actualisation—the soul's need to lead a values- and purpose-driven existence. Next, we feel the pull towards integration—the soul's need to make a difference in the world by collaborating with others who share the same values and purpose. Finally, we feel the pull towards service—we begin to recognise that the real purpose of our existence is to be a vehicle for our soul to give the gifts it came to give.

There are seven stages of psychological development, these are: surviving, conforming, differentiating, individuating, self-actualising, integrating and serving. They are the stages of development we go through when we continually choose growth over safety. When we choose safety over growth or when we allow our secondary motivations to take precedence over our primary motivation, we stop growing and become arrested at the stage of development we have reached.

The job of the evolutionary coach is to find ways to make sure neither of these two things happens, but if they do, the coach must then support their client to get back on track: to choose growth over safety: to build the client's confidence in their ability to cope and find ways to help them satisfy, overcome or come to terms with their unmet needs.

An evolutionary coach needs to instill five qualities in their clients to support them on the journey to full self-realisation—adaptability, emergent learning, the ability to bond, the ability to cooperate and the ability to manage complexity.[12] These qualities are the basic requirements for evolution. Without these qualities, evolution could never have happened.

Adaptability: The ability to take things in your stride—maintain internal stability and external equilibrium when your internal and external environment changes. This implies being able to manage your emotions and taking care of your body in your framework of existence so you can stay fit and healthy.

Emergent learning: The ability to learn by trial and error how to adjust to changes in your internal and external environment so you are able to maintain your internal stability and external equilibrium. This implies a constant focus on learning for the purpose of personal and professional growth and the ability to learn from your mistakes.

Ability to bond: The ability to bond implies: (a) increasing your internal stability by aligning the needs of your ego with the needs of your soul; and (b) increasing your external equilibrium by connecting with others in internally cohesive groups or teams.

Ability to cooperate: The ability to cooperate involves improving your external equilibrium by cooperating with other people, groups or teams who share your values and purpose so you can increase your individual and collective resilience.

Ability to manage complexity: The ability to manage complexity involves activating your intuition and inspiration so you can uncover and understand the underlying causes and patterns that are inherent in a situation and take appropriate action to maintain or enhance your internal stability and external equilibrium. This implies staying calm in the face of danger, remaining committed in the midst of adversity, and being at ease with uncertainty even when you do not know what to do.

Notes

1. Alan Watkins, *Coherence: The Secret Science of Brilliant Leadership* (London: Kogan Page), 2014, p. 95.
2. Roberto Assagioli, *The Act of Will* (New York: Penguin Books), 1973, p. 98.
3. Viktor Frankl, *Man's Search for Meaning* (Boston: Beacon Press), 1946.
4. P. D. Ouspensky, *Tertium Organum: A Key to the Mysteries of the World* (New York: Vintage Books), 1982, pp. 262–263.
5. Abraham Maslow, *Towards a Psychology of Being* (New York: Van Nostrand), 1968, p. 45.
6. Ibid. p. 44.

7. Ibid. p. 46.
8. Ibid. p. 47.
9. Ibid. p. 48.
10. Ibid. p. 48.
11. Ibid. p. 56–57.
12. Richard Barrett, *The New Leadership Paradigm* (Bath: Fulfilling Books), 2010, pp. 75–76.

FOREWORD

No matter what type of coach you are, if you are concerned with the healthy psychological growth of your clients, this is a book you should read. It is not about coaching *per se*, it is about the framework of human development that coaches need to be familiar with in order to facilitate the full emergence of their client's potential; not just helping people become more proficient at what they do, but helping them participate in their own evolution, the evolution of their organisations; the evolution of our global society and the evolution of our species.

If you want to take people on a journey to a place they have never been to before, it is important that you find out as much as possible about the territory before you depart. It helps immensely if you have already explored the territory yourself. You will need to be thorough in your exploration, because everyone you take on this journey will be starting from a different place.

Some will be overladen with baggage: You will need to help them lighten their load. Some will think they know where they are going, only to find when they get there that it is not the paradise they thought it would be: You will need to redirect their energies so they can move forward. Some will be courageous in tackling the obstacles along the way, and some will be fearful: You will need to teach them how to overcome their fears and become the masters of their destiny.

You should think of this book as your travel guide, it provides a detailed map of the territory. It describes each stage of the journey, it tells you what you need to take with you on your journey and how to avoid or overcome the obstacles you may meet on the way.

You don't have to read this book from the beginning. If you are keen to explore the practice of evolutionary coaching you can read this Foreword and Chapter 1, and then jump straight to Part II—the exercises. You should refer to Part I, as and when needed. If you are relatively new to coaching, it would be best to start at the beginning of the book and proceed through to the end.

Individual psychological development

Whatever type of coaching you do, it is important to recognise that every individual you are working with is on evolutionary journey—a natural journey of psychological development that is common to every member of the human race. Every goal your clients are trying to achieve, every challenge they are facing, and every choice they have to make will in some way be related to the needs of the stage of psychological development they have reached[1] or the needs of the stages of psychological development they have passed through that they have not yet mastered—where they still have unmet needs.[2] Understanding where your clients are on their journey will provide you with valuable insights into how you can help them meet their goals and fulfil their potential.

You, the coach, are also on the same journey. Where you are—the stage of psychological development you have reached, and the level of mastery you have achieved in the levels of psychological development you have passed through—will significantly affect your ability to guide your clients on *their* journey. Understanding where *you* are is just as important as understanding where your clients are. If you know where you are then you will know how far you can take your clients before you enter unknown territory.

Once your clients reach the same stage of development that you have reached, you will both be exploring unknown territory. When this happens, you must either hand your client over to someone who is at a higher stage of development than you are or seek the support of this person as a mentor. It will be important to be honest with your client on this matter. It would be advisable early in your relationship with your client, to lay out the full map of emergence, help them understand where they are, explain where you are, and what will happen to the coaching relationship when you reach the limits of your experience.

Cultural context

In addition to recognising that all your clients are on an evolutionary journey, it is important to recognise that all the cultures your clients are embedded in are also on an evolutionary journey. Every client you have is embedded in multiple cultural contexts: a family context, a community context, an organisational context, perhaps a religious context, and most certainly a societal context. In order to facilitate the emergence of your clients, you must understand what stage of development these cultures are at. This is important for two reasons.

First, if the cultures your clients are embedded in are less advanced in their development than your clients are, your clients may find it difficult to explore their full potential. Second, if the cultures they are embedded in are more advanced in their development than your clients are, your clients will feel supported in exploring their development, at least up to the levels of development that these cultures have attained or are willing to tolerate.

When you attempt to move beyond the stage of development of the cultures you are embedded in, you may begin to feel stuck, blocked, frustrated or depressed. You may feel out of alignment with your family, community, society and your work colleagues or even with those with whom you share your religious faith. Your more "evolved" point of view may not be appreciated by other members of these cultures. You may find yourself feeling increasingly isolated.

Eventually you will have to decide what to do—accept the situation (compromise on your values and beliefs) with all the anomalies and inadequacies this may incur, or seek out a new working environment, a new community or even a new society or religion where you can feel supported in your growth and development. The one thing you will not be able to do is seek out a new family.

Feeling out of alignment with your parents, siblings, grandparents and other family members is one of the most difficult issues you may have to face on your evolutionary journey. In this area of your life you will have to be most careful and reach the best accommodation you can. This may result in spending less time with your family, avoiding or holding back your opinions in family discussions, or moving away from the community in which your family is embedded. The family members you will feel drawn to will be those who are at the same stage of psychological development as you. The ones you distance yourself from will be those who are operating at a lower stage of development.

In some cultures, where a religious affiliation is strongly associated with the community or societal culture, changing religion can not only lead to isolation, it can also lead to danger. The fear you experience in such a situation can be a major impediment to personal evolution. Religious intolerance is one of the hallmarks of the early stages of societal development. As societies evolve they become more inclusive, giving less emphasis to the religious side of life and more emphasis to the secular side of life. It is much easier to evolve and grow in a liberal democratic culture than an authoritarian or religious regime.

This discrepancy in evolutionary development between the individual and the cultures the person is embedded in, is one of the reasons people decide to leave the corporate world. As they get further along in their evolutionary journey, they reach a stage in their development where they no longer feel aligned with the values and beliefs of the organisation they are working in. They become gradually more stressed and begin to feel burned out, either because their needs—the opportunities they require to move ahead with their development—cannot be met by the culture they are working in, or because they no longer feel a sense of alignment with the values of the organisation.

Many people put up with such situations for far too long. Because of their loyalty to the organisation or their commitment to their work, they stay longer than they should. They justify their actions by entertaining the dream that somehow the culture will magically change. Others stay because they believe they will not be able to make the same level of income or get the benefits they now enjoy, elsewhere.

They lock themselves into a cultural environment where they feel they have to park their values in the car park every time they enter their place of work. Spending long periods in such a state of misalignment sickens the soul. Eventually, most people get to the point where they cannot stand it anymore. They feel so unhappy that they look for alternative employment, perhaps accepting a lower-paying job, one with fewer benefits, or part-time employment. They will be willing to go anywhere, to get away from the toxic environment of their current place of work. The more talented and courageous among them will start their own businesses.

Coping and letting go

If you are in the middle stages of your psychological development, the questions on your mind, whenever opportunities for professional growth arise, will be: "Do I have the knowledge and competencies necessary to be successful in the new role or position?", "Can I handle the increased responsibility, and will I be able to master the new levels of complexity I will have to deal with?", "Am I good enough?" Behind these fears lie yet more fears—the fear of failure, and behind that the fear of the shame or guilt you may feel if you are not successful in your new position.

Stepping into the unknown to explore your potential not only requires confidence it also requires courage. Often, it is at that this point people seek out the services of a coach or mentor.

For people in the early stages of their development, their principal worry when faced with a professional growth opportunity is not so much about having the knowledge and competencies they need for the job, although these are still relevant factors, but about the fear of losing the carefully woven working relationships that have sustained and nourished them up to this point. If they accept this new opportunity, they fear they may be ostracised by their old friends and not be able to make new friends. Even worse, they may have to supervise or manage their former friends and colleagues. They wonder how they will be able to cope if they can no longer rely on the carefully organised support system in which they have been embedded up to this point in their lives. They worry about isolating themselves.

These concerns about being able to cope in a more complex environment or leaving behind your network of friends occur almost every time you make a significant change in your life. I remember the anxiety I felt when I first went to primary school, when I first went to high school, and later when I went to university. Each of these growth opportunities meant giving up what I had become comfortable with, letting go of friendships, and exploring what was unknown.

The same anxieties came up again when I got my first job, when I had my first intimate relationship, when I got married, when I joined the World Bank, and about seventeen years ago when I left the World Bank to follow my current calling. Every decision required confidence and courage: the courage to face the unknown and explore my potential and the confidence to take on the challenges of a more complex world that I was not familiar with. Accepting such challenges, letting go and leaping into the unknown is how we grow and develop psychologically. We must constantly choose growth over safety if we want to find our full self-realisation.

As I approach my seventieth year, I recognise that I am still on this journey but I am definitely at a different stage than I was at twenty years ago. I know that because my primary motivation has changed. Even so, with all the personal mastery work I have done, and all the wisdom I have accumulated, there are still moments when the unmet needs from the early stages of my development throw me out of equilibrium. Certain situations trigger my subconscious fears causing emotional upsets and reactions. However, because of the willingness I have to take responsibility for these reactions and upsets, these triggering moments have become less and less frequent over time, and they don't last as long as they used to because of the self-mastery techniques I have learned. Emotional self-mastery helps you to get back to a state of calm more quickly because it teaches you how to manage your thoughts.

Even when you reach the higher stages of development, you may from time to time still encounter situations that trigger an unmet need from the early stages of your development—a need you thought you had mastered. Because you have painful memories of trying to meet these needs when you were young, your ego hid them away in the dark corners of your subconscious mind. They became so deeply embedded that you do not know you have them. Often these unmet needs have to do with feelings of abandonment, neglect, sexual abuse, inferiority or a lack of self-worth.

These are not trivial unmet needs. They got hidden away for good reason—they represented such a staggering threat to your internal stability or external equilibrium when you were young, that your mind could not handle them. Your ego hid them away for your protection because they were too painful to deal with when you first experienced them.

Only when you reach the higher stages of development, when you feel safe in the harbor of your soul, will your ego be willing to surrender the keys to the dungeon where your darkest fears and unmet needs are locked. Be aware that if such deeply embedded material bubbles up causing trauma in the minds of your clients, you may have to advise them to seek the professional help of a psychologist or psychiatrist. Some guidelines on this matter are included in Annex 5.

Resonance

One of the most difficult issues we have to deal with when we commit to the journey of evolutionary development is leaving people behind. Every time you shift to a new stage of psychological development, the level of resonance you experience with those who you have been sharing your life with at the old stage of psychological development will begin to wane.

Resonance is a term used in science to denote the tendency of a system to oscillate with greater amplitudes at certain frequencies of vibration. When a system operates at its resonant frequency, significant amounts of energy are released. This is why you feel a pull towards people who are operating at the same level of psychological development as you are. When you come together, you feel resonance, and energy flows between you. You get along with these people, you have similar interests and needs, you share similar experiences and most importantly, you have similar values. When you no longer resonate with someone or with a specific group of people, you have little to say to each other. Conversations become stunted; what matters to them is no longer what matters to you, and you can't wait to remove yourself from their company. There is no mutual exchange of energy when you interact with each other. This is because you are operating at different energetic frequencies: there is no resonance.

Shifting to a new stage of psychological development can affect all your relationships—your relationship to your spouse, to your parents, to your co-workers, to your community, and even the relationship you have with your society.

Each time you shift to a new stage of development, you will feel a pull or an attraction towards those who are operating at the stage of development you are entering. These are the people you will now want to spend your time with because you feel a sense of resonance with them—you will have similar values, similar interests and a similar outlook on life. Those you leave behind will not understand what is happening. Unless you are careful in managing this transition, your friends will feel abandoned.

As I look back over my life, I realise that I have left behind many groups of friends: good people, people I have had great times with, people who nurtured and sustained me, but people I no longer have the same level of resonance with. They either stopped evolving or found themselves on a slower evolutionary trajectory. There is no judgement attached to this statement: it is just what is. Whilst we are all on the same journey, we are all taking different paths. We are all trying to find what makes us happy or what gives our life meaning, and as we shift from one stage of development to the next, our motivations—what we need to make us happy—also change.

When you commit to the evolutionary journey, I mean, really commit, you must understand the further you go, the more isolated and lonely you may feel. Not in a social sense, unless you cut yourself off from the world, but in the sense of really being seen and understood by others. You will find yourself holding back—not saying what you truly think and believe—because what you have to say may be too challenging or threatening for the people around you to hear. You risk being ostracised or being called a weirdo. Not that you will care, but for the sake of your family and your friends you may want to avoid such situations.

The reverse side of this coin is that as you grow and develop you become more deeply connected with your unique self. You find more joy in your life as you explore your innate talents and find your calling. As you do this, you develop deeper more meaningful relationships with the people you come across who share your passion and calling.

What is your story?

We all have a story of how the world works. We need our stories to help us cope with life's challenges. Without a story, life becomes meaningless. Our stories serve two main functions: they help us to place ourselves in the big picture—explain who we are, why we are here, and the purpose of our lives. They also help us to make decisions, so we can navigate more easily through our experiences, they give us a framework of rules, beliefs and values to guide our decision-making, which we believe will help us maximise our happiness and contentment, and minimise our pain and suffering.

As you make progress with your psychological development the scale, scope and depth of your story gets bigger and more inclusive. In order to resonate with another person your stories need to be similar in scale and scope, but not necessarily of the same depth. Depth is an intensely personal dimension which depends on your unique life journey. Whereas people can help each other expand the scale and scope of their stories through the communication of ideas, it is much more difficult to help people increase the depth of their stories: Increasing depth requires experiences.

To counterbalance the increasing loneliness you may feel as you progress on your journey, many people, but not all, look for a spiritual meaning to their lives. They start to connect inwardly as well as outwardly. They don't just want to connect with people who share the same values and purpose, they want to connect with the universal mind—the ground of all being—whatever they consider to be divine. Often this is what sustains people at the higher stages of development. They begin to spend more time in contemplation and meditation because this is how they find the connection they are seeking. We all need a sense of connection to give our lives meaning.

Programming and conditioning

You don't have to reflect for long before you realise that we are all born different. We come into life with inbuilt preferences, qualities and talents. You just have to observe how different siblings can be to know this is true. Differences between siblings are apparent even at a young age. There is no scientific explanation for this. All we know is that we are all different and we all come into this world with our inbuilt preferences and own unique gifts and talents.

It matters not what explanation you may have for why we are all different or whether you have an explanation or not. What matters is that we all get a chance to fully express who we are, become all we can become, and have the opportunities we need to manifest our unique gifts and talents for the good of those who we care about and for humanity in general.

What determines the degree to which we are able to do this is the level of parental programming[3] and cultural conditioning[4] we are exposed to during our formative years.

By the time we become young adults, who we are is a complex mixture of our own unique character overlaid by layers of parental programming and cultural conditioning. You quickly learn during your childhood years that the best way to experience pleasure and avoid pain—physical and emotional—is to follow the desires of your parents and obey the rules of the culture you were brought up in. The programming and conditioning we receive can either hinder us in reaching the individuating and self-actualisation stages of our psychological development or support us.

What happens to most of us is our unique self—the person we were born to become—gets pushed into the background. For this reason, most people only begin to explore who they really are after they leave their parental home or after they engage in some form of higher education and world travel.

In some cases, the parental programming and cultural conditioning we receive may cause us to doubt our capabilities. It may even make us feel unworthy and unlovable. When this happens, we grow up never really understanding who we are, ignorant of our potential, and lacking the confidence to believe in ourselves. Our deepest desires are suppressed to the level of our subconscious, and we become dependent on others for how we feel about ourselves. In this respect, whether we are aware of it or not, and most of us are not, by the time we reach physical maturity, we are the prisoners of our parental programming and cultural conditioning.

The persona we display to the world is not our unique self, but our false self: a self with a socialised mind. If the gap between our false self and our unique self is wide, we will feel uncomfortable—a sense of unease about who we are and what we are supposed to do with our lives. We will feel grossly misunderstood.

Dr. Marc Gafni describes the unique self in the following way:

> *Your Unique Self never was, is or will be every again and expresses itself in your Unique Perspective which fosters your Unique Insight which in turn births your Unique Gift which is the Unique Purpose and Delight of your life.*[5]

Your job as an evolutionary coach is to help your clients break down the bars of the prisons they have constructed for themselves so they can unmask their false selves, discover who they really are, and develop the gifts and talents of their unique selves. This is how you help your clients embark on the journey towards full human emergence.

The importance of individuation and self-actualisation

The process of breaking down the bars of the prison you have constructed for yourself is called individuation. The process of rebuilding your life to reflect your unique self is called self-actualisation. Fully embodying your unique self so you can discover your full potential is called self-realisation.

Individuation involves letting go of the beliefs you assimilated as part of your parental programming and cultural conditioning that you no longer resonate with; self-actualisation involves embracing the values and purpose of your soul.

Self-actualisation represents a major stage in our psychological evolution, because only when we reach this stage are we able to begin to understand the relevance of the experiences we had as we passed through the earlier stages of our development. When you reach the stage of self-actualising you begin to see that there is a meaning to your life. When you look back and join up the dots you see patterns of significance emerging.

Self-realisation gives you this perspective because it gives the capacity to look *at* your life rather than *through it*. Prior to this stage, not only do you not have this ability, you are not even aware that it exists. You are so wrapped up in focusing on the needs of the early stages of development that you are unable to witness your experience. Consequently, only when you individuate and self-actualise—when you allow your ego to blend with you soul—do you begin to understand who you are and your purpose in life.

Let me put it a different way. A caterpillar has no idea of what it can become. It is uniquely focused on satisfying its basic needs. It consumes until it can consume no more. It then moves into a stage of transition and reconstruction. It is only when the butterfly emerges from the cocoon that the butterfly can appreciate, if it has a memory of its caterpillar days, the process that led to its emergence. If the caterpillar had had an evolutionary coach it would have been able to see beyond its own demise. It would have been able to envisage a future beyond satisfying its basic needs. That is the role you can play as an evolutionary coach. With the information contained in this book you can become the catalyst that will help your clients see beyond the stage of development they have reached, to a future that could lead to their full self-realisation.

Herein is the key difference between performance coaching and evolutionary coaching: Performance coaching is about helping people meet the goals they have at the level of psychological development they have reached. This is the domain of the business coach, the sports coach, the voice coach and any other type of coach who is focused on performance with a little "p". As a performance coach, you just have to be good at helping people get better at doing what they do. It does not matter whether you, the coach, have self-actualised or not. Obviously, if you have self-actualised, and coaching is your passion, this will support you in becoming an excellent performance coach.

Evolutionary coaching is also about performance, but performance with a big "P". Performance with a big "P" is about human emergence; not just helping people become more proficient at what they do but helping them to participate in their own evolution and get better at *being* as well as *doing*. This is the domain of the leadership coach, the executive coach and the life coach.

Only when you have lived through your own emergence—completed your individuation and self-realisation—can you bring wisdom to bear on the process your clients are going through.

Finally, I would like to share with you my inspiration for writing this book. When I finished *The Values-Driven Organisation* in the spring of 2013, I realised, more than ever how critical leadership is to creating a high-performing culture. Even though I devoted Part III of *The Values-Driven Organisation* to this topic, and the whole of *The New Leadership Paradigm (2010)*, I realised there was something missing. I needed to bring the ideas contained in these two books to the coaching profession because so many leaders these days are using coaches to help them grow and develop, personally and professionally. So I decided to write a companion volume to these two books especially for coaches.

As I was completing *Evolutionary Coaching*, I also realised that anyone who resonates with the approach outlined in this book can dig even deeper by exploring the content of *What My Soul Told Me*, which I published in 2012.

Richard Barrett
London
March 7, 2014

Notes

1. The satisfaction of these needs represents their primary motivation.
2. The satisfaction of these needs represents their secondary motivations.

3. Parental programming: We all receive conscious and subconscious messages from our parents in the early years of our lives about our strengths and weaknesses, and how we should behave in order to fit into the family environment. The beliefs we learn in our family environment are what I am referring to as parental programming.
4. Cultural conditioning: In addition to the beliefs we learn about who we are and how to fit into our family setting, we also learn beliefs about who we are and how to fit into the culture in which our family is embedded. The beliefs we learn in this larger environment are what I am referring to as cultural conditioning.
5. Marc Gafni, *Your Unique Self* (Tucson: Integral Publishers), 2012.

PART I

The Theory of Evolutionary Coaching

The purpose of Part I of this book is to provide the reader with an overview of a framework of human emergence that can be used in evolutionary coaching. It is not the only framework. There are many others and they are all very similar. The main advantages of the values-based framework are: (a) it is simple to understand and relate to; and (b) it provides a basis for consistent measurement.

After the introduction, which explains why there is a rapidly growing interest in coaching and how evolutionary coaching is different from normal coaching, there are six chapters, each of which deals with different aspects of the framework of human emergence.

Chapter 2 describes the big picture—the three universal stages of evolution and how human emergence fits into this framework. Chapter 3 describes the relationships between the three universal stages of evolution and the seven stages of human psychological development. Chapter 4 describes the relationships between the seven stages of human psychological development and the seven levels of personal consciousness. Chapter 5 explains how the evolution of the human mind/brain affects the way in which our consciousness operates. Chapter 6 describes the evolution of human world views and how they relate to the stages of psychological development. Chapter 7 explains how the evolution of the human mind/brain and the evolution of human consciousness affect how we make decisions.

CHAPTER 1

INTRODUCTION

Another book on coaching! Isn't the market flooded with books about how to support people in achieving their goals? I agree: it is. When I searched Amazon.com for books on Executive Coaching, Personal Coaching and Life Coaching I found more than 4,000 titles. I even found titles such as: Life Coaching for Dummies, Coaching & Mentoring for Dummies and Performance Coaching for Dummies. The implication being, even if you are a "dummy" you can still learn how to coach.

I worry that this increased familiarisation of people with the concept of coaching is making it less of a profession and more of a way for people with a reasonable amount of intelligence to earn a living. This is the bad side. Trivialising coaching potentially lowers the bar of the profession and invites mediocrity. To my way of thinking, a coach cannot guide people on a journey through a territory they have not experienced themselves. To be an effective guide you not only have to know your topic, you have to have lived it. If you are a business coach you need to know about business; if you are a sports coach, you need to know about your sport; if you are a leadership coach, an executive coach or a life coach, you need to know about human emergence.

The good side of the increased visibility of coaching is that it has legitimatised asking for help in meeting our business and life challenges: it has made it OK not to know, and it has made it OK to speak your truth. To say you don't know, to say you need help, to ask: "What can I do?"

Ten-to-fifteen years ago, there were few books on coaching, especially not executive, business or life coaching. Coaching was primarily limited to sports, drama and singing (voice coaching). Now, it seems, everyone is jumping on the bandwagon. Why is that so? Why is there a rapidly growing interest in coaching? What is causing it? More importantly, if you picked up this book you may be wondering: What is *evolutionary* coaching about? How is *evolutionary* coaching different from normal coaching? What problem is *evolutionary* coaching trying to solve that is not addressed by normal coaching? Let me try to answer these questions.

Why is there a rapidly growing interest in coaching?

Coaching as a profession is growing rapidly all over the world, particularly in Asia, South America and the Middle East. The globalisation of the economy that has occurred over the last two decades and the accompanying boost in the economic development of the developing world has opened up new markets and new businesses opportunities, particularly in the BRIC[1] nations. This has led to a large increase in demand for competent people at all levels of management. The owners of these rapidly growing businesses in emerging markets, urgently need effective leaders and managers to run their companies. Consequently, they are willing to do whatever is necessary to help their people grow and develop their managerial skills and leadership capabilities. They see coaching as an effective way forward: a way to grow and develop the talent they have in their organisations.

In the Western world, coaching as a profession is growing, not because of increased demand, but because more individuals at all levels of management are seeking ways to advance their careers. What better way to do this than getting a coach you can trust, to support you in making good choices and wise decisions. Compared to the potential long-term benefits, the costs of getting such help are relatively trivial.

It used to be that having a coach was a sign of failure or under-performance: you were assigned a coach to correct your malfunctions. Whilst this still happens, the majority of people employing a coach do so because they want to get ahead. Nowadays, having a coach is seen as a sign of commitment to improving your performance; it is a way of gaining promotion and becoming increasingly successful. The stigma that was attached to having a coach is no longer there.

The Ridler Report 2013,[2] which examines trends in executive coaching, looked at what qualities clients want from their coaches. The report was based on feedback from 145 organisations employing executive coaches.

The two top-scoring qualities that organisations were looking for in the coaches they employed were: the ability of the coach to raise the awareness of the coachee to their ingrained patterns of behaviour (83% of responses), and the ability of the coach to deliver challenging feedback to the coachee (82% of responses).

Ingrained patterns of behaviour are usually due to preprogrammed responses (good or bad) that enable someone to address their unmet needs. Once a coachee's awareness to an ingrained pattern is raised, they can then consider the impact the behaviours associated with these patterns have on others and whether these behaviours inhibit or support their cause.

To find out what underpins a coachee's ingrained patterns, a coach needs to "probe below the surface." Eighty-three per cent of organisations considered the ability to probe below the surface as an essential ingredient to the success of the coaching experience. This is what evolutionary coaching does. It probes deeply below the surface to find out what is motivating the coachee—what needs they are trying to satisfy at the stage of development they have reached, and what unmet needs they have from the stages of development they have passed through, they have not yet mastered.

How is evolutionary coaching different?

The major difference between evolutionary coaching and normal coaching lies not in the skills and practices, but in the approach and purpose. The skills and practices needed for evolutionary coaching are the same as those used in all other forms of coaching: connecting, listening, clarifying expectations and objectives, suspending judgement, identifying feelings and beliefs, etc. What is different is the understanding that the framework of psychological development brings to the process of coaching. Without this framework we would not be able to understand the deep underlying needs of our clients.

Evolutionary coaching helps people understand what stage of psychological development they have reached, how well they have mastered the stages of development they have passed through, and what stages of development remain for them to master.

The stage of psychological development you are at affects every aspect of your life. It affects your needs, your values, and the relationships you have with your family, your co-workers, and with everyone you interact with on a daily basis. When you understand where you are in your development and what stage is coming up next, you can make choices that anticipate future challenges and thereby accelerate the pace of your development.

When you know your needs and values will change as you grow and develop, it helps you to see your life differently; it gives you an evolutionary perspective. If you know that your needs in the future will be different from the needs you have now, you can look out for opportunities to not just satisfy your immediate needs, but also for opportunities to satisfy your future needs too.

In other words, instead of having just one set of lenses to see the world through—the stage of psychological development you have reached—you can catch a glimpse of what your life might be like if you looked through the lenses of your next stage and subsequent stages of development.

The framework of psychological development also helps you to understand what stages of development the organisation, the community and the society you are embedded in have reached. The stages of development they are at not only affects their values, it also affects the relationships they have with their stakeholders and most importantly their ability to meet your needs at the stage of development you have reached.

It is vitally important for you, as a coach, to explore with the individuals you are coaching the extent to which the culture of the organisation, the community and the society in which they are embedded, support them or hinder them in meeting their needs.

If the cultures they are embedded in hinder them in their developmental journey you may need to help your clients develop an exit strategy: help them find an organisation, community or society that will be better able to support them in their human emergence.

If, on the other hand, the cultures they are embedded in support them in their developmental journey then you should impress on them that their best strategy for success is not to focus on satisfying their *own* needs but on satisfying the needs of organisation, community or society in which they are embedded. This requires a shift in personal focus from caring about the needs of "I" to caring about the needs of "we".

This seems obvious when you consider the western marriage relationship. If you just focus on your own needs, you will not be in a marriage for very long. The shift in focus from "I" to "we" in a marriage is just as important as important as the shift in focus from "I" to "we" in an organisation, community and society.[3] Ultimately the opportunities for personal success are significantly increased if the group, organisation, community and society you are embedded in is successful. Most organisations, communities and societies fail because the individual "I"s consider their well-being to be more important than the well-being of the collective "we". This failure to embrace the needs of the "we" is the main reason we are experiencing a leadership crisis.[4]

In other words, for anyone working in an organisation or some form of partnership, the level of your success will be significantly influenced by the success of the organisation or partnership. The same is true of families, communities and societies. We are all culturally enmeshed in one way or another. Only by focusing on the greater good can we create the conditions which give us the opportunity to find our greatest personal success.

The problem with most approaches to coaching is that they do not take this perspective into account. There is little or no focus on the cultural context that clients are embedded in. Most approaches focus on presenting issues as they relate to the self-interest of the individuals being coached. Not much time or energy is spent on exploring how your clients can help the cultures they are embedded in to become more successful. By failing to get this message across, you are letting your clients down because you are not acting in their best interests.

This is what I meant when I said at the start of this section that the major difference between evolutionary coaching and normal coaching lies not in the skills and practices, but in the approach and purpose. The approach is *evolutionary* and *holistic*; the purpose is *self-realisation* and *human emergence*. Evolutionary coaching not only provides a framework for individual human emergence, it also provides a framework for our collective human emergence.

A leadership crisis

In *True North*[5] Bill George, Professor of Management Practice at Harvard Business School and former Chief Executive of Medtronic, the world's leading medical technology company states:

> *An enormous vacuum in leadership exists today—in business, politics, government, education, religion, and nonprofit organisations. Yet there is no shortage of people with the capacity*

for leadership. The problem is we have a wrongheaded notion of what constitutes a leader, driven by an obsession with leaders at the top.

That misguided stand often results in the wrong people attaining critical leadership roles. When problems surfaced at Enron, WorldCom, Arthur Andersen, Tyco, and dozens of other companies, the severity of the leadership crisis became painfully apparent, creating a widespread erosion of trust in business leaders.

Over the past fifty years, leadership scholars have conducted more than a thousand studies in the attempt to determine the definitive leadership styles, characteristics, or personality traits of great leaders. None of these studies has produced a clear profile of the ideal leader. Thank goodness. If scholars had produced a cookie-cutter leadership style, people would be forever trying to emulate it.

The reality is that no one can be authentic by trying to be like someone else. People trust you when you are genuine and authentic, not an imitation ... You need to be who you are, not try to emulate somebody else ... Leaders are defined by their unique life stories and the way they frame their stories to discover their passions and the purpose of their leadership.

George goes on to say:

What concerns me are the many powerful business leaders who bowed to stock market pressure in return for personal gain. They lost sight of their True North and put their companies at risk by focusing on the trappings and spoils of leadership instead of building their organisations for the long-term ... The result were a severing of trust with employees, customers, and shareholders ... In business trust is everything.

George concludes:

Every successful business leader has to make the shift from "I" to "we".

This, I believe, is where evolutionary coaching comes in. In evolutionary coaching the needs and challenges of the individual are not treated in isolation from the needs of the collective. They are dealt with *in relation to* the needs and challenges of the human group structures in which the individual is embedded. Evolutionary coaching focuses on how individuals can achieve their goals and objectives while at the same time supporting the organisation, the community and the society in which they are embedded to meet their collective needs and goals. In other words, the evolutionary coaching approach focuses not just on the psychological evolution of the individual, but to what extent the individual can contribute to the psychological evolution of the cultures in which the individual is embedded.

A new leadership paradigm

I believe that to survive and prosper in the twenty-first century, business in general, and corporations in particular, will need to find a new leadership paradigm, one that embraces the global common good rather than individual self-interest. This paradigm should be based on values-driven and purpose-driven leadership that targets not only the success of the organisation, but also the well-being of all stakeholders, including employees, customers, investors, partners, society, and the environment: nothing less than full spectrum sustainability.[6]

Over the past century, business has become the most powerful institution on the planet. It is more influential by far than the United Nations (UN), the World Bank, and the International Monetary Fund (IMF) put together. To survive and prosper, the dominant institution in any society needs to be seen to be taking responsibility for the whole.

The real problem with business leaders is not their myopic focus on profits: the real problem is how they identify themselves. They see themselves and their businesses as somehow magically separate from the rest of society. They do not see themselves or their businesses as part of the global collective we call humanity. They see Earth as an infinite resource that can be plundered at will. For them, the planet is just an economic externality, not a life-support system.

They think the only responsibility they have is to their shareholders. They see their shareholders as also somehow magically separate from society. It is as if our business leaders are out of touch with reality. They lead a schizophrenic existence.

When they are at home, they are concerned about their local environment: They want to live in beautiful, clean surroundings. They are concerned about their grandchildren's futures: they want them to live in a better world. They are concerned about ecological diversity: they want to visit wilderness areas or wildlife reserves. They may even support causes that address some of the social injustices that exist in countries around the world.

When they go to work it is as if they step onto a completely different planet. They seem to deny these issues exist, or they see them as impediments to their success. They see the gambling casino of the stock market as their pathway to self-esteem. The share price of their company and the wealth they have accumulated become proxy measures of their self-worth. They are completely driven by their own self-interest—they become addicted to their ego's need for achievement.

In *Liberating the Corporate Soul*[7] and *The Values-Driven Organisation*,[8] I argued that enlightened business leaders know they can only sustain strong positive results if they care about the common good. Enlightened leaders have learned that caring for employees, customers, and the local community is good for the bottom line. They have also learned during the final decades of the twentieth century that it is at their own risk and peril that they ignore their company's larger social responsibilities, such as environmental protection, social justice and ecological diversity. Unfortunately, this message has still not penetrated very far in the business community and hardly at all into our business schools.

Enlightened business leaders are discovering that ethics and values are good for business. Who you are and what you stand for have become just as important as the quality of goods and services that you sell. Companies that knowingly allow tainted or dangerous products to enter the marketplace suffer far more than those that take immediate remedial action. Over the past two decades, a failure to embrace values-driven or ethical leadership has led to the demise of many major corporations and diminishing shareholder returns of others. Events at Enron, WorldCom, Parmalat, Siemens, Bear Sterns, RBS, Northern Rock and Lehman Brothers bear testimony to this fact.

In all of these cases, billions of dollars of shareholder value and employee pension plans were wiped out overnight by the actions of leaders who could not see beyond their own self-interest. The leaders of these organisations were so seduced by the glamour of personal success or consumed by their ego's need for achievement that it seriously impaired their judgement about what constituted good business. They could not see that their strategies for business success were based on strategies of ethical and moral failure. These leaders were operating under the old leadership paradigm where their own short-term self-interests were allowed to take precedence over the long-term interests of the common good.

Many of them underestimated the ability of civil society to mobilise public opinion to destroy their reputations and businesses. The internet-connected world is making what happens at every level of society increasingly transparent. There is nowhere to hide anymore. Society is becoming hypervigilant about its leaders. The masses are demanding their leaders become more accountable and operate with greater self-regulation. In the future, only leaders who embrace the highest levels of ethical conduct will be judged fit to be custodians of shareholder investments or the holders of the reins of political power.

In *Building a Values-Driven Organisation*,[9] I showed how cultural capital has become the new frontier of competitive advantage and that the culture of an organisation is a reflection of the values (levels of consciousness) of the leaders. When these two facts are juxtaposed, it becomes obvious that the values of the leaders are paramount in determining the success of a company.

The values of the leaders determine the culture of the company, and the culture of the company determines its competitive advantage. In *The Values-driven Organisation*[10] I showed how values- and purpose-driven organisations are the most successful organisations on the planet because they address not just the needs of their external stakeholders, but also the needs of their employees at all levels of psychological development.

In the future, values-driven leaders who support the goals of society will naturally rise to the top because they will be the most successful leaders. These are the leaders we need to develop. Evolutionary coaching combined with leadership development programmes based on the new leadership paradigm[11] is how we can make this happen.

I believe there is an evolutionary mechanism at work that encourages and supports values-driven, ethical leadership and punishes ego-driven, self-focused leadership. This mechanism is being driven by the evolving values of society and the increasing transparency provided by the internet. I will show in the following chapter that this evolutionary mechanism, which supports the common good and punishes self-interest, has been present throughout the whole of evolution, ever since the world began.

Summary

Here are the main points of this chapter:

1. The last two decades have seen a massive explosion in coaching.
2. The major difference between evolutionary coaching and normal coaching lie in its approach and purpose.
3. The approach is evolutionary and holistic; the purpose is self-realisation and human emergence.
4. To survive and prosper in the twenty-first century we will need a new leadership paradigm.
5. There is an evolutionary mechanism at work that encourages and supports values-driven, ethical leadership and punishes ego-driven, self-focused leadership.

In the next chapter, I will describe the three universal stages of evolution and explain how they can guide us in building a sustainable future for humanity.

Notes

1. BRIC is an acronym referring to the countries of Brazil, Russia, India and China which are all deemed to be at a similar stage of newly advanced economic development.
2. Ridler Report 2013, *Trends in the use of executive coaching*, Ridler & Co.
3. Richard Barrett, *The New Leadership Paradigm* (Bath: Fulfilling Books), 2010, pp. 8–10.
4. Richard Barrett, *The New Leadership Paradigm* (Bath: Fulfilling Books), 2010, p. 7.
5. Bill George, *True North: Discover Your Authentic Leadership* (San Francisco: Jossey-Bass), 2007.
6. John Mackey and Raj Sisodia, *Conscious Capitalism* (Boston: Harvard Business Review Press), 2013.
7. Richard Barrett, *Liberating the Corporate Soul: Building a visionary organisation* (Boston: Butterworth-Heinemann, 1998.

8. Richard Barrett, *The Values-Driven Organisation: Unleashing human potential for performance and Profit* (London: Routledge), 2013.

9. Richard Barrett, *Building a Values-Driven Organisation: A Whole System Approach to Cultural Transformation* (Boston: Butterworth-Heinemann), 2006.

10. Richard Barrett, *The Values-Driven Organisation: Unleashing human potential for performance and Profit* (London: Routledge), 2013.

11. Richard Barrett, *The New Leadership Paradigm* (Bath: Fulfilling Books), 2010.

CHAPTER 2

UNDERSTANDING EVOLUTION

According to scientists, everything that exists in our universe originated from a Big Bang that occurred about fourteen billion years ago. After that, it has all been about evolution: the evolution of energy into matter, matter into living organisms, and living organisms into creatures. One of those creatures—Homo sapiens—is now involved in attempting to carry the baton of evolution to the next level.

When I say everything in the universe had its origins fourteen billion years ago, I literally mean everything, including not only the physical world of atoms, cells, creatures and Homo sapiens, but also the world of instincts, thoughts, feelings, beliefs and values. Indeed, evolution could not have occurred if the interior realms—the faculties of mind—had not evolved in parallel with the exterior realms—the faculties of the brain.

From an evolutionary perspective, the modern disciplines of physics, chemistry, biology, psychology and sociology when written in this order, represent the chronological order of the different stages of evolution.

Physics provides us with insights into the quantum reality of the energy field that was created immediately after the Big Bang, which eventually led to the creation of electrons, neutrons and protons. Chemistry provides us with insights into the evolution of the atomic world, and the complex molecular structures that led to the creation of the first cells. Biology provides us with insights into the evolution of cells and complex organisms that led to the creation of the first creatures. Psychology/sociology provides us with insights into the personal and cultural evolution of one of those creatures—Homo sapiens.

Each of the entities (particles, atoms, cells, humans) that is studied in these disciplines represent not just a distinct stage of evolution but also a distinct scale and plane of being—the energetic plane, the atomic plane, the cellular plane and the plane of creatures (which includes Homo sapiens).

The most important feature, from an evolutionary perspective, is that each plane of being provides a stable platform for the emergence and subsequent evolution of the next plane of being. If an entity at a particular plane of being is unable to establish itself in its framework of existence—manage its internal stability and external equilibrium—then any attempts it makes to grow and develop by building a group structure, will fail.

Establishing internal stability and external equilibrium are the universal conditions necessary for evolutionary progress. This is just as true for physical evolution as it is for psychological evolution. This is a point we will return to several times during the course of this book.

As far as life on Earth is concerned, evolution progressed by atoms learning how to become viable and independent (establish internal stability and external equilibrium in their framework of existence) and then bonding together to form molecules, which cooperated with each other to form complex molecules and cells. After cells had learned how to become viable and independent in their framework of existence, they bonded with each other to form organisms, and organisms cooperated with each other to form complex organisms and creatures. One of those creatures—Homo sapiens—is now learning how to become viable and independent (establish internal stability and external equilibrium), how to bond with other members of the species to form bands, tribes, city-states and nations, and nations are learning how to cooperate with each other to create higher order regional entities such as the European Union and global entities such as the United Nations.[1] The entities and group structures that formed the different planes of being are shown in Table 2.1.

The continued success of this evolutionary endeavour and our ability to create the next plane of being—the plane of being of humanity—fundamentally depends on human emergence. Without full human emergence, we will not be able to create group structures which are stable enough (have sufficient internal stability and external equilibrium) for humanity to establish itself at a new plane of being.

Table 2.1 Stages of evolution

Planes of being	Group structures
Humanity	Not yet defined
Creatures (Homo sapiens)	Regional groups and global grouping
	Bands, tribes, city-states, nations
	Humans
Cellular plane (Eukaryotic cell)	Complex organisms
	Organisms
	Cells
Atomic plane (Carbon atom)	Complex molecules
	Molecules
	Atoms
Energetic plane: Quantum reality	

Based on the above explanation, we see that each plane of being can be divided into three stages of development differentiated by scale and complexity: the plane of being of an individual entity; the plane of being of the group structures that are made up of that entity; and the plane of being of the groups of group structures, some of which evolve to become the individual entity that becomes the starting point for a new plane of being.

I call this evolutionary progression "the three universal stages of evolution." The higher planes of being are totally dependent on the lower planes of being for their existence. If at any stage of evolution, the lower planes of being are not able to manage their internal stability and external equilibrium, then the higher planes of being that depend on them for their existence will come crashing down when the lower planes of being lose their ability to manage their internal stability and external equilibrium.

Thus, from the individual or collective human perspective, if you are unable to master the lower stages of psychological development, you will not be able to successfully establish yourself or your group structure at the higher stages of development.

We can describe the three universal stages of evolution in the following way:

Stage 1: Becoming viable and independent

In order to survive, the fundamental entity at each scale of existence (atom, cell and creature (Homo sapiens)) must learn how to become viable and independent (be able to maintain internal stability and external equilibrium) in its framework of existence. If the fundamental entity cannot learn how to do this it will perish—cease to exist and disintegrate into its component parts at a lower plane of existence. This is what happens to our bodies when we die: our physical component parts disintegrate into lower planes of existence.

Stage 2: Bonding to form a group structure

When the framework conditions of individual entities become more complex or "life" threatening,[2] the most sustainable "evolutionary" response they can make is to bond together to create a group structure. Bonding increases the resilience of all the entities which form part of the group structure through the sharing of resources. In order for this to happen, the entities that are part of the group structure must learn how to work together for the good of the whole. In other words, each entity must shift from a focus on "I" to a focus on "we" and the group structure as a whole must learn how to become internally stable and maintain a state of external equilibrium with other group structures in its framework of existence.

Once individual entities have bonded—developed a high level of internal cohesion by increasing their capacity for unified decision-making—and a group structure has formed, the ability of individual entities in the group structure to survive and prosper will depend on the ability of the group structure to survive and prosper. Every entity in the group structure must identify with the group structure and work for the common good of the group structure if the group structure is going to maintain its internal stability and external equilibrium.

Entities that fail to put the needs of the group structure ahead of their own needs, not only threaten the survival of the group structure, they also threaten their own survival and the survival of every entity that is part of the group structure.

In other words, when individual entities in a group structure focus too much on their own "self-interest" rather than the good of the whole, the viability of the group structure may be compromised. When this self-interest is left unaddressed or allowed to grow, the group structure will become increasingly dysfunctional.

This is what makes a growing cancer cell so dangerous. The cancer cell's focus on its self-interest rather than the good of the whole eventually compromises the ability of the body to maintain its internal stability.

In human group structures, the focus of individuals on their own self-interest rather than the group interest creates what is known as cultural entropy—a form of internal dysfunction where the needs of the individual take precedence over the needs of the whole. When cultural entropy reaches a critical level, the group structure loses its internal cohesion, breaks down and disintegrates into its component parts.

Stage 3: Cooperating to form a higher order entity

When the framework conditions of a group structure become more complex or "life" threatening, group structures respond by cooperating with other group structures to create a higher order entity, which increases the resilience of all the group structures and every individual entity in each group structure.

In order for this to happen every entity and every group structure in the higher order entity must work together for the good of the whole. In other words, the higher order entity must become internally stable. It must also be able to maintain a state of external equilibrium in its framework of existence if it is going to establish itself as a viable entity at a new plane of being.

Once a higher order entity has developed a high level of internal cohesion—capacity for unified decision-making—the ability of the group structures contained within it to survive and prosper, will depend on the ability of the higher order entity to survive and prosper. For example, the organs in our bodies (group structures) can only "survive and prosper" if we are able to survive and prosper.

Group structures that fail to put the needs of the higher order entity ahead of their own needs not only threaten the survival of the higher order entity, they also threaten their own survival and the survival of every other group structure that is a member of the higher order entity, as well as every individual entity in every group structure. Imagine for a moment what would happen if the organs of your body, decided to compete with each other (focus on their self-interest) rather than cooperate (focus on the good of the whole). You would soon become sick, because the internal stability of your body would be compromised.

Whenever self-interest is left unaddressed or not corrected, either at the individual or group level, the stability of the higher order entity will become compromised.

At every stage of evolution, the most successful group structures always developed high levels of internal cohesion (collective decision-making) and low levels of cultural entropy. By minimising the amount of energy they expend on maintaining internal stability, they maximise the amount of energy they have available for maintaining external equilibrium— communicating and cooperating with other group structures to increase the resilience of the whole.

Bonding and cooperation

It is interesting to note that throughout evolution, among all the different types of entities that existed at each plane of being, there was only one that became the platform for the next stage of evolution. At the atomic plane, it was the *carbon atom*. At the cellular plane, it was the *eukaryotic cell*. Now in the plane of being of creatures, it is *Homo sapiens*.

If you ask the question "What qualities do these specific entities (the carbon atom, eukaryotic cell and Homo sapiens) possess that enabled them to become the platform for the next stage of evolution?" you will begin to see a pattern. The answer to the question "What qualities do these entities share?" is quite simply, *the ability to bond and cooperate*. These abilities are the keys that make internal stability and external equilibrium possible. Without them there can be no internal cohesion.

Carbon atom

The *carbon atom* is the most stable of all elements because it has four electrons available for covalent bonding. Covalent bonding involves the *sharing* of electrons between pairs of atoms. Because of its amazing propensity for bonding, carbon was able to form durable complex molecules. Carbon is the second most abundant element in the human body after oxygen and the fourth most abundant element in the universe after hydrogen, helium and oxygen. There are more compounds of carbon than all of the other elements put together. Carbon atoms form the chemical basis of almost all forms of life known to man.

Eukaryotic cell

The eukaryotic cell differs from its evolutionary predecessor, the prokaryotic cell, because of its internal structure and its ability to form communities of shared awareness. Unlike the prokaryotic cell which has its "organelles" located in the cell membrane, the eukaryotic cell has internal "organelles" (each organelle being a specialised prokaryotic cell). This enabled the cell membrane of the eukaryotic cell to grow in size and develop more sophisticated communication systems than the prokaryotic cell. Consequently, the eukaryotic is able bond and cooperate with other eukaryotic cells to build organisms and specialised physiological structures such as muscles, bones and organs. Eukaryotic cells are the cellular basis of all life.

Homo sapiens

Homo sapiens are potentially the third link in the chain of evolution, having a greater propensity for bonding and cooperation than any other creature, including its now extinct cousins Homo erectus and Homo neanderthalensis. Scientists believe the reason Homo sapiens triumphed over all other members of the genus Homo was due to its superior intellectual powers, and more particularly, to the ability to communicate through language. Communication was the key that made bonding and cooperating possible.

Based on the theory of the universal stages of evolution we can conclude that evolution will only continue to progress if we, the members of the species known as Homo sapiens, can learn how to bond with each other to create human group structures that cooperate with each other to solve the problems of humanity.

In other words, evolution progresses not by becoming the fittest, but by becoming the most stable and most inclusive. There is a definite evolutionary advantage in being able to expand your consciousness (your sense of self or self-identity) to include others.

This idea is backed up by the latest scientific research. Using game theory, two evolutionary biology researchers found that *"evolution will punish you if you're selfish and mean. For a short time and against a specific set of opponents, some selfish organisms may come out ahead. But selfishness isn't evolutionary sustainable."*[3]

This finding has significant implications for our personal psychological evolution and the cultural evolution of the species. If we want to evolve it is vitally important that we learn how to bond and cooperate with others, not just in difficult times but also in good times. To survive and prosper, we need to focus on the interest of the group structures in which we are embedded rather than our own self-interest.

Similarly, if we want the group structures in which we are embedded to evolve, they must learn how to bond and cooperate with other group structures. We must shift from focusing on our own self-interest, to focusing on the interest of the group structures we belong to, and these group structures must shift from focusing on their self-interest to focusing on the interest of the larger common good.

This message is vitally important to all of us at this point in history because the problems of existence we are facing are global but the structures of governance we have for dealing with them are primarily national. We will not solve our problems of existence unless we put away our self-interest and focus on the good of the whole.

We need to develop a new breed of leader, one who realises that their self-interest and the self-interest of the organisations, communities and nations they lead, is wrapped up in the global interest, and that by focusing on the evolution of their own consciousness they are not only fulfilling their own potential, they are also contributing to the evolution of the consciousness of our species.

Your job, as an evolutionary coach, is to support the emergence of the concept of humanity by helping your clients accelerate their psychological development. To do this you will need to have an intimate understanding of the stages of human psychological development.

Summary

Here are the main points of this chapter:

1. Establishing internal stability and external equilibrium are the universal conditions necessary for evolutionary progress.
2. Evolution progresses not by becoming the fittest, but by becoming the most stable and most inclusive. There is a definite evolutionary advantage in being able to expand your consciousness to include others.
3. Selfishness isn't evolutionary sustainable.
4. We will not solve problems of our existence unless we put away our self-interest and focus on the good of the whole.

In the next chapter, I will describe the seven stages of human psychological development and show how they relate to the three universal stages of evolution.

Notes

1. Richard Barrett, *Love, Fear and the Destiny of Nations* (Bath: Fulfilling Books), 2011.
2. Life threatening means challenging the ability of the entity or group structure to maintain internal stability and external equilibrium.
3. Article, Nature Communications, *Evolutionary instability in zero-determinant strategies demonstrates that winning is not everything,* by Christoph Adami and Arend Hintze, published August 1st 2013. See *www.nature.com/ncomms/2013/130801/ncomms3193/pdf/ncom ms3193.pdf.* Beacon Centre for the study of evolution in action.

CHAPTER 3

UNDERSTANDING PSYCHOLOGICAL DEVELOPMENT

From a psychological perspective every person on the planet evolves and grows in the same way. We start by learning how to master our basic needs (physical and emotional), and then, depending on how successful we have been, we gradually shift our focus to learning how to master our growth needs (mental and spiritual).

Because of poverty or cultural and political circumstances, the majority of people on the planet never get to explore their growth needs. They either spend their entire lives working to survive or they live in repressive political or religious regimes that prevent people from exploring their individuality and higher order growth needs.

This is one of the major evolutionary benefits that modern economic development has brought to the world: by alleviating poverty and introducing democratic governance, we have enabled the masses to meet their basic needs and given them educational opportunities that spur them on to pursue their growth needs. Prior to this modern era, only the elites—those with wealth and societal standing—had such opportunities.

To fully embrace your growth needs you must be prepared to let go of the values and beliefs you assimilated from your parents and the culture you were brought up in that no longer serves you or does not align with who you really are. You must begin to embrace the values and beliefs that resonate with your unique self and reflect who you really are.

Before I describe the seven stages of psychological development, I think it is important to get a clear understanding of what comprises a basic need, and what comprises a growth need.

Basic needs

A *basic* need is something that is important to get, have or experience in order to feel physically and emotionally safe in your framework of existence. Abraham Maslow referred to them as "deficiency" needs. We have three sets of deficiency needs—survival and safety needs, relationship or belonging needs, and recognition and acknowledgement needs.

You feel anxious and fearful when you are unable to satisfy these needs, but once they are met, you no longer pay them much attention. The reason you feel anxious or fearful when these needs are not met is because they are intrinsic to your physiological and psychological well-being. Unless you are able to meet these needs, your ego will not be able to experience a sense of emotional internal stability and external equilibrium.

When circumstances arise that allow you to meet a deficiency need, you will feel a surge of happiness—a temporary relief from anxiety and fear. The happiness normally dissipates quickly as your mind refocuses itself on searching for opportunities to meet other deficiency needs.

If you worry a lot—if you have unresolved conscious or subconscious fears—the chances are that you will never get to focus on your growth needs. When you have unresolved conscious and subconscious fears about meeting your deficiency needs, you will always be on the lookout for threats that align with these fears.

The reason fear blocks us from focusing on our growth needs is because our minds are programmed to scan the information we receive from our senses, first for threats that align with our conscious and subconscious fears, and only after that, for opportunities to meet our growth needs. When you have a lot of anxieties and worries about satisfying your deficiency needs, your mind never gets a chance to focus on exploring opportunities to meet your growth needs.

From an evolutionary perspective this makes perfect sense; if we are not able to feed and protect ourselves—stay alive—there would not be much purpose in looking for opportunities to meet our growth needs. Our deficiency needs are always prepotent to our growth needs.

Growth needs

A *growth* need is something that enables you to feel a sense of internal alignment with who you really are; not the false self, created by the ego through your parental programming and cultural conditioning, but your unique soul self. Abraham Maslow referred to these as "being" needs: a way of being in the world, with minimal fear and anxiety that allows you to feel a sense of alignment with who you really are at the deepest level of your being.

When you are able to satisfy your *growth* needs, they do not go away, they engender deeper levels of commitment: you want the feelings you experience when you are in alignment with your soul to become a permanent way of being. The joy of alignment comes from being able to meet your soul's needs—to live a values- and purpose-driven life.

When you are in alignment with your soul, your life has both meaning and significance. Without meaning you feel like your life has little significance, and without significance you feel like your life has no meaning. The feeling of significance arises when you realise you are able to make a difference in the world—to your family, friends, colleagues, humanity or the planet. Finding meaning and making a difference are integral to satisfying your growth needs.

Maslow describes the relationship between our basic needs and growth needs in the following way:

> Man's higher nature rests on his lower nature, needing it as a foundation ... The best way to develop this higher nature is to fulfil and gratify the lower nature first.[1]

This hierarchical dependence of our higher nature on our lower nature is true for all evolution at all planes of being. Complex molecules would cease to exist if the atoms that they are composed of could not maintain their internal stability and external equilibrium; the organs in our bodies would falter if the cells they are composed of were not able to maintain their internal stability and external equilibrium. Nations would cease to exist if the cities and communities they are comprised of were not able to maintain their internal stability and external equilibrium.

This means that throughout evolution the higher is always dependent on the lower: more particularly, as Maslow so rightly points out, our ability to master the higher stages of psychological development is dependent on our ability to achieve internal stability and external equilibrium at the lower stages of development. *We have to become the masters of our basic needs before we can become the masters of our growth needs.*

From basic needs to growth needs

Once you have reached your late twenties you may begin to feel a pull towards satisfying your growth needs. Your ability to move from focusing on your basic needs to focusing on your growth needs will depend on many factors, the most important of which are as follows.

The level of psychological development of your parents

If, for whatever reason, your parents have never had the opportunity to master their deficiency needs, but you have, you may find it uncomfortable to explore your growth needs in your family environment. Your family may not understand why you want to be different or what you think is wrong with their way of being.

The level of cultural evolution of the community you belong to

If, for whatever reason, the culture of your community has not reached the equivalent of the individuation stage of psychological development, then your desire to have the freedom to explore your own values and beliefs, as well as to explore your uniqueness, may be viewed as a threat to the internal stability of your community.

The level of education you attain

Unless you engage in some form of public or private education (or international travel) that is beyond the level attained by your parents, you may not be able to surpass their level of psychological development. You will not have had the opportunity to experience what it is like living in other communities or societies with different values and beliefs: You will not know or appreciate any other way of being than the one you grew up in.

Your will power to explore your full human potential

It takes immense will power as well as courage, to explore the higher stages of psychological development if you are under pressure from your family, community or society to conform to their values and beliefs. If you proceed along the path of growth, you risk isolation and loneliness. This is particularly true for people living in authoritarian or religious regimes, and is especially true for women. Authoritarian regimes and religious cultures have great difficulty in tolerating those who pursue answers to the question who am I, and some of them do not give the same rights to women as they do to men.

Stages of psychological development

The seven stages of psychological development are shown in Figure 3.1 and Table 3.1. Starting at the bottom of Table 3.1, each stage you pass through represents a higher level of maturity. Not only do our needs change as we move from one level to the next, our values and behaviours also change. Speaking of the stages of psychological development, Dr. Alan Watkins states:

> The vertical development journey is the real journey and it can create quantum leaps in development that can immeasurably expand capacity, creativity and productivity.[2]

The first column of Table 3.1 names each stage of development; the second indicates the approximate age range when you would normally experience each stage; the third column describes the developmental task associated with each stage; the fourth describes the needs we are trying to satisfy at each stage; finally, the fifth column describes the opportunities we require from the cultures in which we are embedded to master each stage. These cultures include our family culture, workplace culture[3], our community culture[4] and our societal culture[5].

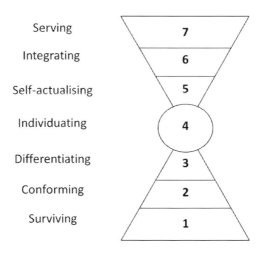

Serving — 7
Integrating — 6
Self-actualising — 5
Individuating — 4
Differentiating — 3
Conforming — 2
Surviving — 1

Figure 3.1 The seven stages of psychological development

Table 3.1 The seven stages of psychological development

Stages of psychological development	Age range of each stage of development	Overview of task	Need requirements	What we need from the cultures in which we are embedded
Serving	Late 50s to early 70s	Fulfilling your destiny by caring for the well-being of humanity or the planet.	Satisfying your need to lead a life of significance by being of service.	Opportunities to serve others or care for the well-being of Earth's life-support systems.
Integrating	Late 40s to early 60s	Aligning with others who share the same values and purpose to create a better world.	Satisfying your need to make a difference by actualising your purpose.	Opportunities to leverage your actions by aligning with others who share the same values and purpose.
Self-actualising	Late 30s to early 50s	Becoming more fully aware of who you are by leading a values- and purpose-driven life.	Satisfying your need to find meaning through activities or work you are passionate about.	Opportunities to learn and grow personally by aligning your work with your values and purpose.
Individuating	Late 20s to early 40s	Letting go of the aspects of your parental and cultural conditioning that no longer serve you.	Satisfying your need for freedom and autonomy by becoming accountable for your life.	Opportunities for adventure, and challenges that allow you to explore and hone your gifts and talents.

Differentiating	8 to early 30s	Distinguishing yourself from the crowd by honing your skills and talents.	Satisfying your need for recognition and acknowledgement for your skills and talents.	Opportunities to learn and grow professionally with feedback and coaching from people you respect.
Conforming	2 to 8 years	Keeping safe and secure by staying loyal to your family, kin and culture.	Satisfying your need for love, respect and belonging at home and work.	Opportunities to live/work in a congenial atmosphere where people respect and care about each other.
Surviving	Birth to 2 years	Staying alive and healthy in the best conditions possible.	Satisfying your physiological and nutritional needs.	Opportunities to earn income or receive benefits that are sufficient to take care of your needs.

The process of growing up takes us quite naturally through the first three stages of psychological development: from the moment we are born to the time we reach our late-20s, we pass through the surviving, conforming and differentiation stages. Depending on our experiences during these formative years, we either move naturally and easily into the individuation stage of our development or we spend a good part of the rest of our life, if not all of our life, trying to find ways to master our deficiency needs (unmet basic needs). Most educated people, brought up in democratic societies, lie somewhere between these two extremes. They are able to satisfy most of their deficiency needs but find it a struggle to move through the individuating and self-actualising stages.

If you are reading this book, you are most likely one of these people. Your parents and the culture you were brought up in probably did a reasonably good job in helping you to satisfy your basic needs, but not good enough to allow you to sail smoothly through the individuation and self-actualisation stages. You are more than likely to have learned some limiting beliefs when you were a toddler, a child or a teenager about not being able to meet your basic needs—not having enough, not being loved enough or not being good enough. Unless you learn to master these needs, later on in life you will not have a strong enough foundation from which to explore your growth needs.

As I pointed out earlier in this chapter, you must build a solid platform at each stage of development before you can establish yourself at the next higher stage of development. This means that the first work you need to do on yourself, as you reach the individuation stage of your development, is to uncover the fear-based limiting beliefs that you learned in your formative years about not being able to meet your surviving, conforming and differentiation needs and replace these limiting beliefs with positive beliefs.

This process is called personal mastery. The purpose of personal mastery is to help you reestablish internal stability and external equilibrium as quickly as possible after one of your subconscious fear-based limiting beliefs has triggered an emotional upset, and eventually to replace your fear-based beliefs with positive beliefs by establishing new neural pathways. What personal mastery helps you to do is reprogramme your mind so you can manage your emotions.

The benefits are significant. In his book called *Coherence*[6] Dr. Alan Watkins states:

> *Mismanaged emotion is "the "superhighway" to disease and distress. Your emotions not only determine whether you are likely to become ill and how happy you feel but also determine whether you will do a good job and get promoted.*

With this understanding of basic needs and growth needs we are now ready to explore the seven stages of psychological development in more detail.

Surviving

The quest for survival starts as soon as a human baby is born. The infant instinctively knows that it must establish itself as a viable entity if it is to remain in the physical world. (We will discuss where this will for survival comes from later.) At this stage, the infant is totally dependent on others to care for its needs. During the first stage of psychological development you have to establish your own sense of identity, separate from your mother, and learn how to exercise control over your environment so that you can get your survival needs met.

If the child is unable to get its survival needs met because its parents are not vigilant enough or it is abused by its parents or siblings, or left alone or abandoned for long periods of time, the child's nascent ego will very likely form subconscious fear-based beliefs that the world is an unsafe place and that other people cannot be trusted.

If, on the other hand, the child's parents are attentive to its needs, and are watchful for signs of distress, then the child will grow up with a sense of security and the feeling that others can be trusted. The feeling of being able to meet your physiological survival needs is the first and most important need of your ego-mind.

Conforming

During the next stage of psychological development, the conforming or self-protective stage, children learn that life is more pleasant and less threatening if they live in harmony with others—particularly their parents. The task at this stage of development is to learn how to feel loved and safe in your family group. Adherence to rules and rituals (conforming) becomes important because they consolidate your sense of belonging and enhance your sense of safety.

At this stage, children also learn beliefs and behaviours that allow them to maximise pleasure and minimise pain. If punishment is used to assure conformity, then the child may adopt a strategy of blaming others to avoid reprimands. If the child believes the reprimands or punishments are unjust or unfair, they may develop a rebellious streak.

If for any reason (usually because of poor parenting) you grew up feeling unloved or you don't belong, your ego may have developed subconscious fear-based beliefs that you are not lovable, not respected and the world is unfair. Later on in life you may find yourself constantly seeking affection and wanting to find a group or community that accepts you for who you are.

If, on the other hand, your parents treat you with respect and consideration, but firmly insist that you live by fair and just rules, you will grow up feeling secure. Feeling loved by others and having a sense of belonging to a group or community, is the second most important need of your ego-mind.

Differentiating

During the next stage of psychological development, the differentiation stage, children want to feel recognised for the things they do well. The task at this stage of development is to develop a healthy sense of pride in your accomplishments and a feeling of self-worth. You want to feel good about who you are by being recognised and acknowledged by your parents and peers.

Your parents are instrumental at this stage of your development for giving you the positive feedback you need. If you fail to get this feedback, you will grow up with the subconscious fear-based belief that you are not good enough. You will feel driven to prove your self-worth. You may become highly competitive, attempting to seek power, authority or status so that you can be recognised as someone important or someone to be feared.

If your ego-mind does not get the reinforcement that it needs, you could grow up with a feeling that no matter how hard you try, recognition escapes you—the successes you achieve will never be enough. Feeling a sense of self-worth or pride in your accomplishments is the third most important need of your ego-mind.

If you were able to successfully transition through these first three stages of psychological development without significant trauma and without developing too many subconscious fear-based beliefs, then you will find it relatively easy to establish yourself as a viable independent adult person in your framework of existence (able to manage your internal stability and external equilibrium), providing you have the opportunities you need to earn a living that meets your survival needs.

Individuating

During the next stage of your psychological development—the individuation stage—which normally occurs once we are adults, in the late 20s or early 30s, we begin to transcend our physical and emotional dependence on our parents and the family, community or cultural group to which we belong, and we start to learn how to release or overcome the subconscious fears we learned about not having enough of what we need to survive, not having enough of what need to feel loved or not being enough to feel good about who we are.

Unlike the previous stages of psychological development that are thrust on us as we move from being an infant to a toddler to a child and then a teenager, individuation is a subconscious choice that depends on our willingness, once we feel secure in ourselves (when we have to a large extent satisfied our survival, relationship needs and self-esteem needs), to respond to the pull we feel inside, to becoming more accountable for our emotions and more responsible for our values and beliefs.

Learning to be accountable for your emotions involves releasing or overcoming the fear-based beliefs you developed during the first three stages of your development, about being able to satisfy your survival, relationship and self-esteem needs. This may require a long-term commitment to personal mastery and reprogramming your neural pathways with new belief structures.

Learning to be responsible for your beliefs and values can be challenging, especially if you grew up in a close-knit kinship or tribal culture, or an oppressive authoritarian regime where people are either dependent on each other for survival or where the pressures to conform are large. If, on the other hand, you grew up in a liberal democratic regime with self-actualised parents who took care of your basic needs and always treated you like a young adult, by teaching you to be responsible and accountable for your life and your emotions, then you will find the process of individuation relatively easy.

Those individuals who have been brought up by self-actualised parents and live in a liberal democracy may reach the individuation stage earlier than those who did not have these benefits. This is because the parental programming they received and the cultural conditioning they experienced supported them in mastering the first three stages of their psychological development while they were young.

Once you have learned how to master your basic needs and have established yourself as a viable independent individual in a larger world than the community you were brought up in, you may, after a certain amount of time, feel a natural pull towards the next stage of your psychological development—self-actualisation.

Self-Actualising

The self-actualising stage of psychological development involves learning to align the needs of your ego with the needs of your soul and leading a values-driven and purpose-driven life free from fear.

Leading a values-driven life means letting go of the decision-making modalities of the ego (beliefs) and embracing the decision-making modalities of the soul (values). The progress you make in this regard could well dictate how quickly you are able to manifest your soul's purpose. You will need to learn to live with trust, empathy and compassion if you are going to achieve your full realisation.

Finding your soul's purpose—your calling or vocation—usually begins with a feeling of unease or boredom with the work on which you depend for your livelihood. You may find your work no longer excites or challenges you. As you begin to discover your calling, you will feel a natural pull towards a new activity or a lifetime interest that you have pushed into the background—something you love to do that when you are doing it totally absorbs your interest. Uncovering your soul's purpose—your personal mission—will bring passion and creativity back into your life and give you a deep sense of meaning and commitment.

Sometimes your soul's purpose unfolds slowly in front of you. You get a feeling or thought about a change you want to make in your life. The thought keeps coming back and won't go away. So you follow your inspiration: you do what it is you feel called to do. This leads to another thought or an opportunity: you follow that, and before too long you find yourself embarked on a journey that brings you into a state of flow: You find work that brings meaning to your life.

Finding your soul's purpose and learning to live a values-driven life represents the first level of soul activation.

Integrating

Making the shift from self-actualisation to integration involves moving from independence to interdependence. The level of fulfilment you feel as you implement this shift will depend on the quality of the connections you establish with other people and your ability to influence or impact the world around you.

The integrating stage of development involves fully activating your sense of purpose so you can make a difference in the world. As you progress down the path of making a difference, you begin to realise that the level of difference you can make could be significantly enhanced if you joined forces with other people who have a similar purpose. For this to happen, you will need to develop empathy.

The people you collaborate with will be people with whom you resonate: people who share your values and your sense purpose—people who are operating at a similar frequency of vibration and stage of development. You may also find yourself coaching those who are younger and less advanced in their development than you. You will be doing this to increase the resilience of the group you are embedded in, because everything you do will be focused on the common good.

Actualising your sense of purpose and integrating with others represents the second level of soul activation.

Serving

The last stage of psychological development involves leading a life of selfless service for the betterment of humanity and the planet. As you enter this stage, you will find yourself getting involved in actions to alleviate suffering and finding ways to preserve the world's life-support systems for future generations—embodying compassion and living sustainably in everything you do.

When you reach this stage, you may find that your job and your workplace become too small for you to fulfil your calling. You may need to find a new and larger role, and more extensive arena for your work. You may become an elder in your community; you may become a mentor to those who are facing life's challenges. You may care for the sick or dying;

or you may find ways to support children or teenagers in dealing with the difficulties of growing up.

It does not matter what you do, when you reach this stage of development your purpose will in some way be focused on helping to improve the well-being of your family, your organisation or the community and society in which you live. Deep down, you will begin to understand that we are all connected energetically, and that by serving others you are serving yourself.

Selfless service represents the third level of soul activation. You fully engage at this stage of development when you become the servant of your soul.[7] When you have mastered this stage of development, and all the previous stages, you will have reached full self-realisation.

The seven stages of psychological development occur more or less in consecutive order. You can jump a stage, but you will, at some point in time, have to come back and learn how to meet the needs of that stage before you can master the higher stages of development.

We begin our psychological journey by learning to survive, and we complete the journey by learning to serve. We start our lives in ego consciousness and if we are successful in meeting our deficiency and growth needs, we end our lives in soul consciousness.

Universal stages of evolution

One of the questions you might ask when you study the seven stages of psychological development is why does human evolution occur in this way. Why do we proceed from being dependent to independent and then interdependent. The answer is as simple as it is profound: it occurs in this way because the seven levels of psychological development align with the three universal stages of evolution described in the previous chapter.

In order to become viable and independent in your framework of existence (maintain internal stability and external equilibrium), you must be able to meet your basic needs: you must learn how to survive; you must learn how to stay safe, and you must learn how to feel good about yourself. Thus, the first three stages of psychological development correspond to the first universal stage of evolution—learning to fend for yourself (become a viable independent entity) within the community you were brought up in.

Whilst you may feel independent in the culture you were brought up in, you will not be experiencing true independence. You are still dependent on your community for your well-being, safety and self-esteem. Your beliefs are mainly those of your parents and their beliefs are mainly the beliefs of the culture they are embedded in. There is nothing truly independent about you—you are the product of your framework of existence. As long as you care about belonging and fitting in, and as long as you care about what others think about you, you cannot individuate—you cannot explore who you really are.

The second universal stage of evolution corresponds to the next two stages of psychological development—individuating and self-actualising. During these stages of psychological development the ego bonds with the soul to create a unified group structure. In other words, your false self—the ego—having mastered its basic needs, starts to align with and embrace the needs of your unique self—the soul. This is the start of true independence. You leave behind the values and beliefs of the community/society you were brought up in that don't serve you anymore. You no longer feel the need to conform, and you are no longer dependent on your parents, your peers and the authority figures in your life for your survival, safety and self-esteem. Only when you embrace your own unique calling and decide to live an authentic life by embracing your soul's values and purpose are you truly independent.

The third stage of evolution corresponds to the last two stages of psychological development—integrating and serving. During these stages of psychological development your soul learns how to cooperate with other souls who share the same purpose, so collectively you can make a bigger difference in the world. You are only able to do this if you have completely put aside your ego's self-interest and you have learned to identify yourself with the group that shares your values and purpose.

As you learn to cooperate with other people, you begin to experience a true sense of interdependence—working together for the common good. The barriers of separation begin to melt away as you unite behind a common cause. You begin to feel a sense of oneness, not just with those whom you are cooperating with, but also with those you are serving. You begin to feel a deep sense of empathy and compassion with the whole human race.

Types of mind

The seven stages of psychological development and the three universal stages of evolution, described in the previous chapter also correspond to three plateaus of adult psychological development described by Harvard researchers Robert Kegan and Lisa Laskow Lahey in their book *Immunity to Change*.[8] Kegan and Lahey call these three stages of development the socialised mind, the self-authoring mind and the self-transforming mind. These three stages of adult development correspond to the dependent mind, the independent mind, and the interdependent mind.

The major differences between the ways people with these three types of mind operate, are how they relate to the world around them, and the level of complexity of their mind function.

At the first level of complexity—the socialised mind:

> *the person … is subject to the values and expectations of his surrounds (be it is his family of origin, his religious or political reference group, or the leaders of his work setting). The perceived risks and dangers that arise for such a person have to do with being unaligned, or out of faith, with that mediating surround; being excluded from it and thereby cut off from its protections; or being evaluated poorly by those whose regard directly translates in his regard for himself.*[9]

This quote perfectly describes the dependent mind. At the next level of mental complexity—the self-authoring mind:

> *a person is able to distinguish the opinion of others (even important others) from his or her self-opinion … The ability to subordinate or relegate opinions, values, beliefs, ideas (our own or others') to a more complex system—to prioritize them, combine them, create new values or beliefs we didn't even know we had—enables us to be the author of our own reality, and look to ourselves as a source of internal authority … This new way of knowing does not remove the spectre of risk and danger … rather it changes the basis or context from which such a sense of alarm arises. Ultimate anxiety is no longer a function of being excluded … but instead may be about the threat of falling short of our own standards, of not being able to realize our agenda, and losing control.*[10]

This perfectly describes the independent mind.

> *And if one is not to be forever captive of one's own theory, system, script, framework, or ideology, one needs to develop an even more complex way of knowing—the self-transforming mind—that permits one to look at, rather than ... through, one's own framework. In such a case that framework becomes more preliminary than ultimate, more in-process than a magnum opus. This breaks through to an even bigger emotional space that can seek out the framework's current limitations rather than merely defend the current draft as a finished product and regard all suggestions to the contrary as a blow to the head.*[11]

This perfectly describes the interdependent mind. Moving from one plateau of knowing to the next, involves disturbing the balance of your life, and learning to *look at,* what before you were *looking through.*[12]

Thus the key to psychological growth is adaptation—a commitment to emergent learning—not just about understanding the world around you, but understanding how you relate to that world and how you derive meaning from your experiences: being willing to modify your world view when you come across new information and look *at* your world view as well as looking through it. This conclusion aligns with the work of other Harvard researchers.

A multi-decade study of one hundred Harvard graduates found that the most successful individuals (those who were most adept at dealing with life's challenges) were those who were able to adapt their thinking to deal with their changing life conditions.[13] Those who could not adapt suffered and found it difficult to find fulfilment.

Summary

Here are the main points of this chapter:

1. From a psychological perspective every person on the planet evolves and grows in the same way.
2. We start by focusing on our basic needs (physical and emotional), and then, depending on how successful we have been, we gradually shift our focus to our growth needs (mental and spiritual).

3. Our ability to master the higher stages of psychological development is dependent on our ability to achieve internal stability and external equilibrium at the lower stages of development.
4. We have to become the masters of our basic needs before we can become the masters of our growth needs.
5. There are seven stages of psychological development.
6. The stages of psychological development tend to occur in fixed age ranges.
7. The first three stages of psychological development are focused on meeting our basic needs.
8. The last four stages of psychological development are focused on meeting our growth needs.
9. The seven stages of psychological development align with the three universal stages of evolution and the three plateaus of adult psychological development.

In the next chapter, I will define consciousness and show how the seven stages of human psychological development align with the seven levels of human consciousness.

Notes

1. Abraham H. Maslow, *Toward a Psychology of Being* (second edition) (New York: Van Nostrand), 1968, p.173.
2. Alan Watkins, *Coherence: The Secret Science of Brilliant Leadership* (London: Kogan Page), 2014, p. 155.
3. Workplace culture: The culture of the organisation or institution where we earn a living.
4. Community culture: The culture of the ethnic or religious group we identify with.
5. Societal culture: The culture of the larger group structure (nation) in which the community we belong to and the organisation we work in is embedded.
6. Alan Watkins, *Coherence: The Secret Science of Brilliant Leadership* (London: Kogan Page), 2014, p. 79.
7. Richard Barrett, *What My Soul Told Me* (Bath: Fulfilling Books), 2012.

8. Reference Kegan and Lisa Laskow Lahey, *Immunity to Change* (Boston: Harvard Business Press), 2009.
9. Ibid. p. 52.
10. Ibid. p. 53.
11. Ibid. p. 53.
12. Ibid. p. 53.
13. George E. Vaillant, *Adaptation to Life* (Cambridge: Harvard University Press), 1977.

CHAPTER 4

UNDERSTANDING THE EVOLUTION OF CONSCIOUSNESS

Having understood how humans grow and develop from a psychological perspective we are now in a position to understand how consciousness relates to human evolution in general and psychological development in particular. We will also explore the question that philosophers have struggled with for millennia: What is consciousness?

The internationally recognised psychologist Carl Jung, writing about consciousness, states the following:

> *Without consciousness there would, practically speaking, be no world, for the world exists as such only in so far as it is consciously reflected and considered by a psyche. Consciousness is a precondition of being.*[1]

If consciousness is a precondition of being, we can define consciousness as the faculty of mind that allows us: (a) to be aware of what is happening around us and experience our feelings; and (b) to derive meaning from what is happening around us and what we are feeling, so we can make decisions about how to react or respond to changes in our environment in a manner that enables us to meet our physiological and psychological needs— to maintain or enhance our internal stability and external equilibrium. Without consciousness we would not be able to recognise either threats to our survival or opportunities for satisfying our needs.

For evolution to have progressed from the energetic plane to the plane of creatures (as shown in Table 2.1), every entity and every group structure at every plane of being had to have been able to sense changes in its internal and external environment and react or respond appropriately, so that it could continue to survive or exploit what was happening in its environment for the purpose of maintaining or enhancing its internal stability and external equilibrium. Anything that reacts to changes in its environment has to have some form of consciousness be it rudimentary and elemental in the case of atoms or complex and sophisticated in the case of human beings.

If the changes that are taking place represent a threat to an entity's or group structure's internal stability and external equilibrium, the entity or group structure has to adapt to the changes or take evasive action. If the changes represent an opportunity for increasing the entity's or group structure's internal stability and external equilibrium, it has to find ways of taking advantage of the presenting opportunities.

The same is true of human psychological evolution. In order to master each stage of development we have to be conscious of what our needs are, recognise threats in the changes that are happening around us that may prevent us from meeting these needs, and also recognise opportunities in the changes that are happening around us that may help us satisfy our needs.

If your life or livelihood is suddenly threatened or you are reminded about any unmet needs you may have from the surviving stage of psychological development, you will automatically start operating from survival consciousness. You will be looking for opportunities to satisfy either your physiological or nutritional needs.

If you find yourself alone without friends or you are reminded about any unmet needs you have from the conforming stage of psychological development, you will automatically start operating from the relationship level of consciousness. You will be looking for opportunities to satisfy your need for love, respect or belonging.

If you are unable to achieve what you want to achieve or you are reminded about any unmet needs you have from the differentiation stage of psychological development, you will automatically start operating from the self-esteem level of consciousness. You will be looking for opportunities to satisfy your need for recognition and acknowledgement.

If you reach the individuation stage of your psychological development you automatically start operating from the transformation level of consciousness. You will be looking for opportunities to satisfy your need for freedom, autonomy and becoming responsible and accountable for your life.

If you reach the self-actualisation stage of psychological development you will automatically start operating from the internal cohesion level of consciousness. You will be looking for opportunities to live your values and satisfy your need to find meaning, by finding activities or work you are passionate about.

If you reach the integration stage of psychological development you will automatically start operating from the making a difference level of consciousness. You will be looking for opportunities to satisfy your need to actualise your sense of meaning, by working with others on projects that align with your sense of purpose.

If you reach the serving stage of psychological development you will automatically start operating from the serving level of consciousness. You will be looking for opportunities to satisfy your need to lead a life of significance, through selfless service to humanity or the planet.

The motivations associated with seven the levels of human consciousness are summarised in Table 4.1. Your primary motivation will always be the need of the stage of psychological development you have reached, and your secondary motivations will always be the needs of the stages of psychological development you have passed through which you have not yet mastered.

Table 4.1 The needs associated with the seven levels of consciousness

Seven levels of consciousness	The needs we are trying to satisfy
Service	The need for selfless service
Making a difference	The need for making a difference
Internal cohesion	The need for meaning and purpose
Transformation	The need for understanding, autonomy and accountability
Self-esteem	The need for recognition and acknowledgement.
Relationships	The need for love and respect
Survival	The need for safety and security

Consciousness defined

Having established the role that consciousness plays in our lives, we can begin to define more precisely what consciousness is.

I propose to define consciousness as *awareness with a purpose:* the primary purpose of consciousness is to maintain the internal stability and external equilibrium of the entity or group structure that possesses the consciousness, so the entity or group structure can survive and thrive. This applies to all entities and all group structures on all planes of being. It also applies to each of the seven stages of psychological development.

As human beings, we maintain internal stability in three ways: our body-mind maintains internal stability through a process known as homeostasis; our ego-mind maintains internal stability through meeting its physiological and emotional needs (deficiency/basic needs); and our soul-mind maintains internal stability through knowledge, understanding and meeting its spiritual needs (being/growth needs).

When our body-mind is unable to maintain internal stability we get sick, suffer and die. When our ego-mind is unable to maintain internal stability we get upset, anxious or stressed. When our soul-mind is unable to maintain internal stability we get sad, despondent or depressed.

When our body-mind is able to maintain internal stability and external equilibrium, we feel vital, healthy and alive. When our ego-mind is able to maintain internal stability and external equilibrium, we feel happy and content. When our soul-mind is able to maintain internal stability and external equilibrium, we feel life has meaning and we experience a sense of joy and inner peace.

It follows therefore that *the key to maintaining internal stability is the ability to satisfy or master our needs at the stage of psychological development we have reached and the stages of development we have passed through, where we still have unmet needs.*

In addition, we also have to be able to remain in external equilibrium with our surrounding physical and social environment at every stage of psychological development. Any changes that disturb our external equilibrium that we believe could prevent us from meeting our needs will bring up feelings of fear, thereby disturbing our internal stability. Fear is the feeling that arises when we believe our needs will not be met.

Thus we can define fear as the *feeling that arises when the situation we are in triggers a limiting belief about our ability to meet our future needs.*

Fears (limiting beliefs) can be instinctual—that snake might kill me—a DNA encoded survival fear; subconscious and learned—I am not good enough—a self-esteem fear based on early childhood experiences; or conscious and learned—I will burn myself if I get too close to the fire.

We only return to internal stability after the energy associated with the fear we are experiencing about not getting our needs met is no longer present in our conscious mind. Every time we let fear into our minds, we disturb our internal stability; every time we remove fear from our minds, we increase our chances of experiencing internal stability and external equilibrium.

The answer to living in internal stability and external equilibrium is not to eliminate fear from our lives, only the fear that no longer serves us—the subconscious fear we learned about surviving physically and emotionally in the parental and cultural framework of existence we experienced during our formative years.

In general, we could say that our instinctual (DNA encoded) fears are good fears: we don't want to get rid of them because they help us to stay alive. We could also say some of our learned conscious fears are also good fears, such as the fear of getting burned by fire.

The fears that are bad—those that no longer serve us but disturb our internal stability—are our subconscious learned beliefs that represent the unmet needs from the first three stages of our psychological development—not having enough, not being loved enough and not being enough. When we are able to remove, overcome, master or bypass these fears by building new neural pathways, they lose their power over us. They no longer disturb our internal stability because they are no longer used as filters to scan our environment for threats.

There are two sets of circumstances that cause our minds to experience fear: (a) when you encounter a situation that *directly threatens* your ability to meet one of your deficiency/basic needs; and (b) when you encounter a situation that *triggers* a subconscious fear-based limiting belief you have about not being able to meet one of your deficiency needs.

For example, if you are at the individuation stage of psychological development and suddenly find yourself in a situation where your savings are used up and you no longer have a job your consciousness will revert to the survival level.

Similarly, if you are holding onto a subconscious fear-based limiting belief that you learned in childhood about not feeling loved or not being good enough, and you encounter a situation that triggers you (reminds you of that unmet need), you will immediately revert to the relationship or self-esteem level of consciousness.

The reason for this is that our reptilian and limbic minds/brains have been programmed to focus on what we regard as potential threats (fears) before they focus on potential opportunities. If you are holding onto any fear-based beliefs, these will be used as filters to make meaning of what is happening around you. Wherever your fears lie, your consciousness follows.

At the species level these fear-based filters (instincts) are programmed into our reptilian mind/brain by our DNA. At the human level, these fear-based filters are learned, and are programmed into our limbic mind/brain during childhood and teenage years.

When you have subconscious fear-based beliefs regarding the unmet needs of your childhood, and we all have them to some extent, you will find yourself fluctuating back and forth between the level of consciousness that corresponds to the stage of psychological development you have reached and the levels of consciousness where you still have these unmet needs.

As you make progress in mastering your fear-based beliefs or "engineering" new neural pathways, you will find yourself being triggered less and less by your subconscious fears: you will become more resilient, and more able to rebound to your normal operating level of consciousness (the stage of psychological development you have reached) more quickly. You will spend less time in internal instability and external disequilibrium.

As you progress with your psychological development, eventually, when you reach the latter part of your life, you may be able to master all your needs. This is called full-spectrum consciousness. When you operate from full spectrum consciousness you are able respond appropriately to all situations that life throws at you without fear, upset or anxiety.

The body-mind

There are two major implications that we can draw from the above. First, that wherever you have an entity or group structure that is attempting to maintain internal stability and external equilibrium, you have consciousness; second, wherever you have consciousness you have a mind.

Thus we can say that an atom, which is attempting to keep its energy field in internal stability and external equilibrium, is not only conscious, it also has a mind, and since the mind is not a physical entity, the only place the atom's mind can exist is in its energy field.

The same is true of a cell and a human body. A cell, which is made up of molecules, which are made up of atoms, has a mind, and its mind exists in the energy field of the cell. The mind of the cell manages the cell's internal stability and external equilibrium. The body, which is made up of organs, which are made of cells, which are made up of molecules, which are made up of atoms, has a mind, and its mind is comprised of the minds of all its components (atoms, molecules, cells, organs) located in the energy field of the body. Consequently, the body also has a mind. The purpose of the body-mind is to keep your body in a state of internal stability and external equilibrium (homeostasis).

As you aware, we are more than our bodies; we are bodies with a personality, and our personality also has a mind. So where is the mind of the personality? The mind of the personality is also in the energy field that surrounds the energy field of the body: The body-mind and the personality mind are interlocking energy fields.

The ego-mind and the soul-mind

The human personality is made up of two components—the ego-mind and the soul-mind. The energy field of the ego-mind surrounds the energy field of the body-mind, and is itself surrounded by the energy field of the soul-mind but separated from it by the mental field. The mental field, lying as it does between the ego-mind and the soul-mind, is the part of the mind used by the neo-cortex to rationalise and bring logic to the decisions you make.

When your fear-based beliefs are triggered and you react emotionally to a situation, your emotional field (limbic mind/brain) disturbs the etheric field (body mind/brain) causing you to react according to your conscious and subconscious beliefs. It is only later, approximately half a second later, that the mental field comes into play.

Thus the human body is surrounded by four energy fields: the etheric field—which penetrates and surrounds the human body and is home to the body-mind; the emotional field—the home of the ego-mind; the mental field—a rational, dispassionate information processing facility; the spiritual field—the home of the soul-mind. The mental field—let us call it the rational mind—is available to both the ego-mind and the soul-mind; however, the ego-mind can only access the mental field when it is calm and relaxed. When it is in a state of agitation or excitement it cannot make use of the mental field. Consequently, whenever you are upset, anxious or afraid, your ability to use your neo-cortex—your mental field—to make rational, logical decisions disappears, and you cannot connect with your soul-mind in the spiritual field.

Whereas the purpose of the conscious awareness of your body-mind is to regulate the functioning of your body, the purpose of the conscious awareness of your ego-mind is to protect itself and your body, and whatever entities it strongly identifies with, as well as seeking out opportunities to meet its needs and the needs of those with whom it identifies.

Although we may not realise it until we reach an advanced stage of psychological development, the ego is not who we are: it is the temporary agent of the soul. Its job is to learn how to keep the body safe from harm and help your soul navigate its way through the cultural and social environment of your framework of existence so the soul can fulfil its purpose. The ego is unaware of this role. The problem the ego has is that it thinks it is separate and alone. Because it identifies with the physical body, it thinks it can die. The soul, on the other hand, feels connected to everyone and everything. It exists in the quantum world of energy fields. Because it identifies with the energy field, it knows it cannot die.

The ego has three basic needs: to keep the body (and the bodies of those it cares about) safe from harm; to love and be loved, so that it can feel a sense of safety and does not feel alone in the world; and to be recognised by others for its gifts and talents so it can feel a sense of self-worth. When the ego is able to satisfy these needs it feels at ease—you feel a sense of internal stability. When the ego is unable to satisfy these needs it feels a sense of anxiety—you feel internally unstable. It is the anxieties you feel and the underlying fears that create the instability in your energy field.

The soul also has three needs: for the ego to align its beliefs and motivations with the values and motivations of the soul, so that it can fulfil its purpose in the world; to make a difference by collaborating with others who share the same values and purpose; and lead a life of selfless service for the good of humanity and the planet.

Unlike the ego, the soul does not have any anxieties about fulfilling its needs; it just waits in the background for the ego to learn how to meet its basic needs, and then individuate and self-actualise. But the soul will only wait for so long. If, by the time you reach middle age, your ego has not been able to master its needs you will begin to feel a growing sense of unease. Your energy field will become unstable. You may even become depressed. This instability arises from the lack of energetic alignment between the ego and the soul: the fears and anxieties of the ego preoccupy the mind to such an extent that the mental field is unable to focus on meeting the needs of the soul.

In *Modern Man in Search of a Soul*, Carl Jung the founder of analytical psychology expresses a similar thought:

> I have treated many hundreds of patients. Among those in the second half of their life—that is to say over thirty-five—there has not been one whose problem, in the last resort, was not that of finding a religious outlook on life.[2]

I believe, when Jung uses the word "religious" in this context he means "spiritual". In my interpretation, he is saying that the major issue in the second half of our lives is to establish a connection with our soul.

In order for your ego to bond with your soul, you must do two things: relinquish your fears and anxieties about meeting your survival, relationship and self-esteem needs, and abandon the aspects of your parental programming and cultural conditioning that do not align with the values of your soul. This is the work of the individuation stage of psychological development. Only when progress has been made on these tasks is it possible to fully explore the self-actualisation stage.

For a more complete understanding of the ego and the soul, and the interplay between them, as the soul wrestles with your ego to get your attention during the individuation and self-actualisation stages of psychological development, please refer to *What My Soul Told Me*.[3]

The seven levels of consciousness

The following text provides a brief description of the seven levels of personal consciousness associated with the seven levels of psychological development. You can use these descriptions to help you determine what stage of psychological development you and your clients have reached, and what stages of development you have passed through, where you still have unmet needs (see Chapters 9 and 10).

Level 1: Survival consciousness

The first level of personal consciousness is concerned with your body's physiological survival and your ego's self-preservation. We need clean air, food, and water to keep our bodies alive and healthy. We also need to keep ourselves safe from harm and injury and defend ourselves from physical or verbal attacks.

Whenever you feel threatened or insecure, physically or financially, you shift into survival consciousness. How you deal with survival situations, as an adult, depends on the programming and conditioning you received as a child. If you never felt abandoned and your parents did not display any anxiety about survival issues, then the chances are that your ego developed a healthy relationship to survival consciousness. In this case, you would approach survival situations from a rational perspective rather than an emotional perspective. You would respond rather than react to survival situations. You would simply get on with the actions you needed to take in order to survive without getting overly upset, anxious or fearful.

If, on the other hand, your parents ignored you when you were a child or were constantly stressed or anxious about their survival or your survival during your early years, then it is likely that whenever you feel you have been abandoned by others or encounter a survival situation, your repressed hurts and fears will be triggered, causing you to react emotionally to the situation you are experiencing rather than staying cool, calm and collected.

When you hold deep insecurities about survival or abandonment, anxiety becomes pervasive in your life. You easily get upset or angry when things get out of control. Whenever something goes wrong, you ego sees it as a personal threat. You believe you live in a hostile, uncaring world where no one can be trusted. You are always cautious or on guard; you feel that, if you don't look out for yourself then no one else will. Consequently, to feel safe, and get your needs met you must control everything around you. You plan carefully, leaving nothing to chance. If you are in charge of a team or an organisation, you micromanage those around you.

Because of your anxieties, you usually want what you want, when you want it. You will have little patience with people who are slow. As soon as you think you have the answer to a problem you are facing, you will stop listening to the opinions of others. You will be focused on your own thoughts and needs, never on the needs of others.

If you display any of these traits, then you will need to uncover and work on releasing or reprogramming your limiting survival- and safety-based fears.

Level 2: Relationship consciousness

The second level of personal consciousness is concerned with establishing and preserving relationships that engender a sense of emotional belonging. As young children, we learn very quickly that, if we don't belong, we cannot survive. We also learn that, in order to belong, we need to be loved. When you are loved unconditionally, you develop a healthy sense of relationship consciousness. You feel secure in yourself because you grew up feeling loved for who you are.

When the love you receive from your parents depends on your behaviour, you learn that love is conditional and has to be earned. When this happens, you grow up with the subconscious belief that you are not liked or not worthy of love unless you fulfil certain requirements. This programming gets hard-wired into your mind as beliefs about how to fit in, how to get love, and how to be accepted. You learn that, if you want to avoid punishment and get the love you want, you need to conform to the wills and desires of those whose love you depend on and the authority figures in your life. Consequently, your consciousness is constantly focused on looking for signs of affection, acceptance, or inclusion because, subconsciously, you want to be liked and you want to fit in.

People who suffer in this way will avoid telling the truth if they think it will any way prevent them from getting the love or acceptance they want. They will blame others to avoid facing punishment for mistakes they have made. They may even put up with verbal or physical abuse as long as they feel they have a place in the world where they belong.

The most frequent manifestation of fear-based relationship beliefs shows up in conflict avoidance and excessive harmony seeking. Conflicts are hard to deal with when you believe that speaking up could cause the other person to be angry and hold back their love. So you learn to avoid conflicts/disputes and diffuse potentially upsetting situations by changing the subject or staying neutral—never expressing what you feel. The last thing you want to do is ruffle any feathers or disturb the carefully engineered status quo. If you find it difficult to make lasting relationships, you may sometimes use humour to diffuse emotionally charged situations or as a way of getting the attention you crave.

The underlying issue in all these cases is that you were never taught how to handle the emotions of others. Consequently, you try to avoid situations where emotions are involved. You will never tell those you are close to how you are really feeling, especially your significant other: You would rather walk around on egg shells than risk all by telling your truth. If you display any of these traits, then you will need to uncover and work on releasing or reprogramming your relationship-based fears.

Level 3: Self-esteem consciousness

The third level of personal consciousness is concerned with establishing and maintaining your sense of self-worth. In order to feel good about ourselves we need to feel recognised and acknowledged by others, not just our immediate family, but also by our peers and the authority figures in our lives. You build a healthy sense of self-worth when you are young by spending quality time with your parents; being praised for your accomplishments no matter what they are, and encouraged to keep trying even when things go wrong.

People with a healthy sense of self-esteem take pride in themselves and their performance. They excel at what they do. They are reliable and responsible. Because they don't need to prove anything to themselves or others, they are good team players. They just feel good about who they are.

When you don't feel recognised or are ignored by your parents, or when acknowledgement is given only when you win, you grow up believing you need to prove to others that you are worthy of their love or attention. Such individuals seek the recognition they need through wealth, status, power or authority. They can be highly competitive and extremely focused on winning. Their self-esteem is built around their status and achievements. They need to look good and project a positive image. They want to stand out from the crowd and be noticed. They want to be the best so they can receive the recognition they were denied when they young. Taken to an extreme, they want fame and glory. They want to bask in the adulation of others.

People with a poor sense of self-worth often mask their feelings of inferiority by dropping the names of famous people they know or bump into. They do this to make you think they are well connected. They want to feel superior. If you display any of these traits, then you will need to uncover and work on releasing or reprogramming your self-esteem fears.

Mastering Your Deficiency Needs

Our minds get locked into the first three levels of personal consciousness because of the subconscious fears we have about not being able to satisfy our deficiency needs. The only way out is to become responsible and accountable for every aspect of your life, including your emotions. You must learn how to manage, master, release or reprogramme your limiting survival, relationship, and self-esteem beliefs if you are to fulfil your potential and become all you can become.

Level 4: Transformation consciousness

The fourth level of human consciousness is concerned with the search for your true identity. At this stage of development the questions you are asking yourself are "Who am I?", "Who is the 'I' that lies beyond my parental and cultural conditioning?", and "Who is the 'I' that wants to break out and be seen in the world?" Only when you answer these questions, can you discover your authentic self.

Fully expressing who you are without fear of what others may think, particularly your parents, your peers, your spouse, your children and the authority figures in your life, gives you the opportunity to make choices that are more in alignment with who you are; choices that allow you to express your unique self. The prize that comes with the pursuit of self-knowledge is freedom: the freedom to express yourself with honesty and integrity. When you discover and express who you really are, you no longer have to hide behind a façade. You will be able to march to your own tune, not the tune others have imposed on you. To find out who you are, you will want to embrace adventure; you will want to discover and hone your skills and talents: you will want to become all you can become.

The work of transformation is a lifelong process of self-discovery, and the fine-tuning of your values and beliefs. If you grew up with self-actualised parents in a liberal democracy you will already have a head start. You will have few limiting subconscious fear-based beliefs (deficiency needs) to master. You will feel free to express your true nature.

Level 5: Internal cohesion consciousness

The fifth level of human consciousness is concerned with finding meaning in your life—what you came into the world to do. At this level of consciousness, the question is no longer "Who am I?" but "Why am I here in this body, and in this situation?" For some, those who do not feel any sense of purpose, this is a daunting inquiry. For others, who are gifted with a particular talent, your purpose may seem more obvious. If you are not sure of your purpose, simply focus on what you love to do and pay attention to what is immediately in front of you. Do it to the best of your ability. Alternatively just follow your joy, develop your talents, and pursue your passion. This will lead you eventually to where you need to be to fulfil your soul's destiny.

The road to your destiny may have many twists and turns. You need to recognise that it is a journey. Many people do not find their purpose until mid-life or later. However, when they look back, they realise that all the twists and turns had a purpose—to prepare them through their experiences to give the gift they were born to give.

When you find your purpose, it may feel like something small, or it may feel like something large. Whatever it is, you need to recognise that it is what your soul came here to do, and if you follow your inspiration—the promptings of your soul—you will eventually find the sense of fulfilment you seek.

When you stay open to the influence of your soul, you will find that you are guided along the paths you need to take. When you are fully in your flow, you will find that your needs are met even before you know you have them. Life will become a journey of synchronicity; it unfolds easily in front of you. Be assured that when you commit your energy to your soul purpose, all manner of unexpected events will occur to support you on that journey.

When the needs of the soul are ignored over long periods of time, depression, sadness and frustration result. You will begin to feel uncomfortable with your life. You will feel bored. You may even feel lost. You can't explain exactly what is wrong. You just know your life feels empty and you are not fulfilling your potential.

Level 6: Making a *difference* consciousness

The sixth level of human consciousness is to make a difference in the world—in the immediate world that surrounds you, in your community or nation, or in the global society. Once you have found a purpose that gives your life meaning, you quickly learn that the difference you can make is much bigger if you collaborate with others who share a similar purpose or are aligned with your cause. This is where all the work you have done in learning how to manage, master, or release the emotions associated with your subconscious fears pays off. The more easily you are able to connect and empathise with others, the easier it is to collaborate and thereby leverage your impact in the world.

When you are a leader operating at this level of consciousness, you realise that your ability to fulfil your purpose and make a difference is conditioned by your ability to facilitate the work of those who are supporting your cause. You begin to realise that it is through others—your followers— that you make your impact on the world. You need to understand that it takes courage to be a follower, particularly an early follower. This is why you must support and nurture your followers, to help them become all they can become.

If, by the time you reach the making a difference level of consciousness, you still have emotional deficiency needs or have an exaggerated sense of your self-importance, you will give people the impression you are operating out of self-interest and they will not be drawn to you. They will keep their distance, they will be reluctant to give assistance, and you will lose your opportunity to fulfil your soul's potential.

This is why the transformation level of consciousness is so important. As you continue to uncover deeper levels of your insecurities—the fears associated with your unmet needs—you will need to return to the transformation level of consciousness to manage, master, release or reprogramme your limiting conscious and subconscious fear-based beliefs and build new neural pathways.

The focus of making a difference consciousness is on action. Finding the right avenue to express your purpose may not be straightforward. It may mean giving up a way of life that brings you comfort, stability, and certainty. It may mean moving location, giving up friends, and letting go of financial stability. It might feel very scary. But it is not something you can avoid. You will never be at ease with yourself—you will not find internal stability—if you do not follow your passion. There is no real alternative. You either follow your soul's purpose, or you spend the rest of your life living in regret.

Level 7: Service consciousness

The seventh level of human consciousness is selfless service to the cause that is the object of your soul purpose. You reach this level when making a difference becomes a way of life. You are now fully imbued with your soul purpose and living the life of a soul-infused personality. You are at ease with uncertainty and embrace whatever comes your way, without judgement. You are always looking for opportunities to grow and develop.

When you reach this stage of development you may find yourself needing time for quiet and reflection. You will be seeking the inspiration you need from your soul so you can live and breathe your purpose every moment of the day. You will know when you are operating from this level of consciousness because there will be nothing else to do. You will not want to "retire" because that would stop your life from having any meaning. There will be no division between work and the rest of your life. What you considered before as your work now becomes play.

The danger you now face is losing balance: you will want more and more of the exhilaration you feel as you experience yourself in flow. You must never forget that you have physical, emotional, mental and spiritual needs, and to experience internal stability all these needs must be met. Don't neglect yourself. Exercise regularly, eat healthy meals, have deep nurturing friendships, stay interested in current affairs, and maintain the disciplines that support your spiritual life. This is the only way you will be able to sustain working on your soul purpose over a long period of time. If you don't, you will get burned out; your body will wear out before you do.

Another danger to watch out for at this level is over committing yourself. This can also contribute to losing balance. Successful people are attractors. Everyone wants to be near them, talk to them and work with them. If you are not careful, all this attention will cause you to lose your focus. You will know when you this is happening when you are no longer enjoying yourself. The best advice I can give you is, do the things that bring you joy and design your life the way you want it.

Finally, it is important that you learn to detach from outcomes. Think about this, by setting goals, you may be limiting what you can achieve in the world. Your job at this stage of development and this level of consciousness is to surrender to the inspiration of your soul. That is how you fulfil your destiny and achieve maximum impact in the world. Your soul will never ask you to do more than you can. Your soul wants you to care for your physical, emotional, mental and spiritual needs. It needs you to live a long and healthy life so it can live out its purpose.

Full spectrum consciousness

Individuals who have learned how to master all of their needs operate from full spectrum consciousness. They display all the positive attributes of the seven levels of personal consciousness:

- They master their survival needs by staying healthy, assuring their physiological survival and their financial security and keeping safe from harm and injury.
- They master their relationship needs by building friendships and family connections that create a sense of emotional belonging based on unconditional love.
- They master their self-esteem needs by building a sense of pride in themselves and their performance and acting responsibly and reliably in everything they do.
- They master their transformation needs by having the courage to embrace their authentic selves and letting go of the fears that keep them focused on their deficiency needs.
- They master their internal cohesion needs by uncovering their soul's purpose and aligning the beliefs of their ego with the values of their soul.
- They master their making a difference needs by actualising their sense of purpose and leveraging their actions, and by collaborating

with others who have a similar purpose or are aligned with the same cause.

- They master their service needs by leading a life of selfless service for the good of humanity and the planet.

Summary

Here are the main points of this chapter:

1. Anything that has the ability to sense and react to changes in its environment is conscious.

2. The primary purpose of consciousness is to maintain the internal stability and external equilibrium of the entity that possesses the consciousness.

3. Humans maintain internal stability by learning how to master the needs of the stage of psychological development they have reached and the stages of development they have passed through, where they still have unmet needs.

4. We operate with three minds—the body-mind, the ego-mind and the soul-mind.

5. When our body-mind is no longer able to maintain internal stability we get sick, suffer and die. When our body-mind is able to maintain internal stability and external equilibrium, we feel vital, healthy and alive.

6. When our ego-mind is unable to maintain internal stability we get upset, anxious or stressed. When our ego-mind is able to maintain internal stability and external equilibrium, we feel happy and content.

7. When our soul-mind is unable to maintain internal stability we get sad, despondent or depressed. When our soul-mind is able to maintain internal stability and external equilibrium, we feel life has meaning and we experience an inner sense of joy and peace.

8. The ego has three basic needs: to keep itself and the body free from harm, to love and be loved, and to be recognised by others for its gifts and talents.

9. The soul also has three needs: for the ego to align its beliefs and motivations with the values and motivations of the soul, to make a difference in the world, and lead a life of selfless service.
10. There are seven levels of consciousness that correspond to the seven stages of psychological development.
11. Individuals who have learned how to master all their needs operate from full spectrum consciousness.

In the next chapter, I will describe the stages of evolution of the human mind/brain and the implications this has on how we make decisions.

Notes

1. Carl Jung, *The Undiscovered Self*, 1958 p. 48.
2. Carl Jung, *Modern Man in Search of a Soul*, 1933. p. 229.
3. Richard Barrett, *What My Soul Told Me* (Bath: Fulfilling Books), 2012.

CHAPTER 5

UNDERSTANDING THE EVOLUTION OF THE MIND/BRAIN

In order for consciousness to do its job—identify threats to an entity's or group structure's internal stability and external equilibrium, or opportunities to enhance an entity's or group structure's internal stability and external equilibrium—it has to be able to do four things:

- *Recognise* potential threats and opportunities when it perceives them.
- *Remember*, based on past experiences, what actions to take when faced with specific threats or opportunities it has encountered before so it can minimise the threat or maximise the opportunity.
- *Analyse* options for dealing with a potential threat or an opportunity that has never been encountered before.
- *Decide*—choose between options—figure out what to do to allow an entity or group structure to meet either its safety or growth needs.

In other words, in order to stay present in the physical world an entity must possess some form of physical "hardware"[1] for *data gathering* (sensing mechanisms), some form of "operating system"[2] for *information processing, memory making and pattern recognition*, and some form of "software"[3] for *meaning-making* and *decision-making*.

Hardware

Data Gathering is the ability of an entity to sense changes in its internal and external environment and pass this data on for information processing.

Operating system

Information processing is the ability to synthesise the streams of data gathered from the different senses into comprehensive and meaningful information packages.

Memory-making is the ability to store information packages along with the reactions and responses to these information packages that enabled the entity to maintain its internal stability and external equilibrium in the past.

Pattern recognition is the ability to identify incoming information packages and compare them to those stored in memory to find a match that would then precipitate a reaction or response that would enable the entity to maintain or enhance its internal stability and external equilibrium.

Software

Meaning-making is the ability to find matches between incoming information packages and information packages stored in memory for the purpose of understanding what is happening—to what extent the information package represents a threat to the entity's internal stability and external equilibrium or an opportunity for enhancing its internal stability and external equilibrium.

Decision-making is the ability to formulate appropriate reactions or responses to incoming information packages based on the meaning given to them: to take evasive actions if the incoming information package represents a threat, ignore or relax if the information package is neutral, or exploit the situation if the information package presents an opportunity for meeting the entity's immediate or future needs.

I call these diverse functions the six vectors of consciousness.

For evolution to have progressed, each stage of evolution required an increase in the level of sophistication of each vector. The reason for this was simple: as entities evolved, their frameworks of existence became larger and more complex, and they needed more specialised hardware, more complex operating systems and more sophisticated software to make meaning of the situations they encountered.

Based on this understanding, we can describe evolution as:

> *The ever-increasing ability of physical entities and their group structures to derive information from their environments so they can maintain or enhance their internal stability and external equilibrium in increasingly larger and more complex frameworks of existence.*

This definition of evolution could also be used as a basis for defining intelligence—*intelligence is the ability to derive information from our internal and external environment and use this information to enhance our own internal stability and external equilibrium and the internal stability and external equilibrium of the group structures to which we belong.*

On this basis, we can say that for the moment, Homo sapiens represents the pinnacle of evolution because we have proven without a doubt we are capable of mastering more complex environments than any other species or sub-species including all the extinct branches of the genus Homo.

Let us now explore how we were able to achieve this supremacy by looking at the evolution of the human mind/brain and exploring the way it operates.

The human mind/brain

In evolutionary terms, we could say that the human mind/brain is the product of approximately 500 million years of evolution.[4] It is comprised of three different physical complexes, known as the reptilian brain, the limbic brain and the neo-cortex. This trio of interwoven complexes is sometimes referred to as the triune brain.[5]

In evolutionary terms, each complex represents a significant "hardware upgrade" over previous brains. Accompanying each of these hardware upgrades were "operating system" or mind upgrades. New operating systems were necessary for two reasons: to integrate the workings of the new part of the brain with the old brain(s); and provide a higher level of functionality, more congruent with maintaining internal stability and external equilibrium at an increased scale and more complex framework of existence.

In the following text you may get the impression that I am referring to hardware, operating system and software upgrades as if they occurred in new releases at specific moments in time. This of course is a gross over-simplification of evolution. In reality, the hardware, operating system and software improvements that occurred would have emerged as incremental improvements over millions or years.[6]

Carl Jung describes the evolution of the human psyche in a similar way:

> *Every civilized human being, whatever his conscious development,*
> *is still an archaic man at the deeper levels of his psyche. Just as*
> *the human body connects us with the mammals and displays*
> *numerous relics of earlier evolutionary stages going back to even*
> *the reptilian age, so the human psyche is likewise a product of*
> *evolution which, when followed up to its origins, show countless*
> *archaic traits.*[7]

Hardware and operating system upgrades

The reptilian mind/brain

From an evolutionary standpoint the first brain to emerge was the reptilian mind/brain. It regulates our physiology—the body's vital functions such as heart rate, breathing, body temperature and balance—and is the home of our survival instincts. This type of mind/brain is found in all living creatures. The reptilian mind is closely associated with the body-mind and the etheric energy field.[8]

The principal driver of the operating system of the reptilian mind/brain is an uncompromising impulse for *self-preservation* at the individual and species level. The reptilian mind/brain scans incoming information packages for threats to its physical survival and also for opportunities to satisfy its hunger and procreation needs. It has no social impulses or motivations. Typical behaviours associated with the reptilian mind/brain are aggression, dominance, territoriality, lust and ritual displays.

The reptilian mind/brain operates exclusively at the survival level of consciousness and together with the limbic mind/brain is the main repository for our species memories. It makes meaning out of what it senses by pattern recognition based on species memories transmitted from one generation to another through DNA.

The limbic mind/brain

The second mind/brain to emerge in evolution was the limbic mind/brain. The limbic brain is built on top of and surrounds the reptilian brain and is closely associated with the ego-mind and the emotional energy field.

The limbic mind/brain is found in all mammals and regulates our affiliation instincts. Whereas neither male nor female creatures with reptilian mind/brains are involved in raising their young, male and female mammals not only raise their young but also bond with each other to form families and social networks that support group preservation. Typical behaviours associated with the limbic mind/brain are caring, nurturing, protecting, and educating.

In addition to the affiliation instinct, the other major upgrade that came with the limbic mind/brain was the drive to *seek physical and emotional pleasure and avoid physical and emotional pain.*

Whereas the reptilian mind/brain scans incoming information packages for threats to its physical survival and opportunities to satisfy its hunger and procreation needs, the limbic mind/brain scans incoming information packages for threats which could result in physical and emotional pain and opportunities that could result in physical and emotional pleasure. In other words, the limbic mind/brain focuses on its physical and emotional safety needs and the reptilian mind/brain focuses uniquely on its survival needs.

In most situations the limbic mind/brain will override the overly aggressive self-preservation, hunger and species procreation reactions of the reptilian mind/brain in order to meet the ego's social motivations. The limbic mind/brain protects others, shares food with others, and restrains from fornicating with the partners of other members of its group. This is why mammals teach their young rules to regulate their social interactions. The rules are intended to curb the instinctive reactions of the reptilian mind/brain that threaten the harmony and cohesion of the family or community on which the ego depends for its survival, relationship and self-esteem needs.

Unlike the reptilian mind/brain, which makes meaning of what it senses through pattern recognition based solely on species memories, the limbic mind/brain is able to make meaning of what it senses through species *and* personal memories—in particular the personal memories of childhood when most of the brain's neural pathways are formed.

The neo-cortex

The third mind/brain to emerge from an evolutionary standpoint was the neo-cortex. The neo-cortex physically sits on top of and surrounds the limbic brain. The neo-cortex is our rational thinking mind/brain. It is found in all higher order mammals and primates. It is most developed in the genus Homo, which appeared 2.3–2.4 million years ago. The subgenus Homo sapiens (modern man) reached anatomical maturity about 200,000 years ago and began to exhibit full behavioural maturity around 50,000 years ago.

Because of the limited size of the human birth canal, the neo-cortex is not fully formed when we are born. In fact, it is not until we reach the age of seven or eight that we have a fully functioning human brain. This means that the first neural pathways to be built in the neo-cortex are those that depend on the reptilian and limbic minds' interpretation of our ability to meet our survival and relationship needs during the surviving and conforming stages of our psychological development.

The principal function of the neo-cortex mind/brain in the human adult is to support us in our *search for meaning*. This happens at two levels: meaning, as in understanding what is happening in the world around us, so we can decide what to do to best meet our ego's survival, relationship and self-esteem needs; and meaning, as in understanding our life purpose, so we can satisfy our soul's internal cohesion, making a difference and service needs. The neo-cortex is therefore the servant of both the ego-mind and the soul-mind.

The principal function of the neo-cortex is to scan incoming information packages from our senses for logical consistency and clarity. It automatically alerts us (grabs our attention) when it senses changes in our framework of existence that deviate from normal and in situations that are unusual. The neo-cortex, which is associated with the mental energy field, also helps us to determine how we can best respond to changes in our environment or unusual situations so we can continue to meet our deficiency needs and explore opportunities for increasing our internal stability and external equilibrium at the level of psychological development we have reached.

Compared with the reptilian and limbic mind/brains, which react instinctively to situations, the neo-cortex operates more slowly, but more accurately.[9] It does not use pattern recognition to create meaning: rather, it uses data, facts and beliefs to works things out in a logical manner. It reflects, calculates, reasons and uses logic to find meaning.

Once the neo-cortex has helped us to figure out what is happening in our environment and how the changes it has noticed may affect us or afford us opportunities, we then use the mental faculties of the neo-cortex to make decisions about how we can best meet our needs in the prevailing circumstances.

In evolutionary terms, pattern recognition which is used by the reptilian and limbic mind/brains is a perfect survival mechanism because it operates almost instantaneously. The reptilian and limbic mind/brain complexes enable you to react to threats or opportunities well before your neo-cortex has had time to understand what is happening and how to respond.

There is one big problem with pattern recognition: it is not very accurate. Immediately your reptilian and limbic mind/brains recognise a few data points it fills in the blanks with assumptions based on your beliefs.

Beliefs are simply well-worn neural pathways. When limiting fear-based subconscious beliefs are used to fill in the blanks, you risk reacting inappropriately to whatever is happening, because your reptilian and limbic mind/brains are filling in the blanks and jumping to conclusions.

More often than not your reactions will be based on emotionally charged conscious or subconscious beliefs formed before the age of eight, when you were laying down your first neural pathways. This was a time when you were least able to defend yourself and negotiate with your parents to get your needs met. Unless you do something to correct the limiting beliefs you learned while your neo-cortex was still growing, you will find them showing up in your adult life as the neural pathways that condition your fast thinking. These beliefs, formed in childhood, may no longer be appropriate when you become an adult. They can easily lead to misinterpretations and misunderstandings.

Fast thinking

Pattern recognition, as practised by our reptilian and limbic mind/brains is the cause of our fast thinking—thinking that our conscious mind (the neo-cortex) is not even aware of.

Fast thinking is helpful if you are living in dangerous situations where your survival is constantly threatened (in a battle field or living in the jungle), but in everyday modern life, with all its complexities, jumping to conclusions can get you into a lot of trouble and undermine your chances of survival. Here is an example of how our fast thinking jumps to conclusions. Study the following text for a few seconds and then read it.

7H15 M3554G3

53RV35 7O PR0V3

HOW OUR M1ND5 C4N

DO 4M4Z1NG 7HING5!

1MPR3551V3 7HINGS!

IN 7H3 B3G1NN1NG

17 WA5 H4RD BU7

NOW, ON 7H15 LIN3

YOUR M1ND 1S

R34D1NG 17

4U70M471C4LLY

W17H OU7 3V3N

7H1NK1NG 4BOU7 17

In this example, we have nothing to lose. Whether we can read this or not will not undermine our chances of survival.

> *Jumping to conclusions is efficient if the conclusions are likely to be correct and the costs of an occasional mistake acceptable, and if the jump saves much time and effort. Jumping to conclusions is risky when the situation is unfamiliar, the stakes are high, and there is no time to collect more information.*[10]

This is why the neo-cortex is so appropriate for our modern times: It helps us to navigate through the complexity of our modern world more accurately than the reptilian and limbic mind/brains. However, this advantage can only be realised if you are able to move beyond the fear-based programming that occurred when you were young, because the limiting beliefs you learned at that time are the neural pathways that condition your fast thinking. Whenever your limiting fear-based beliefs trigger an emotional reaction, the neo-cortex cannot be accessed. We cannot bring reason to bear on a situation when we are in the midst of an emotional upset. We become *unreasonable* because we lose our ability to reason. Only when the fear-based reaction has subsided and the emotions dissipated are we able to access our neo-cortex again.

Dr. Alan Watkins describes fast thinking in the following way:

> *In that half second [between sensing a threat and thinking] our physiology has changed; the emotion emerged and whether we were aware of that emotion as a feeling or not it has already initiated a response that the neo-cortex is not yet even aware of. This biological phenomena means we are all living half a second behind reality, and also explains why feeling dominates thinking and not the other way round. Feeling is faster than thought and sets the context in which thoughts even occur. ... Thoughts wouldn't have emerged had our physiology and emotion not changed first.*[11]

Slow thinking

Slow thinking comes in two "flavors": ego-driven slow thinking and soul-driven slow thinking. In ego-driven slow thinking, we use our conscious *beliefs to* decide what actions to take to deal with a threat or exploit an opportunity for meeting our needs. We do what we *think* is required to meet our needs. In soul-driven slow thinking, we use our positive *values* to decide what actions to take to deal with a threat or exploit an opportunity for meeting our needs. We do what we *feel* is required to meet our needs.

Whenever you make a difficult decision it is always worthwhile asking yourself, does the decision you have reached make you feel good inside or does it make you feel uneasy—does it leave you with some level of internal instability. If the actions you came up with based on your ego's beliefs do not align with the values of your soul, then you will feel internally unstable.

You have two choices in such a situation: you can ignore how your decision makes you feel and go ahead with your plan of action based on your beliefs or you can reevaluate your decision about what actions to take based on your values and choose to focus on your soul's needs.

Needless to say, soul-driven slow thinking only begins to occur when we have reached the higher stages of psychological development. Whilst we are still operating at the surviving, conforming, differentiating stages of development and the early stages of individuating our decision-making is usually a prisoner to our beliefs. Only when you begin to make progress at the individuating and self-actualisation stages of your development, do your deeply held values begin to take precedence over your beliefs in the decision-making arena.

Values versus beliefs

Values-based decision-making is well suited to our complex modern world. The reason for this is that belief-based decision-making is based on information from the past which we use to decide on our future. This is all well and fine in a stable, non-evolving world, where what happened in a previous time period is a good predictor of what will happen in a future time period. But this is not the situation we are living in.

We are living in a world that appears to get more complex by the day. In such a situation, decisions based on information from the past are not a good predictor of the future. The only other guidance system we have, if we cannot trust our beliefs, is our values. Values enable us to make decisions that feel right. Such decisions are in alignment with the needs of our souls.

Chapter 7, which explores the six evolutionary modes of decision-making, describes in detail the differences between belief-based and values-based decision-making. Needless to say, you can only make values-based decisions if you know what your values are. Hence the reason for including the values exercises contained in Part II.

The rule of thumb is this: If you are operating from the first three or four stages of psychological development, you will more than likely make a decision that aligns with the beliefs of your ego. As you shift from the individuation stage of development to the self-actualisation stage of development you will increasingly use your values to make decisions. Eventually, values-based decision-making will become automatic. You may still use your beliefs to understand the implications of the situation you are in, but you will naturally use your values to decide what to do. Using our values to make decisions is how we maintain internal stability at the soul level of consciousness.

> We should not pretend to understand the world only by the intellect; we apprehend it just as much by feeling. Therefore, the judgment of the intellect is, at best, only the half of truth, and must, if it be honest, also come to an understanding of its inadequacy.[12]

Just as the limbic mind/brain enables us to override the primal reactions of the reptilian mind/brain so we can increase our ability to survive in a social context, the neo-cortex enables us to override the ego-driven reactions of the limbic mind/brain so we can increase our ability, if we so choose, to live in soul consciousness. However, we can only do this if we insert a pause between the events that trigger our emotions and our reactions to those events. The pause gives us a space to reflect and bring the logic of our neo-cortex into service. Whether we then use our beliefs or our values to drive the thinking of the neo-cortex, depends on which stage of development we have reached.

Software upgrades

In summary, we can say that the evolutionary hardware and operating system upgrades that have occurred to the mind/brain complex during the past 2.3–2.4 million years reached their culmination with the arrival of Homo sapiens about 200,000 years ago. Since that time, evolution has continued to advance, not through hardware and operating system upgrades but through individual and collective *software* upgrades.

Software upgrades at the individual level occur at each stage of our psychological development and are reflected in the shift in focus of our needs and values. The most significant shift occurs during the individuation stage of development, when we begin to move from belief-based, ego-driven decision-making to values-based, soul-driven decision-making—the shift from the satisfaction of our basic needs to the satisfaction of our growth needs.

Up until about one hundred years ago the possibility of experiencing all individual software upgrades in a lifetime (full psychological development) was the purview of the rich or religious elites. Nowadays, anyone living in a liberal democracy with a good education and a reasonable income that allows them to take care of their basic needs can experience all the individual software upgrades in a single lifetime. The achievement of full spectrum consciousness is now more available to the masses than at any other time in history.

Software upgrades at the collective level occur at each stage of our cultural development and are reflected in our changing world views. Since the time of our hunter/gatherer ancestors there have been six world view upgrades and a seventh is now unfolding. Five of these world views are actively present in various societies and communities around the world; the sixth world view is finding a strong foothold in some of the most democratically advanced nations; the seventh is just unfolding among the thought leaders of our age who are wrestling with the global problems of existence that our species is now experiencing. A description of all these cultural world views can be found in the following chapter.

Summary

Here are the main points of this chapter:

1. There are six vectors of consciousness.
2. For evolution to have progressed, each stage of evolution required an increase in the level of sophistication of each vector.

3. Evolution is the ever-increasing ability of physical entities and their group structures to derive information from their environments so they can maintain or enhance their internal stability and external equilibrium in increasingly larger and more complex frameworks of existence.
4. The human mind/brain is made up of three physical complexes— the reptilian mind/brain, the limbic mind/brain and the neo-cortex mind/brain.
5. The reptilian and limbic mind/brains are capable of fast thinking (instantaneous reactions).
6. The neo-cortex is only capable of slow thinking.
7. The limbic mind/brain is capable of overriding the reactions of the reptilian mind/brain.
8. The neo-cortex is capable of overriding the reactions of the limbic mind/brain after an emotional upset has ceased.

In the next chapter, I will describe the stages of evolution of our collective human world views and how these world views impact our psychological development.

Notes

1. I have borrowed the term "hardware" from computer technology. In this instance it is meant to indicate the human brain and the physical senses that enable decision-making.
2. This term is also borrowed from computer technology. In this instance, the term "operating system" refers to the protocols that link the mind/brain to the parts of the body that it has under its control. A computer operating system manages the way the different pieces of the computer work together and control the computer peripherals such as printers, scanners and facsimile machines.
3. This term refers to the programming instructions (beliefs and values) that cause feelings, emotions, thoughts and motivations to arise in the human mind/brain. These impact the physiology of the human body through the operating system.

4. Approximately from the time of the emergence of the first arthropods—invertebrate animals such as insects having an external skeleton, a segmented body, jointed appendages.

5. A term coined by the American physician and neuroscientist, Paul D. MacLean in the 1960s. Whilst the triune brain model is useful in that it brings simplicity to complexity, modern science and particularly neuroscience is teaching us that this strict division of hierarchical brain function should not be taken too literally. What we can say, is that some structures of the brain are older than others, and the newer parts are designed to support creatures living in increasingly complex life conditions.

6. For example, the first brain (reptilian) formed over 500 million years ago: the limbic brain (present in all mammals) emerged about 130 million years ago, and the proto-type of the neo-cortex (present in all hominids) emerged about 10 million ago. The neo-cortex continued to grow in size up to about 200,000 years ago when the modern human brain emerged.

7. Carl Jung, *Modern Man in Search of a Soul*, 1933, p. 126.

8. The reptilian mind fulfils similar functions to the body-mind.

9. For more information on the speed of thinking please consult: Daniel Kahneman, *Thinking Fast and Slow*, (London: Penguin), 2011.

10. Daniel Kahneman, *Thinking Fast and Slow* (London: Penguin), 2011. p. 79.

11. Alan Watkins, *Coherence: The Secret Science of Brilliant Leadership* (London: Kogan Page), 2014, p. 105.

12. Carl Jung, *The Undiscovered Self*, 1958, p. 628.

CHAPTER 6

UNDERSTANDING
CULTURAL EVOLUTION

During the early years of our lives, while we are passing through the surviving, conforming and differentiating stages of our psychological development, we have to do two important tasks: develop a sense of self—an image of who we believe we are, and build our story—establish a set of beliefs that we can use to explain how the world around us operates. The image we create becomes our identity and the story we tell becomes our cosmology.

Our identity and our cosmology are conditioned by two factors: our parents, and the culture of the community/society in which we live. By the time we become young adults, who we think we are is a complex mixture of our own unique character overlaid by layers of beliefs we have learned about ourselves from our parents, other close family members, and the community/society in which we are embedded.

If parental programming[1] and cultural conditioning[2] was all there was to our character and story, then all children born into the same family in the same community and the same society would turn out the same. But this is not the case.

You don't have to reflect for long before you realise that as far as our characters are concerned, we are all born different. We come into this physical life with inbuilt preferences, qualities, gifts and talents. You just have to observe how different siblings can be to know this is true. These differences are apparent even at a very young age. There is no scientific explanation for this: All we know is that every one of us is unique, special and different.

The parental programming and cultural conditioning we experience can either suppress our uniqueness, in which case we develop a false sense of our self, or can support us in discovering our uniqueness.

This is what evolutionary coaching is about—helping your clients examine and, as necessary, remove or reduce the layers of parental programming and cultural conditioning that have led to the creation of their false sense of self (the ego), so they can uncover and examine and explore their unique sense of self (the soul).

In other words, evolutionary coaching is about helping people find out who they really are and become all they can become—helping them to individuate and self-actualise—so they can be truly independent unique human beings and live the life their souls intended.

Cultural conditioning

There are two aspects to cultural conditioning: the internal aspect—the world view we adopt (the beliefs and prominent values of the culture we live in), which tells us how to manage our internal stability and external equilibrium in the community or society to which we belong; and the external aspect—the ethnic artefacts of the culture—the language, the dress, the rituals and the religion of the community or society to which we belong.

Although there are thousands of ethnic cultures in the world, there are only a limited number of world views. The diversity of ethnic cultures is clearly evidenced by the multiplicity of languages, dress codes and cultural norms displayed by the peoples of Sub-Saharan Africa, who despite their ethnic differences embrace the same tribal world view. This is also true of the western world, where many different ethnic cultures embrace the same capitalist/democratic world view.

The world view we adopt influences the beliefs and values we use when making decisions, and the artefacts and rituals we adopt, influence our behaviours and our sense of identity. Neither the world view nor the identity we adopt is who we really are. It is just who we believe we are based on the conditioning we receive and the circumstances of our birth. If the level of conditioning is extremely strong it can prevent us from finding our uniqueness.

Cultural evolution framework

The framework of the evolution of world views I am about to describe is based on the pioneering work of Clare Graves (1914–1986). Graves' theory was originally known as The Emergent Cyclical Levels of Existence Theory. It is now popularly known as Spiral Dynamics.[3]

Graves research was motivated by his desire to create a theory that would reconcile the various approaches to understanding human nature and questions about psychological maturity that existed in the middle of twentieth century. He saw the evolution of collective world views in the same way that Kegan sees the stages of adult development—as a series of emergent plateaus interspersed with periods of change.

According to Graves, cultural evolution can be regarded as a never ending spiral of accommodation between our evolving beliefs and values (world views), and the problems of existence that our beliefs and values create. We can either advance or regress in our world views, depending on the life conditions we are experiencing.

As one might expect, the stages of psychological development and the evolution of world views are not only related, they interact with each other. When people experience a significant change in their life conditions, a new world view can emerge which supports a new stage of psychological development. It also works in reverse: when a critical mass of people reach a new stage of psychological development, a new world view can emerge which creates a new set of life conditions.

Implementing the new life conditions can pose significant problems because in its initial stages the proponents of new world view must dismantle the artefacts (structures, hierarchies, rules and laws) of the old view before they can build the new artefacts reflecting the new values. In other words, structural realignment must accompany values realignment.

The correlation between new stages of psychological development and new world views is not always one-on-one. Sometimes several changes in world views are needed for a critical mass of people to experience a new stage of psychological development, and sometimes a single change in world view can open up opportunities for multiple stages of psychological development. In other words, the world view of the culture someone is brought up in can either support or inhibit their psychological development. As an evolutionary coach, this is important for you to know. I will show at the end of this chapter which world views support which stages of psychological development, and which world views block which stages of psychological development.

The evolution of world views

The survival world view

The first world view that Graves identified is referred to in Spiral Dynamics terminology by the colour beige. This world view was prevalent among our earliest ancestors. The survivalist world view represents how hunter gatherers viewed the world. People operating from this world lived in bands and had few possessions. The only people left in the world operating from this world view live in the remote jungle territories of the Amazon and Papua New Guinea.

The tribal world view

The second world view to emerge is referred to in Spiral Dynamics terminology by the colour purple. This world view began to emerge when bands of hunter gatherers settled in tribes and began cultivating crops and keeping herds of animals. The tribal world view is less concerned with survival and more concerned with safety and protection. People operating from this world view give great importance to belonging to the tribe. For them, the tribe is more important than the individual. The resilience of the tribe depends on people conforming to the rules of the tribe. People who are unwilling to conform are cast out or excommunicated.

The reason people are loyal to the tribe is because their safety depends on it. Everything that is owned by the tribe belongs to the tribe. Members of the tribe are not allowed to stand out or be different; their individuality is held in restraint by the culture. In other words, in this type of culture the possibilities of exploring the differentiation stage of psychological development are extremely limited.

Up to this point, there is a clear correspondence between the first two stages of psychological development and the first two world views. The first stage of psychological development and the first-world view are both concerned with survival. The second stage of psychological development and the second world view are both concerned with conforming: Not conforming for the sake of getting along, but conforming for the purpose of belonging. It is vitally important for our development to feel part of a group where we can feel safe and experience psychological security.

We find the tribal world view in groups that share a common heritage or identity, and bond together to protect or differentiate themselves from other groups. Such groups usually have rituals of membership and rules of behaviour that must be adhered to. Your "pedigree"—who your ancestors were—determines whether you are granted admission to the group.

The power world view

The third world view to emerge is referred to in Spiral Dynamics by the colour red. This world view began to appear around 9,000 years ago at the time of the creation of city-states. The red world view is one of chiefdoms, power and empire building. It can be characterised by the statement "the more power I have the more respect I will get". People operating from this world view stand tall, call the shots and demand loyalty; they have no sense of guilt. This world view allowed the elites and their close supporters to experience differentiation—something that had been frowned upon in the tribal world view.

The problem with this world view was that no leader was safe. There was intrigue and plotting everywhere. You could not trust anyone, not even the members of your inner circle. As a leader, you had always to be alert to threats and dangers from potential competitors. The only way to stay on top was to rule by fear. You had to remove, annihilate or be extremely wary of those around you who you could not absolutely trust, and you had to distribute the spoils of your empire building with your lieutenants in order to keep their allegiance.

This world view precipitated constant changes in governance, because allegiances were always changing. Only the most powerful, the most fear-inducing and the most scheming survived.

We find the modern-day equivalent of this world view in the mafia, street gangs and drug barons. We also see it in any group or community that is led by a "big man" who rules by fear. You can recognise a big man because he wants what he wants when he wants it, and you had better beware for your life if you cannot deliver.

The authority world view

The fourth world view to emerge is referred to in Spiral Dynamics by the colour blue. It brought a sense of order and safety to the chaos created by the power world view by creating hierarchies of authority. This world view began to appear about 5,000 years ago.

The impulsiveness of the power world view was brought under control in the authority world view by the establishment of rules and laws that everyone, even the elites, were obliged to obey. However, by modern day standards, the punishments were severe: you could be hanged for stealing a sheep and have a hand removed for picking a pocket.

Where there was chaos, there was now order and a simplistic form of justice. Everyone had their place in society. The stability the authority world view meant there was far less fear in the world. The masses, in theory, now had an avenue to appeal against the injustice of the elites.

In modern times, we find the authority world view in group structures that are governed though hierarchies—the civil service, the military, organised religions, and certain schools and universities. In this world view you advance your position through, sacrifice, self-discipline and loyalty. Higher positions, awards and decorations are reserved for those who have given the longest service.

The authority world view brought order and hierarchy to the world through the establishment of rules based on moral authority. Whereas in the power world view leaders did what they wanted, now they were required to submit themselves to rules, laws and the will of a God.

The status world view

The fifth world view to emerge is referred to in Spiral Dynamics by the colour orange. This world view began to appear about 1,000 years ago. The status world view gradually opened up the possibility of differentiation to everyone who was prepared to study and engage in hard work.

The status world view began to gain acceptance when the scientific interpretation of the world gained more acceptance than the religious interpretation. First knowledge and then wealth became the determinants of status. It did not matter what age you were, you could gain respect through your achievements. The more you achieved the more respect you gained in the eyes of society. The keys that opened the door to recognition in the status world view were education and the possession of unique, qualities, gifts or talents that could be used to add economic value to society. What mattered now was not how righteous you were but how rich and famous you were.

The status world view gave people the opportunity to become the masters of their own future, but it created increasing levels of inequality and led to the exploitation of the global commons for private self-interest. Economic development paid little attention to preserving Earth's life-support systems and the needs of future generations. In the status world view, people and ethical and moral principles tended to get pushed into the background; winning was more important.

This was the last world view that focused on differentiation. In this world view everyone could find recognition. All you had to do was to develop your skills and talents, and become responsible and accountable for your life. This world view created the ground conditions that would allow the masses to individuate and self-actualise.

The people world view

The sixth world view to emerge is referred to in Spiral Dynamics by the colour green. This world view began to assume importance towards the end of the nineteenth century. In this world view, everyone is treated with respect because everyone is considered equal. No one is considered inferior or superior: everyone is allowed to have their own beliefs and values as long as they do not undermine or compromise the needs of the group (the common good). Indigenous communities and aboriginal populations that had been dominated, exploited and cheated out of their territories under the previous world views began to have their rights returned.

This was also the era of the adoption of democratic principles. In this world view, we all have a voice in how we are governed. In theory, no one is left behind. The poor and disadvantaged are cared for by taxing the rich. This world view has contributed greatly to the reduction of fear in society.

Although many societies have accepted living by democratic principles, few fully reflect the people world view. Most so-called democracies are in effect pseudo-democracies because those in charge mostly operate from the power, authority or status world view. Consequently, not everyone is treated equally and not all values and beliefs are tolerated, especially if they run counter to the values and beliefs of the "elected" leaders.

The potential downside of the people world view is its extreme focus on equality. As a consequence, groups that operate from the people world view can become overly participative, leading to consensus management that slows down the process of decision-making and leads to ineffective compromises. A few people in the group who are operating from the power or authority world views can easily undermine or disrupt the smooth operation of groups operating from the people world view.

Because the people world view gives emphasis to freedom and equality, it strongly supports the individuation and self-actualisation stages of psychological development.

The integrative world view

The seventh world view which is now in the early stages of emergence represents a major shift in world views. It is known in Spiral Dynamics as the yellow world view. It began to appear about 50 years ago.

The yellow world view sees the problems of existence through a systems perspective. It approaches issues in a pragmatic way. The focus is on competence and what works. Power, authority and status are not considered important in the integrative world views.

Unlike the previous world views, the integrative world view sees societal development from an evolutionary perspective. People with this world view are able to look at their world view alongside other world views. They see their world view as a work in progress. They are willing to adopt approaches from other world views to solving problems if these world views provide practical solutions, something earlier world views found it difficult to do.

The integrative world view closely aligns with the stage of adult development that Kegan refers to as the self-transforming mind. We find this world view among some of our more prominent business leaders, especially those who are embracing the concept conscious capitalism. Respect in this world view is earned not from age, status, authority or power but from competence.

The integrative world view allows people to express who they are but never at the expense of others. People operating from the integrative world view feel they cannot be successful if the group they identify with is not successful. This is the first world view to truly embody an awareness of the bigger picture in positioning our own needs.

In the integrative world view chaos and change are seen as natural, and difficulties are regarded as opportunities for learning, rather than problems to be solved. People with this world view may be anxious about the future but they are not fearful.

I believe this world view will lead to a new form of democracy which is not dominated by power and status hungry elites that run our political parties, but by people working together collaboratively to find solutions which truly focus on the good of the whole. Decision-making will be decentralised to local self-organising communities.

The holistic world view

The eighth world view to emerge is referred to in Spiral Dynamics by the colour turquoise. We catch glimpses of this world view in the writings of modern philosophers, and ecological groups that are looking for ways to improve the health of our planet and provide a sustainable future for mankind. People with this world view look for patterns in the chaos to help them make decisions. They consider the long-term effects of their decisions and the impacts they may have on future generations. Only a small fraction of the global population operates with this world view.

The deeper mental and spiritual capacities are awakened in this world view. People are able to call on their intuition and inspiration to understand and resolve the issues they are facing. This leads to an expansiveness of thinking that goes beyond all previous world views. People operating with this world view see the embedded nature of things: they see individuals embedded in families, which in turn are embedded in communities.

They see communities and organisations embedded in nations, which in turn are embedded in the living organism we call Earth. They see the interconnectedness of all things. They look at the world and see the interplay of forces and energies. They understand how all the other world views operate.

World views and stages of psychological development

Table 6.1 shows a possible correlation between the universal stages of evolution, stages of psychological development and world views. Let me stress that this mapping is approximate. However, I believe it is sufficiently accurate for the purpose in hand—evaluating the extent to which a particular world view can support or hinder a particular stage of psychological development.

Table 6.1 Universal stages of evolution, stages of psychological development and world views.

Universal stages of evolution	Stages of psychological development	World views
Cooperating to form a higher order entity	Serving	Holistic
	Integrating	Integrative
Bonding to form a group structure	Self-actualising	People
	Individuating	
Becoming viable and independent	Differentiating	Status
		Authority
		Power
	Conforming	Tribal
	Surviving	Survival

I would like to make the following comments on Table 6.1.

First, whereas it took three shifts of world views (power, authority and status) to gradually open up the possibility of the differentiation stage of psychological development to the masses, it took only one shift of world view (from status to people) to open up the possibility of the masses experiencing the individuation and self-actualisation stages of psychological development.

Second, whereas there are no societies operating with the integrative world view, some communities are beginning to experiment with this world view. This is something we can expect to see emerging in the communities of the most advanced democratic nations in the next few decades.

Third, the bonding that takes place in the tribal world view is different from the bonding that takes place in the people world view. Bonding in the tribal level world view is exclusive; it happens only in groups that share the same ethnicity or heritage. People of different ethnicities or with a different heritage are excluded from the group. Bonding in the people world view is inclusive; everyone in the same community and society, including people of different ethnicities is included as part of the group.

Fourth, viewed in its entirety, the framework of collective human emergence described above contains some evolutionary patterns. Each world view is progressively more inclusive: the criteria for community or society membership become less focused on ethnicity and religion and more focused on character or competence. Each world view progressively reduces the level of cultural fear and reflects a higher stage of psychological development and higher level of consciousness.

This finding is confirmed by my own research. In *Love, Fear and the Destiny of Nations* I show that there is a strong link between the level of cultural fear in a nation and the level of democracy (as measured by the Economic Intelligence Unit's Democracy Index).[4] As the level of democracy increases, the level of cultural fear decreases: and as fear decreases, the levels of equality and trust increase.[5]

Also, in *The Values-Driven Organisation* I show that the level of cultural entropy (impact of fear-based behaviours) reduces as organisations embrace the values associated with the higher stages of psychological development.

The shift in world views is now accelerating at a rapid pace. Whereas previously it took several millennia, and then centuries for new world views to appear, when the conditions are right (basic needs met and democracy established) new world views are now emerging in just a few decades. The impact of this is that consciousness can evolve at a faster pace than ever before in human history because the barriers to psychological development have been removed.

As more and more communities or societies are able to meet the basic needs of their people, more and more people in those communities or societies feel called to move from the differentiation stage of their psychological development to the individuation stage. This in turn creates pressures to implement democratic governance. Once democratic governance and principles are well established, people no longer experience the cultural fears that prevented them from individuating and self-actualising.

Summary

Here are the main points of this chapter:

1. Cultural evolution can be regarded as a never ending spiral of accommodation between our evolving beliefs and values (world views), and the problems of existence that our beliefs and values create.
2. The evolution of world views can interact with the stages of psychological development to support or inhibit human emergence.
3. The correlation between the stages of psychological development and the evolution of world views is not always one-to-one.
4. Sometimes a single change in world view can open up opportunities for multiple stages of psychological development.
5. Sometimes it takes multiple changes of world views to facilitate one stage of psychological development which is available to all.
6. Although there are thousands of ethnic cultures in the world, there are only a limited number of world views. To date, Homo sapiens have experienced the emergence of eight world views.

In the next chapter, I will describe the six modes of decision-making, how they evolved and the relationship between modes of decision-making and the stages of psychological development.

Notes

1. Parental programming: We all receive conscious and subconscious messages from our parents in the early years of our lives about our strengths and weaknesses, and how we should behave in order to

fit into the family environment. The beliefs we learn in our family environment are what I am referring to as parental programming.

2. Cultural conditioning: In addition to the beliefs we learn about who we are and how to fit into our family setting, we also learn beliefs about who we are and how to fit into the culture in which our family is embedded. The beliefs we learn in this larger environment are what I am referring to as cultural conditioning.

3. The name Spiral Dynamics was created by Don Beck and Christopher Cowan, who were students of Graves. After Graves died, Beck and Cowan continued to develop the concept of Spiral Dynamics and assigned colours to each of the world views. For more information see, Beck and Cowan, *Spiral Dynamics* (Malden: Blackwell), 1996.

4. Richard Barrett, *Love, Fear and the Destiny of Nations* (Bath: Fulfilling Books), 2011, p. 157.

5. Ibid. p. 241.

CHAPTER 7

UNDERSTANDING THE EVOLUTION OF DECISION-MAKING

One of the subtle but more important changes that occur as we move through the seven stages of psychological development is how we make decisions. The predominant mode of decision-making at the survival stage is *instincts*. At the conforming and differentiating stages we primarily use *subconscious beliefs*, supplemented by conscious beliefs. When we reach the individuating stage *conscious beliefs* start to predominate. At the self-actualising stage we shift to *values-based* decision-making. Values are supplemented by *intuition* at the integrating stage, and by *inspiration* at the serving stage.

The relationship between the universal stages of evolution, the seven stages of psychological development and the six modes of decision-making are shown in Table 7.1.

The shift from one mode of decision-making to the next takes place gradually—at the same pace as the shift from one stage of psychological development to the next. Once you reach a new stage of development and have started using a new mode of decision-making, the previous modes of decision-making are still available to you; you just use them less often.

Table 7.1 Universal stages of evolution, stages of psychological development and modes of decision-making

Universal stages of evolution	Stages of psychological development	Modes of decision-making
Cooperating to form a higher order entity	Serving	Inspiration
	Integrating	Intuition
Bonding to form a group structure	Self-actualising	Values
	Individuating	Conscious beliefs
Becoming viable and independent	Differentiating	Subconscious beliefs
	Conforming	
	Surviving	Instincts

Sometimes, even in the lower stages of development, you may experience the higher modes of decision-making. For example, you may get a sudden flash of intuition or an inspirational thought may suddenly occur. The frequency of occurrence of these two higher modes of decision-making—intuition and inspiration—which are not under your conscious control, increase significantly once you reach the self-actualising stage of development.

The shift from one stage of development to the next and from one mode of decision-making to the next, is also reflected in the shift that takes place in the use of the reptilian mind/brain—surviving (instincts), the limbic mind/brain—conforming and differentiating (subconscious and conscious beliefs) and the neo-cortex—individuating and self-actualising (conscious beliefs and values). When you move beyond the self-actualisation stage towards full self-realisation, the decision-making modalities of the soul begin to take over: intuition at the integrating stage, and inspiration at the serving stage. These modes of decision bypass conscious thought, you just know what it is you have to do. Once you have this knowing, you can then use your rational neo-cortex to work out the best way to achieve what you have to do. Each of the six modes of decision-making is now described in more detail.

Instinct-based decision-making

Instinct-based decision-making is more or less the exclusive domain of the reptilian mind/brain complex and is found in all living creatures. Decisions are automatic and immediate. The reactions of the reptilian mind/brain are triggered by pattern recognition in our species memory banks encoded in our DNA. Instinct-based decisions mostly relate to three factors: self-preservation, the satisfaction of physiological needs, and the perpetuation of the species. The basic reptilian mind/brain reaction to a threat is either fight or flight.

The main features of instinct-based decision-making are:

> *Actions always precede conscious thought. There is no pause for reflection between meaning-making (pattern recognition) and decision-making.*
>
> *The decisions that are made are always based on past experiences—what species history has taught us about how to survive, keep physically safe, and seeking out opportunities to procreate.*
>
> *Reactions are automatic—you have no opportunity to reflect before you act.*

When you are involved in instinct-based decision-making, you are not consciously in control of your words, actions, behaviours or your body functions. The decisions made originate from the DNA instructions contained in the body-mind.

Subconscious belief-based decision-making

Subconscious belief-based decision-making is the exclusive domain of the limbic mind/brain complex and is found in all mammals. As with instinct-based decision-making, subconscious belief-based decisions are automatic and immediate. However, instead of being triggered by pattern recognition at the level of species memories, they are triggered by pattern recognition at the level of the personal memories.

Subconscious belief-based decisions are always about the protection of the body or ego (avoidance of physical or emotional pain), or the exploitation of opportunities to get more of the basic needs that your ego believes are missing in your life—more security, more love or more recognition (seeking of pleasure).

Whenever you feel impatient, frustrated, and angry or get into a rage, you know that subconscious fear-based beliefs are dominating your decision-making. These emotions, which are being triggered by a present moment event, are linked to your memory of an event in the past when you failed to get one of your needs met at the surviving, conforming or differentiating stages of your psychological development.

Whereas the self-preservation instinct of the reptilian mind/brain concerns only the self, the self-preservation instinct of the limbic mind/brain can include other people with whom close attachments have been formed—those with whom you identify. For example, a mother will instinctively protect her child; a soldier will instinctively protect his comrades.

The main features of subconscious belief-based decision-making are:

> *Actions always precede conscious thought. There is no gap for reflection between meaning-making and decision-making.*
>
> *The decisions that are made are always based on past experiences—what your personal history has taught you about maximising pleasure and minimising pain in the framework of existence of your childhood.*
>
> *Reactions are automatic—you have no opportunity to reflect before you act.*

When you are involved in subconscious-based decision-making, you are not consciously in control of your words, actions and behaviours. They are in control of you. When you are experiencing a love-based or fear-based emotional reaction triggered by a subconscious belief, the only way to get back into control is to take the time you need to release your emotions.

Releasing your emotions helps you to clear your mind. If, for whatever reason, you feel you are unable to release your emotions, because you are afraid of what might happen if you do, then the emotional energy will accumulate below the surface of your conscious mind like water vapour in a pressure cooker. Eventually, the stress you feel from these supressed emotions will either make you sick or cause you to burst out into a fit of anger or rage.

The basic limbic mind/brain reaction to a perceived threat is not fight or flight, but avoidance. The main way this shows up is in the shunning of conflict. We avoid conflict because of a learned belief, usually from our childhood, about our ability to deal with what might happen to our emotional or physical safety if we express how we feel. This is one of the ways the ego tries to protect itself: blame is another.

We blame others, not just to avoid punishment, but also because we want to avoid conflict. In our ego-mind, conflict represents separation, and separation for children triggers fears for their safety. In extreme cases, the ego-mind of a child will dissociate from a painful experience by forming a sub-personality—one that is able to function in the world without the memory of the painful experience.

Conscious belief-based decision-making

Conscious belief-based decision-making is the exclusive domain of the neo-cortex mind/brain complex and is found in its most advanced form in human beings. Conscious beliefs, like subconscious beliefs, are assumptions we hold to be true. They may not be true, but we assume they are, and our mind acts on them as if they were true. Beliefs show up in the brain as neural pathways—connections between events and outcomes (feelings and emotions) that have been learned through repetition in the past. The most deeply engrained neural pathways are those that we learned in our childhood when the reasoning power of the neo-cortex was not available to us.

If you want to make rational decisions, you have to move beyond subconscious belief-based decision-making and shift to conscious belief-based decision-making. This means you have to insert a pause between the event that triggers your subconscious belief and your reaction to it. The pause allows the emotion associated with the belief to subside and gives you time for reflection, so you can use logic (slow thinking) to understand the meaning of what is happening and then make a choice about how to respond. By inserting a pause, you also have time to discuss the situation with others and get advice about the best way to get your needs met. Unlike the reptilian and limbic mind/brains which *react* to threats (fast thinking), the neo-cortex *responds* to threats by analysing the situation to understand what is happening (slow thinking) and find the meaning.

The main features of conscious belief-based decision-making are:

> *Conscious thought precedes action. A pause is inserted between an event and the response. The pause allows logic or reason to be used to determine the best way of getting your needs met.*

> *Decisions are based on past experiences—what your personal history, your culture or your religion has taught you about maintaining internal stability and external equilibrium in your framework of existence. You make decisions based on what you believe you know.*
> *You are in control of your actions and behaviours.*
> *You can consult with others, who you trust, to support and enhance your decision-making.*

Conscious belief-based decision-making has one thing in common with subconscious belief-based decision-making and instinct-based decision-making: it uses information from the past to make decisions about the future.

Consequently, conscious belief-based decision-making does not serve you well in understanding and navigating complex situations which you have never experienced before. For that, you need a more sophisticated decision-making modality: a decision-making modality that focuses not on what you want to happen to meet your ego's needs but on what you want to happen that allows you to live in alignment with your soul's values.

Values-based decision-making

The shift from conscious-belief based decision-making to values-based decision-making is not easy. You have to complete the process of individuation before values-based decision-making is fully and naturally available to you. Until you individuate, your decision-making will be primarily influenced by the beliefs you learned from your parents and your community during your childhood and teenage years.

The process of individuation involves examining the beliefs you learned during your formative years and letting go of those that no longer serve you and those you no longer consider to be true. Once you begin to reflect on your beliefs, you will start to think about what is important to you and you will naturally start to reflect on your values.

Whereas beliefs are the context-related guidance system of the ego, values are the universal guidance system of the soul. Beliefs are always contextual and values are always universal. Everyone on the planet shares the same deeply held human values, but not the same beliefs. Consequently, when people start to make decisions using their values they find themselves drawn together. When they make decisions based on their beliefs they find themselves separated. In other words, values unite and beliefs separate.

When you shift to values-based decision-making, you can effectively throw away the rulebooks you learned when you were young. Every decision you make is sourced from what you consider to be "right action"—actions that are fully aligned with who you really are—your soul-self.

Values-based decision-making allows you to create an authentic way of operating in the world because you no longer hide your feelings. That is not to say there is no place for conscious belief-based decision-making based or logic or rational thinking: there is. However, you will quickly realise as you proceed with your self-actualisation and get in touch with your deeply held values that all the critical decisions you need to make in your life need to pass the values test.

If a decision seems logical, but goes against your values you will feel uncomfortable. You need to give precedence to decisions that make you feel good rather than decisions that focus on getting what your ego thinks it needs. You want to know that you did the right thing. You know if you did the right thing by how it makes you feel. What makes you feel good is when you are living in internal stability—in other words, when the decisions you make align with your soul's values.

The main features of values-based decision-making are:

> *When you first begin, conscious thought precedes action. You carefully consider what values you want to guide your decisions. The decisions you make are not based on your past history. They are based on who you truly are and who you want to become.*
>
> *You are in control of your actions and behaviours.*
>
> *You do not need to seek guidance from others. You will know what is right from the way that you feel.*
>
> *After a while, when you have become practised in values-based decision-making, you do not have to reflect anymore: It becomes automatic.*

Values-based decision-making has another advantage: it allows you to consciously create the future you want to experience. For example, if you value trust, you will make decisions that display trust and you will be trusted by others. If you value accountability, then you make decisions that display accountability and those around you will be encouraged to be accountable. You create the future you want to experience because the quality of the energy you put out into the world through your decision-making is the quality of the energy you receive back. Honesty breeds honesty. Trust breeds trust. Conversely, fear breeds fear.

Intuition-based decision-making

The shift from values-based decision-making to intuition-based decision-making does not happen overnight: it develops gradually as you move through the higher stages of psychological development. Although you can experience intuition at all stages of development, it is not until you begin to focus on satisfying your higher order psychological needs that you can count on it showing up in your life.

Intuition allows you to access the collective unconscious—the universal intelligence that resides in the quantum energy field. You access this field through your soul. Consequently, intuition-based decision-making only really begins to kick-in when you reach the integrating stage of your psychological development. The principal characteristics of intuition-based decision-making are as follows:

> *Thoughts, beliefs, and agendas are suspended.*
> *No meaning-making takes place.*
> *The mind is still and empty.*
> *The mind is free to make a deep dive into the mind-space of the collective unconscious and emerge with a thought or understanding that provides an answer to a question that has been on your mind.*

Intuition arises suddenly out of nowhere, usually when your mind is resting, often in the middle of the night. Even though intuition-based decision-making is not logical, it is the principal source of our most important breakthrough ideas. When you are totally present to a situation without thought, belief or judgement, you create the conditions that allow your mind to intuitively recognise what wants to emerge. When we work with others to create a collective, non-judgemental mind space, intuition can become even more powerful. It can result in new ways of approaching old problems that have never been considered before.

Inspiration-based decision-making

Inspiration is the term I use to describe thoughts and prompts you receive from your soul about what you need to do with your life.

Inspiration is always very personal and directive. You will recognise it as a persistent thought that will not go away. It delineates the next steps you have to take in your life journey. Inspiration keeps prompting you until you listen and follow through. It is about what your soul wants you to do. Not surprisingly, therefore, the purpose of inspiration is to support you in living your soul's values and fulfilling your soul's purpose.[1]

Even though the voice of inspiration can come through at any stage of your psychological development, you will not begin to recognise it as such until you reach the stage of self-actualisation. Up to that point, it will seem like just another thought. Discerning the difference between a thought originating from ego and a thought originating from soul is quite difficult at first. It gets easier as time goes by and you devote your life to serving the needs of your soul.

Some people ask: "How is inspiration different from intuition?" Intuition is non-directive. It is an idea or insight that arises from nowhere at an undetermined moment that provides a solution or a clue to resolving a problem or issue that you are currently facing. Intuition can best be described as a *"eureka"* moment.

Inspiration, on the other hand, is a definitive prompt. It can best be described as *guidance for keeping your life in a state of flow*. You know you are living in soul consciousness and receiving soul inspiration when synchronicity rains down on you. Your life takes on a magical quality. Don't expect the magic to happen every day. It may appear for several weeks at a time, disappear, and then re-emerge again when you are least expecting it.

When you receive soul-driven thoughts about an action or direction you need to take, and you do not follow this directive, you will eventually have to deal with the consequences. For example, when you continually allow your fears about satisfying your basic needs to take precedence over fulfilling your growth needs, you may find yourself getting increasingly depressed. You will feel stifled and out of alignment because you are not fulfilling your soul's potential.

The principal characteristics of inspiration-based decision-making are as follows:

Thought appears to arise from nowhere.
The thought is persistent.
The thought is linked to actions or a direction you need to take.
There are emotional consequences for not following your inspiration.

In the preface of *The New Leadership Paradigm*,[2] I speak about my calling to write a book on leadership. I tried to resist the idea, but I could not: it would not go away. For me, that was inspiration in action. When I began to write the book, ideas and insights just kept flooding my mind. Synchronicity was with me almost every day for a full year. Whenever I was stuck with my writing, I would get out of my logical intellectual mind and seek assistance from my higher self. Soon thereafter I would find words streaming into my consciousness without need of editing. At those moments, I was aware that I was experiencing a state of flow.

When you reach this stage of development you begin to realise that your life does not belong to you: your life belongs to your soul. Your ego needs disappear as your soul takes charge of your life. Life is not something that happens to you, it happens through you. To experience this way of being you must learn to befriend, trust and then become one with your soul.

Summary

Here are the main points of this chapter:

1. One of the subtle but more important changes that occur as we move through the seven stages of psychological development is in how we make decisions.
2. Instinct-based decision-making is more or less the exclusive domain of the reptilian mind/brain complex and is found in all living creatures.
3. Subconscious belief-based decision-making is the exclusive domain of the limbic mind/brain complex and is found in all mammals.
4. Conscious belief-based decision-making is the exclusive domain of the neo-cortex mind/brain complex and is found in its most advanced form in human beings.

5. Values are the universal guidance system of the soul.
6. Although you can experience intuition at all stages of development, it is not until you begin to focus on satisfying your higher psychological needs that you can count on it showing up in your life.
7. Inspiration is always very personal and directive. You will recognise it as a persistent thought that will not go away. Inspiration comes in the form of thoughts or prompts from your soul about what you need to do with your life.
8. There are consequences for not following the inspiration of your soul.

In the next part of the book, I will introduce and describe exercises that allow you to identify your client's primary motivation, their secondary motivations and the stage of development the organisation they are embedded in has reached.

Notes

1. For a full account of inspiration-based decision-making consult: Richard Barrett, *What My Soul Told Me* (Bath: Fulfilling Books), 2012.
2. Richard Barrett, *The New Leadership Paradigm* (Bath: Fulfilling Books), 2010.

PART II

The Practice of Evolutionary Coaching—Exercises

The purpose of Part II of this book is to provide the reader with tools and exercises for the practice of evolutionary coaching.

Chapter 8 provides an introduction to tools and exercises that are used for evolutionary coaching and explains why it is important for coaches to first carry out these exercises on themselves, before using them on their clients. Chapter 9 explains how to uncover the primary motivation of your clients by determining what stage of psychological development they have reached. Chapter 10 explains how to uncover the secondary motivations of your clients by determining what stages of psychological development they have passed through, where they still have unmet needs. Chapter 11 explains how to assess the extent to which your clients feel supported by the culture they are working in, by identifying what stage of psychological development the organisation they are working in has reached.

CHAPTER 8

INTRODUCTION TO THE EXERCISES

The exercises included in the second part of this book have three objectives:

- To uncover your client's primary motivation.
- To uncover your client's secondary motivations.
- To assess to what extent the culture of the organisation your client is working in is able to support them in meeting their primary motivation.

With this information, you will be able to get a complete picture of where your clients are on their evolutionary journeys, what is motivating them to move forward, and what is holding them back, personally and organisationally.

Assessing yourself

Before you start helping your clients on their journey of human emergence, you should begin by assessing where you are—what stage of psychological development you have reached; and, what stages of psychological development you have passed through, where you still have unmet needs.

The best way to do this is familiarise yourself with Part I of this book and then complete the exercises here in Part II. There are several important reasons you should begin by exploring your own evolutionary journey:

1. The first and most obvious reason is to get a deeper personal understanding of the concept of human emergence.
2. The second reason, which is just as important as the first, is to experience what it feels like to do the exercises that you will be asking your clients to do.
3. The third reason is to become aware, if you are not already, of your primary motivation and your secondary motivations, and to what extent your secondary motivations are preventing you from meeting your primary motivation.
4. The fourth reason is to know your limits. Once you know your limits you will know how far you can take your clients in their evolutionary journey, before you enter unknown territory.

It is incumbent upon you as an evolutionary coach to display the utmost integrity in this matter. You will not only be doing your clients a disservice if you try to lead them through a territory you are not familiar with, you will also be doing yourself a disservice. Simply having an understanding of the theory of human evolution is not sufficient: to be of real service to your clients you will need to have experienced the journey.

In practical terms, this means, to become an evolutionary coach, you must, at a minimum, be well advanced in your own self-actualisation. Once you have self-actualised, you will be able to help clients move through the differentiation, individuation and self-actualisation stages of their development—by far the most frequent developmental stages you will come across in your coaching career. To coach people through the integrating and serving stages of psychological development you will need to become a master evolutionary coach. It is most likely you will not be able to operate at these levels until your late 50s or early 60s.

Your ability to help your clients go beyond the self-actualisation stage to full self-realisation, will not only depend on your age, it will also depend on your commitment to your soul's journey. You cannot reach the higher stages of development without aligning your ego's motivations with your soul's motivations and fully committing yourself to living a values-driven and purpose-driven life. This means that if you want to guide people to the highest levels of psychological development, you will need to become the servant of your soul.

This is not something that happens overnight, no matter how much you may desire to reach this state. Learning to become the servant of your soul can take several decades of life experiences, study, reflection and meditation. It requires courage and faith—a willingness to leave the safety of your ego identity and step into the unfamiliar world of your soul identity. You have to get beyond your ego's perspective—living in a three-dimensional physical world, and embrace your soul's perspective—living in a multidimensional energetic world. In *What My Soul Told Me*[1] I describe the four stages of this journey—connecting with your soul, befriending your soul, trusting your soul and becoming one with your soul. I also describe the skills you will need to master at each stage of this journey.

Once you have explored where *you* are on your journey and discovered your primary and secondary motivations, you are now ready to implement your evolutionary coaching practice.

The first step in working with your clients is to identify what stage of psychological development *they* have reached and hence their primary motivation. This is important for two reasons:

1. When you know what stage of psychological development your clients have reached you will know what needs are uppermost in their conscious minds—what is driving them, and what they feel they need to achieve in order to feel a sense of internal stability and external equilibrium.
2. When you know what stage of psychological development your clients have reached you will be able gauge to what extent you will be able to help them. If they are operating at a stage of development beyond where you are at, you may need to consider asking someone who is more advanced in their development, to act as their coach. If your client is at the same level as you, you may want to seek advice from a mentor as and when you feel the need for support.

The New Leadership Paradigm

Many of the evolutionary coaching exercises included in this book are taken from the New Leadership Paradigm (TNLP) learning system.[2] This is a state-of-the-art leadership development programme which includes four learning modules:[3]

- Leading self

- Leading a team
- Leading an organisation
- Leading in society

Each of the learning modules contains between 30 and 40 exercises; the exercises in each learning module are organised in six sections:

Journey: The journey section explores the past to the present. Where you (team, organisation, society) have been and, where you are now.

Potential: The potential section explores the possibility for the future—who you (your team, organisation, society) can become, and where you want to go.

Challenges: The challenges section explores the reality of where you (team, organisation, society) are now and the hurdles you have to overcome.

Mastery: The mastery section explores the way you manage your day-to-day reality (team, organisation, society) so you can get the outcomes you need and get to where you want to go.

Evolution: The evolution section explores your (team, organisation, society) evolutionary progress—your latest feedback/performance measures, and your commitments to continued growth and learning.

Self-coaching: The self-coaching section supports your (team, organisation, society) evolutionary progress by providing a checklist of actions you can take when you are confronted by specific issues.

One of the ways you can accelerate your client's progress on their evolutionary journey is to systematically take them through the exercises of the Leading Self module of The New Leadership Paradigm learning system. When they have completed that module, you can then take them through the exercises in the Leading a Team module, and if appropriate, the Leading an Organisation module.

Summary

Here are the main points of this chapter:

1. Before you start helping your clients on their journey of human emergence, you should begin by assessing where you are.
2. The best way to do this is familiarise yourself with Part I of this book and then complete the exercises in Part II.
3. To become an evolutionary coach, you must, at a minimum, be well advanced in your own self-actualisation.

In the next chapter of the book, I will describe the tools and exercises you can use to help you to identify the primary motivation of your client.

Notes

1. Richard Barrett, *What My Soul Told Me* (Bath: Fulfilling Books), 2012.
2. Richard Barrett, *The New Leadership Paradigm* (Bath: Fulfilling Books), 2010.
3. Information on TNLP can be found at *http://newleadershipparadigm. com*

Chapter 9

Identifying
Primary
Motivations

There are several ways you can approach finding out the primary motivation of your clients (what level of psychological development your clients have reached). The first approach is to consider their age. For most people, this will give you a reasonably accurate reading.

Age exercise

This is not so much an exercise as simple method you can use for identifying your client's most likely stage of psychological development. If your client is somewhere between the ages of 30 and 60, they are most likely to be in either the differentiating, individuating, self-actualising or integrating stages (see Figure 9.1).

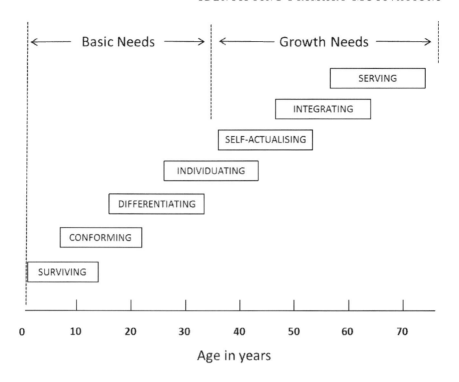

Figure 9.1 Age versus stage of psychological development

You begin your life as a baby at the surviving stage. Two-to-three years later, once you have learned how to speak, you enter the conforming stage. If all goes well, by the time you reach your teens, you will have entered the differentiating stage.

Although your primary motivation in your teens and 20s will normally be linked to the differentiating stage—wanting to feel good about who you are by being recognised or acknowledged by your parents and peers—you will still be learning how to conform (feel a sense of belonging) and survive (feel a sense of security) in increasingly larger frameworks of existence as you move from school, to university, to finding work that enables you to become a productive member of society. If all goes well, by the time you reach your late 20s you will be giving your full attention to your differentiation needs.

If, however, you had a difficult time growing up and were subject to negative parental or cultural conditioning, you may not be able to give your full attention to your differentiation needs when you reach your late 20s.

Your unmet needs from previous stages of development may be hijacking your conscious awareness, preventing you from learning the skills that would allow you to master your differentiating needs. This could delay or block the individuating stage of development.

Assuming your clients have had a relatively normal and healthy upbringing and were able, for the most part, to satisfy their surviving, conforming and differentiating needs, they will start the process of individuating in their 30s, and again if all goes well, they will start the process of self-actualising in their 40s. They will move to the integrating stage in their 50s and the serving stage in their 60s.

You may find some clients—those who have been raised by self-actualised parents in a liberal democracy—who reach the individuation stage somewhat earlier than their 30s. This is primarily because the world view they grew up in was supporting their psychological development. On the other hand, you may find yourself working with clients—those who have significant unmet needs from the early stages of their development—who are still struggling to get beyond the differentiating or individuating stage of their development, even in their 40s.

Primary motivation exercise

Having roughly identified what stage of development your client is at, based on their age, you should confirm this by getting them to complete the primary motivation exercise described in Annex 1 so they can discover it for themselves.

In most instances, your clients will identify one primary motivation. If they are transitioning from one stage of development to the next, they might identify two motivations. Normally the motivations they identify will be adjacent to each other. If they are not, you should focus on the lower motivation, because until that motivation is satisfied, they will not have a significantly strong foundation to master the next higher stage of psychological development.

Sometimes you will come across people in their 20s and 30s who are unconsciously feeling their soul's impulse to make a difference in the world. Because of their devotion to a cause, they may believe themselves to be operating at the integrating level. This is extremely unlikely. You can tell the difference between someone who is truly operating from the integrating stage of development and someone operating from a lower stage of development by how they approach what they do.

Someone who is truly at the integrating stage will be operating with a self-transforming mind—they will be able to appreciate different points of view. They will not just be aligning themselves with other people who share the same values and vision, they will also be actively collaborating with other people to create a better world. They will not be fighting against something but fighting for something. They will be engaged in constructive dialogue rather than destructive behaviour. They will not buy into the "us" and "them" scenario. They will approach what they are doing from the perspective of inclusion—finding solutions that address everyone's needs. They will be operating with a self-transforming mind.

People in their 20s and 30s are more likely to be operating with a self-authoring mind. They will find it difficult to see the world from other people's points of view. If someone at the differentiating stage feels their soul's impulse to align with a cause they will tend to take a more strident activist approach—they will usually be rebelling. At the individuating stage of development, they will still be operating with a self-authoring mind but they may be more willing to listen to other points of view and enter into a debate, arguing strongly for what they believe.

Other exercises that your client can do to find the level of psychological development they are operating from include the following:

My in-flow days exercise: The purpose of this exercise is to discover what needs are being met when your clients feel as if they are in a state of flow.

My level of happiness exercise: The purpose of this exercise is similar to the previous one, except, instead of focusing on needs, the focus is on what makes them happy.

My level of identity exercise: The purpose of this exercise is similar to the previous two: instead of focusing on flow or happiness, it focuses on your client's sense of identity. As we grow and develop through the seven stages of psychological development, we experience an increasingly inclusive sense of identity.

Each shift to a higher level of development requires you to adopt a larger sense of self and results in an expansion of consciousness. You are always operating from self-interest, but as you increase your level of consciousness, the self that has the self-interest assumes an increasingly larger sense of identity. When this larger sense of self makes decisions, it does so with the well-being of the groups you identify with, in mind. For detailed information on all these exercises, see Annex 1.

Summary

Here are the main points of this chapter:

1. The first step in evolutionary coaching is to identify your clients' primary motivation. This will tell you what stage of psychological development they have reached.
2. There are several ways you can approach finding out the primary motivation of your clients. The first approach is to consider their age.
3. Having roughly identified what stage of development your clients are at, based on their age, you should confirm this by getting them to complete the exercises described in Annex 1 so they can discover it for themselves.

In the next chapter of the book, I will describe the tools and exercises you can use to help you identify the secondary motivations of your clients.

Chapter 10

Identifying Secondary Motivations

The next step in evolutionary coaching is to identify your clients' secondary motivations. These will tell you what conscious and subconscious unmet needs your clients have at the stages of psychological development they have already passed through. Your secondary motivations may be conscious or subconscious. The most commonly experienced secondary motivations are the unmet needs of the first three stages of psychological development.

Conscious secondary motivations

Conscious secondary motivations can arise from the particular circumstances of your current life situation or from the unmet needs of previous stages of your psychological development.

No matter what stage of psychological development you have reached if you lose your job and have no income for several months, you will find yourself automatically focusing on the survival level of consciousness. Alternatively, let's say you find yourself taking an assignment in a foreign country where you do not speak the language and have no friends, you will automatically find yourself focusing on the relationship level of consciousness.

If you are entering the self-actualising stage of psychological development but still have unmet needs from the individuating stage, you may find yourself continually seeking the thrills of new adventures or new challenges. If you are at the integrating stage of psychological development but still have unmet needs from the self-actualising stage, you may find yourself spending more time exploring the meaning of your life or pursuing your spiritual understanding of the world, than actually participating in making a difference.

Subconscious secondary motivations

Subconscious motivations can affect your behaviours just like conscious motivations, but they are more subtle, and because they are subconscious, they are less easy to identify. You can experience subconscious motivations at any stage of psychological development.

The soul's subconscious secondary motivations

Because we are not consciously aware of our souls, the soul's needs are communicated to us from the subconscious realms of our minds. Because they lie beneath our conscious awareness we are not aware of their origin. Unlike our secondary motivations, which come from the stages of development we have passed through, the soul's motivations come from the stages of development we have not yet reached. They come into our lives as prompts about what our souls want us to do in order to get into alignment with their purposes and values.

When you first become aware that you have a soul and it has motivations, you may have some difficulties distinguishing between the thoughts that arise from your ego-mind and the thoughts that arise from your soul-mind. The main difference is, your ego thoughts will in some way serve your own survival, relationship or self-esteem needs, whereas your soul thoughts will serve your higher order growth needs. The problem of distinguishing the difference between ego thoughts and soul thoughts usually only occurs during the early stages of self-actualisation. As you become more fully self-actualised and move into the integrating stage of psychological development you will no longer have any ego needs—your ego's motivations will have blended with your soul's motivations.

The ego's subconscious motivations

The ego's subconscious motivations have to do with satisfying your unmet needs from the first three stages of psychological development—surviving, conforming and differentiating—the stages of development we experience in our childhood and teenage years. If we had difficulties satisfying our deficiency needs during these years, the ego-mind will develop subconscious fear-based beliefs about not having enough safety or security, not being loved or respected enough, and not being recognised or acknowledged enough.

Practically everyone in the world grows up with some of these subconscious fears. The extent of these fears will depend largely on the quality of the parental programming and cultural conditioning you received as you were growing up—the extent to which you were able to satisfy your deficiency needs in your family environment and the community you grew up in.

When we are young and unable to meet our needs for safety and security, love and respect, and recognition and acknowledgement, we develop what are known in psychological parlance as early maladaptive schemas (EMS). Dr. Jeffrey E. Young, Founder and Director of the Schema Therapy Institute, describes EMS in the following way:

> Early Maladaptive Schemas [beliefs] seem to be the result of dysfunctional experiences with parents, siblings, and peers during the first few years of an individual's life. Most schemas [beliefs] are caused by on-going everyday noxious experiences with family members and peers which cumulatively strengthen the schema [belief]. For example a child who is constantly criticized when performance does not meet parental standards is prone to develop the incompetence/failure schema.[1]

These early negative experiences may never occur again, but their effects remain—they become hard-wired into our brains. The reasons they become hard-wired are: (a) when you are young, your brain is in the process of building neural pathways to help you understand and make meaning of the world around you; and (b) up to the age of eight, your neo-cortex, the part of the brain that allows you to use reason and logic, is not fully developed. The only parts of the brain that are fully available to us in childhood for processing our experiences are the reptilian and limbic mind/brains. These are the parts of the human mind/brain that deal with emotions.

Consequently, when we are young we learn to navigate in our world based on how what is happening makes us feel. We attach emotions to the beliefs we learn about what gives us pleasure and what gives us pain.

When we are able to satisfy our deficiency needs (the needs arising from the first three stages of psychological development) we feel physical and emotional pleasure; when we are not able to satisfy our deficiency needs we feel physical or emotional pain.

The emotions formed during our early years are stored in our memories and become a permanently embedded stimulus which shapes or distorts our present reality in line with the past. This means that our reptilian and limbic mind/brains—the fast thinking parts of our brains—have become "hard-wired" to search for threats that correspond to our most painful personal experiences—the experiences of not getting our deficiency needs met.

As an adult, whenever we experience a situation that reminds of these memories, the old neural pathways (beliefs) are triggered and the emotions associated with these memories flood into the body and the mind. What we do with them depends on our conscious fears—we can let our emotions out or we can hide them away.

If your clients have significant secondary ego motivations, you will need to help them find ways to address these unmet needs before you address the needs associated with their primary motivation. The reason you need to spend time on helping them resolve their secondary ego motivations is the energy they expend on satisfying these needs is energy that is no longer available for focusing on their primary motivation. In other words, if they are unable to master their past unmet needs they will find it difficult to work on their current needs.

Our secondary motivations not only distract us from focusing on our primary motivation they also inhibit our evolutionary progress and can also undermine our family life and our professional progress. The reason they do this is because they result in behaviours that affect other people in negative ways. This is because the majority of our subconscious fear-based limiting beliefs are focused on the serving the needs of the "I", rather than serving the needs of the "we". Consequently, our fear-based subconscious beliefs almost always create separation rather than connection.

Humans are basically social creatures: We depend on each other for our individual and collective survival, progress and success. When one person in a family or team appears to be focused more on their own needs or success rather than the group's needs or success, discord and conflict will ensue, causing the family or team to become dysfunctional.

Unless they are able to establish healthy psychological functioning at the lower stages of development, your clients will find it difficult to master the higher stages of development. They will be attempting to build on an unstable foundation. Whenever their unmet deficiency needs are triggered, their psychological foundations will quake, causing internal instability.

Let us now take a brief look at the three types of limiting beliefs we learn during childhood and teenage years that could limit our progress or success in adult life.

Limiting survival beliefs

The limiting beliefs we learn at the surviving stage of development are about not having enough to feel safe and secure. These beliefs result in the display of potentially limiting values such as control, manipulation, greed, excessive caution, impatience and generally result in a lack of trust.

During the first stage of your psychological development, the surviving stage, your primary task is to establish a separate sense of identity from your mother, and learn how to exercise control over your environment so you can get your survival needs met. If, for whatever reason, you had difficulties accomplishing this task, either because your parents were not vigilant enough to your needs, or you were left alone or abandoned for long periods of time, or your parents were fearful for their own survival, your nascent ego will likely have formed subconscious fear-based beliefs (early maladaptive schema) that the world is an unsafe place and that other people cannot be trusted. This either leads you to want to control and manipulate your environment, so you can get what you want, or operate with excessive caution and become risk-averse, to make sure what you already have does not get taken away.

If, on the other hand, your parents were attentive to your needs, and were watchful for signs of distress, then you will grow up with a sense of security and the feeling that others can be trusted. You will feel confident about being able to meet your survival needs, and consequently, will not spend much time or energy worrying about having enough. Feeling safe and secure is the first and most important need of the ego-mind.

Limiting relationship beliefs

The limiting beliefs we learn at the conforming stage of development are about not being loved enough to feel accepted or protected—feeling separate and not belonging. These beliefs result in the display of potentially limiting values such as jealously, blame and being liked. Being liked is potentially limiting because your overriding need to be accepted may cause you to embroider the truth so people do not think badly about you or do not get upset by what you have to tell them. The desire to be liked can also lead to dishonesty and blame. You lie about your actions and deflect responsibility for your "wrongdoings" onto other people to avoid punishment and stay in good favour. If as a child, you were constantly blamed for things others did, you will grow up wanting to be treated fairly and strongly concerned about justice.

During the second stage of psychological development, the conforming or self-protective stage, your primary task is to learn how to feel loved and safe in your family or social group. Adherence to rules and rituals (conforming) becomes important, because they consolidate your sense of belonging, and enhance your sense of safety. If for any reason you grow up feeling unloved or unaccepted, not getting your share of love or not belonging, your ego may have developed a subconscious fear-based limiting belief that you are not lovable, not accepted, not preferred or that you are an outsider. Later on in life, you may find yourself constantly seeking affection or searching for a group or community that accepts and welcomes you as you are.

If on the other hand, you always felt loved no matter what you did, and that love was given unconditionally, then you will grow up with a sense of being accepted. You will feel confident about being able to meet your relationship needs, and consequently not spend much time or energy worrying about being loved enough. Feeling loved, accepted and a sense of belonging is the second most important need of the ego-mind.

Limiting self-esteem beliefs

The limiting beliefs we learn at the differentiating stage of development are about not being enough—not feeling confident in your capabilities and not feeling recognised or acknowledged. These beliefs result in the display of potentially limiting values such as status seeking, power-seeking, political manoeuvring, being highly competitive and wanting to be top dog.

During the third stage of psychological development, the differentiation stage, your primary need is to be recognised by your parents or peers for excelling or doing well. The task at this stage is to develop a healthy sense of pride in your accomplishments and a feeling of self-worth. You want to feel good about who you are and you want to feel respected by your peers. If, for whatever reason, you are denied this recognition, you will grow up with the subconscious fear-based belief that you are not good enough. You will always feel driven to prove your self-worth. You may become a workaholic. You will want to be acknowledged by your peers or those in authority as someone who is important or someone to be feared. If your ego-mind does not get the reinforcement that it needs, you could grow up with a feeling that no matter how hard you try, recognition escapes you: The successes you achieve may never be enough to satisfy your needs.

If, on the other hand, your parents encouraged you to try out new things, and praised your efforts no matter how well you did, you will feel a sense of self-worth or pride in your accomplishments. You will feel confident about who you are and your abilities, and consequently, not spend much time worrying about being enough. Feeling a sense of self-worth is the third most important need of the ego-mind.

Dr. Jeffrey E. Young of the Schema Therapy Institute has identified eighteen common negative schema or limiting beliefs that he has come across in his patients. These are listed in Annex 3 under three subheadings—survival and safety needs, relationship and belonging needs, and self-esteem and recognition needs. These correspond to the first three stages of development. The allocations of the schema described in this annex to the three stages of psychological development are mine.

Becoming aware of your secondary motivations

Up to and including the individuation stage of psychological development, people are not usually aware of their secondary motivations, nor are they aware of how these motivations are getting in the way of satisfying their primary motivation: they are unable to see or appreciate the impact their behaviours are having on others and how their behaviours can act against them in a detrimental manner. Only when we reach the self-actualisation stage do we start to become aware of how our unmet psychological needs are preventing us from finding happiness and success, and how the pursuit of these needs can have hurtful repercussions on close family members and colleagues.

Usually what gets our attention is the emotional pain we feel when the pursuit of our unmet needs injures or upsets our most important relationships and inhibits our professional progress. It is the frustration we feel about our inability to meet our primary motivation and the deleterious impact our behaviours have on our relationships that causes us to stop and reflect, and then identify, understand and explore our subconscious secondary motivations.

If you are able to identify your unmet needs before they create too much havoc in your life, then your passage to and through the self-actualisation stage of your development will be immensely facilitated.

The first time you recognise the impact that an unmet need is having on your life, through feedback from others or through the pain you are experiencing in your own life, you realise that you have been living unconsciously—insensitive to the needs of others, and primarily focused on your own needs. This can be an emotionally shocking experience, unleashing feelings of guilt and inadequacy, especially if you have always prided yourself on trying to live an honest, ethical and caring life. Receiving such feedback can be a blow to your self-image. You will feel a high level of inner turmoil as you realise the degree of hurt your insensitivity to the needs of others has caused.

Experiences like this help you to realise that not only have you been living unconsciously, you are also incompetent at meeting your needs. Once you have experienced the pain and you recognise your culpability, you shift from being *unconsciously* incompetent to being *consciously* incompetent. This is usually when you take action to find ways to master your unmet needs. The pain you felt and don't want to experience again encourages you to become accountable for the way you live your life, in particular the way in which your words, actions and behaviours impact other people.

The first task you have to undertake if you want to become accountable for your actions is to identify the subconscious fear-based beliefs you are holding on to that are causing the behaviours preventing you from finding happiness and success. Only when you have identified these beliefs and named them, can you understand how they originated and take the necessary measures to overcome them or replace them with a belief that will cause you to behave differently in the future.

Your job as an evolutionary coach is to help your clients uncover their unmet needs—help them to move beyond being *unconsciously* incompetent to being *consciously* incompetent. Then, you have to help them master their unmet needs so they become consciously competent. The best way to do this is to help them build the new neural pathways so these needs no longer divert their attention from their primary motivation. This reprogramming can take several months or even a year to implement.

It is quite possible to help most people to deal with their unmet needs using the techniques described in this book. However, in some cases, where the trauma associated with the unmet need has significantly destabilised your client, you may have to refer him or her to a psychologist or psychotherapist. Knowing where these boundaries lie is important. Some guidelines on this matter are provided in Annex 5.

Exercises for identifying secondary motivations

There are two approaches you can use to uncovering your clients' secondary motivations: self-reporting, which reveals their *conscious* motivations, and feedback reporting (from others), which reveals their *subconscious* motivations as well as some of their conscious motivations. Our conscious motivations represent what we know about ourselves. Our subconscious motivations represent what we probably don't know about ourselves that others know about us—our blind spots.

There are several exercises/surveys you can ask your clients to do to help them identify their secondary motivations. Let's start with an exercise that enables your clients to identify their *conscious* secondary motivations.

Personal values assessment

One of the ways you can identify your clients' conscious secondary motivations is by asking them to carry out a personal values assessment (PVA).[2] This free survey, which takes about five minutes to complete, and provides a short report that shows your clients what levels of consciousness they are operating from. Their primary motivation will usually be the highest level of consciousness/stage of development where they have two or more values. Their secondary motivations will be the levels of consciousness where their other values are located. You can compare the results of this survey with the primary motivation exercises to get further clarity on their primary motivation.

This exercise is similar to the "My values/behaviours exercise" used for identifying primary motivations which can be found in Annex 1. The differences are: (a) the personal values assessment has more values for your clients to choose from; and (b) the list of values in the PVA includes some potentially limiting values such as "being liked". Being liked is potentially limiting, because when you operate with this value it may cause you to hide things about yourself from other people in order to stay in their favour.

The most important thing to remember about this self-reporting exercise is that results err on the side of your clients' aspirations. It tells you how they see themselves: not how others see them. To find out how other people see your clients they will have to do a feedback assessment.

Here are some self-reporting exercises that can help your clients uncover their subconscious motivations. More information on these exercises can be found in Annex 2.

My out-of-flow days exercise

This exercise is similar to "My in-flow days exercise" described in Annex 1. The difference is that instead of helping you to identify your clients' primary motivation, it helps you identify their *subconscious* secondary motivations. It does this by asking them to probe deeply into what is happening to them when they are having a bad day.

My anxieties exercise

This exercise along with the next three, takes the previous exercise to a deeper level. This exercise helps your clients understand what unmet needs they have by identifying what they are anxious about. Anxiety arises from your limiting beliefs about not being able to cope with the demands that you have put on yourself or others have put on you, and the potential consequences of failure. Underlying these anxieties are fear-based beliefs.

My stressors exercise

This exercise helps your clients to identify their points of stress. Stress occurs when worries associated with your anxieties begin to impact your body's and mind's ability to function in a normal way. If you feel stressed over a long-period of time, you can develop physical conditions such as ulcers, diabetes and malfunctions of the digestive and cardiovascular systems, as well as mental illness.

My upsets exercise

All upsets—feelings of resistance, impatience, frustration, anger or rage—are signs of internal misalignment of the ego with the soul. The causes of these upsets are the conscious and subconscious fear-based beliefs you hold about not being able to get your deficiency needs met.

My conflicts exercise

All conflicts are sourced from a difference of opinion about how to get a specific need met or from competition for resources for getting needs met. They cause a sense of separation and estrangement that undermines the cohesion and efficacy of a couple, a team or a group.

My fear/needs inventory

Many of the challenges you have in life are of your own making. They arise from the thoughts that are driven by your conscious or subconscious fear-based beliefs about not being able to satisfy your deficiency needs. These fears about not getting your needs met are the primary cause of your anxieties, stress, upsets and conflicts.

This exercise consolidates the fears and needs you have identified in the previous four exercises so that you can more clearly identify the subconscious fear-based beliefs that cause you to experience internal instability and external disequilibrium.

Feedback from others

Having had your client complete the anxiety, stress, upset and conflict exercises, and then consolidated their understanding of their secondary motivations by doing the fear/needs inventory, it is time now to confirm these findings by getting feedback from others.

One of the ways to do this is to carry out a 360° feedback exercise such as a Leadership Values Assessment (LVA) or a Leadership Development Report (LDR). These two surveys, used by coaches all over the world, form part of the Barrett Values Centre's Cultural Transformation Tools. You can find out more about these surveys by reading Chapter 10 of *The Values-Driven Organisation*[3] or referring to the following website: *http://valuescentre.com/products__services*

The purpose of the LVA and LDR is to get feedback from your client's peers, subordinates and superiors on how they see your client operating, and compare their perspective on your client's values with your client's perspective on thier values. The advantages of this approach are that it uncovers your client's blind spots, and it enables you to get an objective measure of your clients' level of personal entropy. Personal entropy is the amount of fear-driven energy that a person expresses in their day-to-day interactions with other people.

Almost everyone, except perhaps for some of the most highly evolved souls, operates with some level of personal entropy. The problem with personal entropy is, if you don't learn to master it, it becomes counterproductive to meeting your individual short-, medium- and long-term goals. If you are a leader, manager or supervisor, you will find your personal entropy showing up in your organisation, department or team as cultural entropy. It will undermine the performance of your team, reduce their level of commitment and decrease their level of engagement.

Personal entropy arises from your early life experiences about not being able to meet your deficiency needs—not being able to get enough of what you need to feel safe and secure (the survival level of consciousness); not being able to get enough of what you need to feel loved and respected (the relationship level of consciousness); and not being able to get enough of what you need to feel acknowledged and recognised (the self-esteem level of consciousness). It is a reflection of the parental and cultural programming you received while you were growing up which led to the development of your early maladaptive schema.

The LVA process begins with the customisation of the leadership values template for the organisation. Leaders are then asked to go to a password-protected website to select ten values that most represent their operating style. They also list what they believe are their strengths, and the areas of improvement they are currently working on. Fifteen to 20 assessors, chosen by the leader, also go to the password-protected website to select ten values that represent the leader's operating style, the behaviours they believe the leader needs to stop, start or improve, and any other comments they may wish to give as feedback to the leader. Assessors can choose whether to provide their name with their feedback or take the survey anonymously. The LVA report is then generated and feedback based on the report is given by a coach in a two-to-three hour one-on-one session with the leader. Based on the feedback, the leader and the coach together develop a detailed action plan to improve the leader's performance.

When a group of leaders in the same leadership team are having LVAs produced at the same time, a collective Group Leadership Plot can be produced. This plot shows the amalgamated values of the group and how they are seen by others. The group plot highlights the common strengths and issues of the group. It uncovers their collective blind spots.

The main difference between the LDR and LVA is that the LDR is automated. It uses a standard leadership values template based on the most common values that have been recorded for hundreds of leaders over a period of several years. Clients can choose to customise this template at an additional cost. Once the survey website is open, and leaders have logged on using a personal password, they are asked to select ten values that most represent their operating style. They are then asked to rate themselves against 26 leadership behaviours, indicating to what extent each of the statements represents an existing strength or area for development. Fifteen to 20 assessors, chosen by the leader, also go to the password-protected website to select ten values that represent the leader's operating style, and ten values they believe are important for the leader to integrate into their operating style. They then rate the leader against the 26 leadership behaviours and provide any other comments they wish to give as feedback to the leader.

The results of the LDR, like the LVA, are delivered by a coach in a two-to-three hour one-on-one feedback session. Based on the feedback, the leader and the coach together develop a detailed action plan to improve the leader's performance.

Here are two examples of LVA results, one for a low-entropy leader (see Figures 10.1 and 10.2) and one for a high-entropy leader (see Figures 10.3 and 10.4).

Low-entropy leader

This leader is in her 50s, so you would expect her primary motivation to be at the making a difference level of consciousness. On the left of the figure you find the ten values that the leader picked to describe her leadership style, and on the right you will find the top values picked by her 19 assessors.

There are four matching values between the leader's value choices and the assessors' choices—listening, open to new ideas, team builder and vision. The assessors see this leader as an authentic, enthusiastic, caring individual who coaches and mentors her staff. She collaborates with others to make a difference. She is appreciated by her staff because she is open to new ideas, listens to people and operates with integrity.

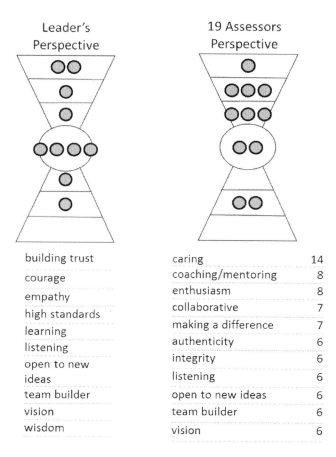

Figure 10.1 LVA: Low personal entropy leader

You will immediately notice from the distribution of top values (dots) on Figure 10.1 that the assessors consider this leader's values to be focused at Levels 5 and 6, whereas the leader sees herself operating mainly from Level 4. This underestimation of her abilities or show of modesty, is relatively typical of leaders who are operating from the higher levels of consciousness.

If you look carefully at the values distribution diagram of the assessors in Figure 10.2, you will see that 27 per cent of the leader's values as observed by the assessors are at the level of a self-transforming mind, 43 per cent at the level of a self-authoring mind and 30 per cent at the level of a socialised mind.[4] The overall level of personal entropy is in the healthy range at 4 per cent.

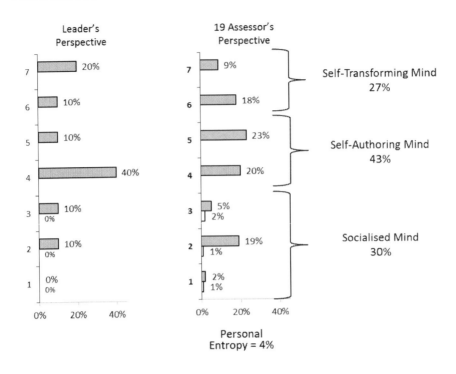

Figure 10.2 LVA: Low personal entropy leader distribution

Based on the feedback this leader received from her assessors, we can say that this leader's primary motivation is to satisfy her need to make a difference—the integrating stage of development, as we would have expected, given her age.

She is also working on her need to find meaning through her work—the self-actualisation stage. Her secondary motivations are mainly at the transformation and relationship levels of consciousness. We can regard these motivations, not as unmet needs, but rather as positive expressions of her character because the needs she has at these levels are represented by positive values. She appears to have very few (4 per cent) entropic values to prevent her from moving forward with her psychological development.

High-entropy leader

This leader is in his 40s, so you would expect his primary motivation to be associated with the individuation or self-actualising stages of development.

He is the founding partner of a small organisation. At the time of the assessment, the organisation had been running for about five years and was modestly successful. The results of the LVA are shown in Figures 10.3 and 10.4.

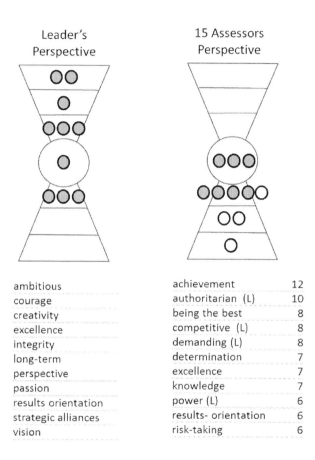

Leader's Perspective	15 Assessors Perspective	
ambitious	achievement	12
courage	authoritarian (L)	10
creativity	being the best	8
excellence	competitive (L)	8
integrity	demanding (L)	8
long-term	determination	7
perspective	excellence	7
passion	knowledge	7
results orientation	power (L)	6
strategic alliances	results- orientation	6
vision	risk-taking	6

Figure 10.3 LVA: High personal entropy leader

The first point to notice in Figure 10.3 is that the leader's perspective and the assessors' perspective are very different. The leader sees himself mainly focused in the upper levels of consciousness and the assessors see him focused in the lower levels of consciousness.

When you take a close look at the leader's perspective of his own values, you would have to agree that the values he chose are excellent for getting an organisation up and running.

The leader brings both his ambition and his passion to bear on his vision. He has courage, he is creative and he is focused on getting results. He builds strategic alliances, operates with integrity and focuses on excellence. An important clue to the way he is viewed by his colleagues is that he has no positive relationship values in his top ten; he is not a people person.

Whilst the people in his organisation recognise many of his strengths, particularly his focus on results and excellence (matching values), he comes across as an authoritarian, demanding, competitive and power seeking.

When you look at the values distribution diagram (Figure 10.4) you will see that this is a person whose behaviours are driven by his fears. He gets his drive from his self-authoring mind (27 per cent of values), but uses the fear-based values of his socialised mind (36 per cent entropic values (9% + 18% + 9%)) to bully people into getting what he wants: None of the values chosen by the assessors fall into the self-transforming mind category. The fact that this leader has very little self-awareness is evident from the difference between the leader's perspective of his values and the perspective of his assessors.

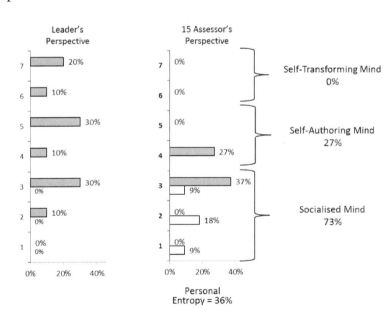

Figure 10.4 LVA: High personal entropy leader distribution

In discussing this feedback with the client, the question naturally came up as to how he could best use his energies and talents for the good of the company? The client quickly recognised that he was less suited to managing the company, and more suited to meeting with clients and building the business. The feedback in the LVA did not come as a surprise to him. He was aware of his limitations regarding his people management skills, and although a little disappointed with the result, recognised that his talents lay elsewhere.

Based on the feedback this leader has received from his assessors, we can say that this leader's primary motivation is to satisfy his need for recognition and acknowledgement, and also satisfy his need for freedom and autonomy. He appears to be in the process of moving from the differentiation stage of development to the individuation stage. Based on his age we would expect him to be more advanced in his individuation. His impression of himself is that he is operating from the differentiating, self-actualising and serving stages of development; very different from how is assessors see him. Based on the personal entropy scores (9% at the survival level of consciousness, 18% at the relationship level, and 9% at the self-esteem level) we can say that this leader has significant secondary motivations generated by his limiting fear-based beliefs at the first three levels of consciousness. These motivations (unmet needs) are preventing him from advancing in his psychological evolution.

Summary

Here are the main points of this chapter:

1. Having identified your clients' primary motivation the next step is to identify your clients' secondary motivations. These will tell you what conscious and subconscious unmet needs your clients have at the stages of psychological development they have already passed through.
2. There are two types of secondary motivations—conscious and subconscious.
3. Conscious secondary motivations can arise from the particular circumstances of your clients' life situation or from the unmet needs of previous stages of psychological development.
4. There are two types of subconscious motivations—ego motivations and soul motivations.

5. Almost everyone on the planet has some subconscious fear-based ego motivations—limiting beliefs.

6. There are three types of limiting beliefs—limiting survival beliefs, limiting relationship beliefs and limiting self-esteem beliefs.

7. Up to, and including, the individuation stage of psychological development, people are not consciously aware of their secondary motivations.

8. There are two approaches you can use to uncovering your clients' secondary motivations: self-reporting, which reveals their *conscious* motivations, and feedback reporting, which reveals their *subconscious* motivations as well as their conscious motivations.

9. One of the ways to get feedback reporting is to have your clients carry out a Leadership Values Assessment (LVA) or a Leadership Development Report (LDR), which measures their level of personal entropy.

In the next chapter of the book, I will describe how to assess what stages of psychological development the cultures your clients are embedded in are operating from.

Notes

1. Jeffrey E. Young, *Cognitive Therapy for Personality Disorders: A schema-focused approach (revised edition)* (Sarasota: Professional Resource Press), 1994, p. 11.
2. *http://valuescentre.com/pva*
3. Richard Barrett, *The Values-Driven Organisation* (London: Routledge), 2013.
4. The allocation of values to the three types of mind is my interpretation of Kegan's conceptual framework.

CHAPTER 11

ASSESSING CULTURAL COMPATIBILITY

As I explained in the preface, if the cultures your clients are embedded in are less advanced in their development than your clients are, your clients may find it difficult to explore their full potential.

If, on the other hand, the cultures they are embedded in are more advanced in their development than they are, your clients will feel supported in exploring their development, at least up to the levels of psychological development that these cultures have attained or are willing to tolerate. There are four levels of culture that you need to consider in this regard.

- The family culture
- The community culture
- The society culture
- The organisational culture

There are two ways you can evaluate these four cultures: by determining the predominant world view of the culture or by carrying out a values assessment of the culture.

Because carrying out a values assessment involves costs, the cheapest and quickest way to assess these cultures is to ask your client to read the descriptions of the world views provided in Chapter 6 and determine which world views they believe to be the most prevalent in the family, community, society and organisation to which they belong.

When you have done this, use Table 11.1 to make a correlation between the world views identified and the stages of psychological development. Based on the result, determine to what extent the stage of psychological development of your clients aligns with the stage of psychological development of the cultures in which they are embedded.

Table 11.1 Stages of psychological development and world views

Stages of psychological development	World views
Serving	Holistic
Integrating	Integrative
Self-actualising	People
Individuating	
Differentiating	Status
	Authority
	Power
Conforming	Tribal
Surviving	Survival

If, the results of the analysis of family, community and society world views show these cultures to be at a lower stage of development than your client, there is not much they can do to change the situation, unless they are able to move to another community or immigrate to another country which is operating at a higher stage of psychological development.

Their scope of action is much greater if they find the organisational culture they are embedded in is at a lower stage of development than they are. For this reason, one of the most important things you can do for your client is to help them evaluate if they are in the right organisation for the stage of development they have reached. The key question is: "Does the culture of the organisation in which they are embedded support or inhibit the level of development they have reached?"

Whilst you can use the world views from Chapter 6 to analyse the organisational culture in which your client is embedded, a better way of doing this is to use the descriptions of the stages of organisational development provided in this chapter to determine the primary and secondary stages of development of the organisation.

You can also carry out what is known as an Individual Values Assessment (IVA) or alternatively a Cultural Values Assessment (CVA).[1] The difference between these two types of assessment is as follows: The IVA represents your client's perspective on the organisational culture, whereas the CVA represents the amalgamated perspective of all the employees of the organisation or the team or business unit in which your client is embedded.

If you are coaching someone in an organisation that has done a CVA, then you may be able to use these results to assess the stage of psychological development of the organisation. If you are coaching someone in an organisation that has not done a CVA, then your best plan is to ask your client to carry out an IVA.

Ideally, having the results from an IVA *and* a CVA would give you the best outcome, especially if the CVA represents the particular functional group (team, unit or division) or hierarchical level (supervisor, manager or executive) that your client belongs to.

The reason it is best to have both an IVA and a CVA of the group your client is embedded in is because your client's perspective (IVA) may not be the same as the group's perspective (CVA). If your client's IVA is similar to the group or company-wide CVA, then you know your client's perspective is not biased. If, on the other hand, the IVA of your client is significantly different from the group or company-wide CVA, then you will need to explore with your client why their perspective is different. This will give you some insights into the biases your client has in the way they perceive their reality.

Stages of development of an organisation

Organisations grow and develop in the same way as individuals—by successfully mastering their needs. The most successful organisations are those that develop full spectrum consciousness—the ability to master the needs associated with every level of organisational consciousness. They are able to respond and adapt appropriately to all the challenges that the market place throws at them or in the case of public sector organisations, whatever conditions and vagaries are present or occur in their institutional environment.

The seven existential needs that constitute the seven stages of organisational development/levels of consciousness are shown in Table

11.2 along with the associated developmental tasks. The developmental tasks represent the stages that an organisation goes through from start-up to full spectrum performance. These are similar to the development tasks associated with the seven stages of personal psychological development.

Table 11.2 Stages of organisational development

	Stage of psychological development/ Levels of consciousness	Actions and needs	Developmental tasks
7	Serving/Service	Creating a long-term sustainable future for the organisation by caring for humanity and preserving Earth's life-support systems.	*Serving*: Safeguarding the well-being of the planet and society for future generations.
6	Integrating/ Making a difference	Building the resilience of the organisation by cooperating with other organisations and the local communities in which the organisation operates.	*Collaborating*: Aligning with other like-minded organisations and the local community for mutual benefit and support.
5	Self-actualising/ Internal cohesion	Enhancing the capacity of the organisation for collective action by aligning employee motivations around a shared set of values and an inspiring vision.	*Bonding*: Creating an internally cohesive, high-trust culture that enables the organisation to fulfil its purpose.
4	Individuating/ Transformation	Increasing innovation by giving employees a voice in decision-making and making them accountable for their futures and the overall success of the organisation.	*Empowering*: Empowering employees to participate in decision-making by giving them freedom and autonomy.

3	Differentiating/ Self-esteem	Establishing structures, policies, procedures and processes that create order, support the performance of the organisation and enhance employee pride.	*Performing*: Building high-performance systems and processes that focus on the efficient running of the organisation.
2	Conforming/ Relationship	Resolving conflicts and building harmonious relationships that create a sense of loyalty among employees and strong connection to customers.	*Harmonising*: Creating a sense of belonging, loyalty and mutual respect among employees and caring for customers.
1	Surviving/ Survival	Creating financial stability, profitability and caring for the health and safety of all employees.	*Surviving*: Becoming financially viable and independent.

The focus of the first three levels of organisational consciousness is on the basic needs of business—financial stability and profitability, employee and customer satisfaction, and high-performance systems and processes.

The focus of the fourth level of consciousness is on adaptability—continuous renewal and transformation—a shift from fear-based, rigid, authoritarian hierarchies or silos to more open, inclusive, adaptive and democratic systems of governance that empower employees to operate with responsible freedom (accountability).

The focus of the upper three levels of consciousness is on organisational cohesion, building mutually beneficial alliances and partnerships, and safeguarding the well-being of human society.

Organisations that focus *exclusively* on the satisfaction of their basic needs are not usually market leaders. They can be successful in their specific niche, but in general they are too internally focused and self-absorbed, or too rigid and bureaucratic to become innovators in their fields. They are slow to adapt to changes in market conditions and do not empower their employees. There is little enthusiasm among the workforce and innovation and creativity get suppressed. Levels of staff engagement are relatively low. Such organisations are run by authoritarian leaders who operate by creating a culture of fear. They are not emotionally healthy places to work. Employees feel frustrated or disempowered and may complain about stress.

Organisations that focus *exclusively* on the satisfaction of the higher needs lack the basic business skills necessary to operate effectively and profitably. They are ineffectual and impractical when it comes to financial matters, they are not customer oriented and they lack the systems and processes necessary for high performance. They are simply not grounded in the reality of business.

Developmental tasks

The first task when you create an organisation is to find ways of surviving financially. If you cannot survive—achieve an income stream that is larger than your expenses—then you will go bankrupt or fail.

Once a sustainable income stream has been achieved, the next task is to focus on relationships—managing internal conflicts, creating a sense of harmony and ensuring customers feel cared for and are happy with your products or services. If harmony cannot be achieved, frictions, frustrations and fragmentation will appear that undermine the organisation's performance. If your customers are not happy they will quickly migrate to other providers.

The next developmental task is to create order and efficiency in the structure and operations of your organisation by focusing on values such as excellence, quality and professionalism. You want to be productive, and you want your employees to feel a sense of pride in the organisation. You need to develop a reputation for reliability and agility so you can be responsive to the needs of the market place.

To be responsive, you need to innovate. To innovate, you need to engage the minds of your employees. To engage the minds of your employees, you have to involve them in decision-making—give them a sense of ownership.

An organisation cannot move to the transformation stage of development if it does not give its employees a voice in decision-making. This means empowering your employees by giving them responsible freedom—a felt sense of accountability for their contribution to the organisation. This stage of development is critically dependent on the degree to which the leadership group chooses to embrace democratic governance principles.

Once you have empowered your employees by giving them responsible freedom, the next step is to get everyone heading in the same direction and living the same values. To do this, you need to create a shared vision to give clarity to your purpose, and a shared set of values to guide decision-making. The vision should embrace a higher purpose—a purpose that supports the well-being of humanity or the planet. The values should be values that resonate with the hearts and minds of employees.

Only when the organisation has achieved a strong sense of internal cohesion (a high-trust culture) will it be able to successfully move to the next stage of development—collaborating with other like-minded organisations, partners and communities for mutual well-being and support. The purpose of this stage of development is to ensure the long-term resilience of the organisation.

Finally, the last stage of development is to support our human society. The organisation must become a responsible global citizen by doing what it can to support and create a sustainable future for the local communities where it operates, and for humanity in general, by helping the poor and disadvantaged and protecting the planet's life-support systems.

Each of these developmental tasks corresponds to a different level of consciousness—the focus of each of the seven levels of organisational consciousness is explained below.

Surviving

The first and most basic need of all organisations is to ensure their financial survival. Without profits or access to a continuing stream of funds, organisations quickly perish. Every organisation needs to make financial stability a primary concern. A precondition for success at this level of consciousness is a healthy focus on cash flow and the bottom line. When companies become too entrenched in survival consciousness they develop an unhealthy short-term focus on shareholder value. In such situations, making the quarterly numbers—satisfying the needs of the financial markets—can preoccupy the minds of the leaders to the exclusion of all other factors including the needs of employees. This leads to excessive control, micro-management, caution and a tendency to be risk-averse.

Businesses that operate from survival consciousness are not interested in strategic alliances; takeovers are more their game. They will purchase a company and plunder its assets. They see people and the Earth as resources to be exploited for gain. When asked to conform to regulations, they do the minimum. They have an attitude of begrudging compliance.

The key to success at the first level of consciousness is strong financial performance and a focus on employee health and safety. Without profits, companies cannot invest in their employees, create new products or build strong relationships with their customers and the local communities where they work.

Harmonising

The second basic need for all organisations is to create harmonious interpersonal relationships and good internal communications. Without good relationships with employees, customers and suppliers, a company's survival will be compromised. The critical issue at this level of consciousness is to create a sense of loyalty and belonging among employees, and a sense of caring and connection between the organisation and its customers and suppliers. Preconditions for creating a sense of belonging are open communication, mutual respect and employee recognition. Preconditions for caring are friendliness, responsiveness and listening. When these are in place, loyalty and satisfaction among employees and customers will be high. Traditions and rituals help cement these bonds.

Fears about belonging and lack of respect lead to fragmentation, dissension and disloyalty. When leaders meet behind closed doors, or fail to communicate openly, employees suspect the worst: Cliques form and gossip becomes rife. When the leaders are more focused on their own success rather than the success of the organisation, they begin to compete with each other. When leaders display territorial behaviours, blame, internal competition and internal politics ensue. Family businesses often operate from the second level of consciousness because they are patriarchal, built on family connections and are unable to trust outsiders in management positions.

Performing

The focus of the third level of organisational consciousness is on performance, excellence, quality and professionalism. It is about keeping a balanced and watchful eye on all the key performance indicators. At this level of consciousness, the organisation is focused on staying agile, becoming the best it can be through the adoption of best practices and focusing on productivity and efficiency. Systems and processes are strongly emphasised and strategies are developed to achieve desired results. Re-engineering, Six Sigma and Total Quality Management are typical responses to issues of performance at this level of consciousness.

Organisations that operate from the third level of consciousness tend to be structured hierarchically for the purposes of central control. Top-down is the primary mode of decision-making. The hierarchical structure also provides opportunities for rewarding individuals who are focused on their own personal success. Steep hierarchies often serve no other purpose than to cater to managers' needs for recognition, status and self-esteem. To maintain central control, organisations that operate from the third level of consciousness tend to formulate rules to regulate and bring order to all aspects of their business. Companies that are predominantly focused at this level of consciousness can easily degenerate into power-based silos or rigid authoritarian bureaucracies. When this happens, failure or collapse will eventually occur, unless the organisation can shift to the next level of consciousness.

Empowering

The focus of the fourth level of organisational consciousness is on adaptability, employee empowerment, continuous renewal and continuous learning. The critical issue at this level of consciousness is how to stimulate innovation so that new products and services can be developed to respond to market opportunities. This requires the organisation to be flexible and take risks. To fully respond to the challenges of this level of consciousness, the organisation must actively garner employees' ideas and opinions. Everyone must feel that their voice is being heard. This requires managers and leaders to admit they do not have all the answers and invite employee participation. For many leaders and managers this is a new role, requiring new skills. That is why it is important to develop the emotional and social intelligence of managers. They must be able to facilitate high performance in large groups of people who are looking for equality and responsible freedom. Employees want to be accountable—not micro-managed and supervised every moment of every day.

One of the dangers at this level of consciousness is to become overly biased towards consensus. Whilst some level of consensus is important, ultimately decisions must get made. Too much consensus can be the death knell of innovation.

A precondition for success at this level of consciousness is encouraging all employees to think and act like entrepreneurs. More accountability is given to everyone and structures become less hierarchical. Teamwork is encouraged and more attention is given to personal development and relationship skills. Diversity is seen as a positive asset in exploring new ideas. This shift, which brings responsible freedom and equality to workers, cannot fully achieve the desired results unless all employees and teams share similar values, have a common purpose and a shared vision of the future. This requires a shift to the fifth level of consciousness.

Bonding

The focus at the fifth level of consciousness is on building an internally cohesive organisation that has a capacity for collective action. For this to happen, leaders and managers must set aside their personal agendas and learn to work for the common good. The critical requirements at this level of consciousness are developing a shared vision of the future that inspires employees, a shared set of values that provides guidance for decision-making, and an organisational purpose that is more than making a profit. The shared vision, values and purpose should clarify the intentions of the organisation with regard to all its stakeholders. The values should be translated into behaviours so they can be used for performance management. The values should be reflected in all the systems and processes of the organisation, with appropriate consequences for those who are unwilling to conform.

A precondition for success at this level of consciousness is to build a climate of trust that engenders responsible freedom. In order to build commitment and enthusiasm, every member of the organisation should understand how their contribution relates to the overall success of the organisation. In organisations that operate from the fifth level of consciousness, failures become lessons, and work becomes fun. The key to success at this level of consciousness is the establishment of a strong, positive, unique cultural identity that differentiates the organisation from its competitors. The culture of the organisation becomes a reflection of the brand. This is particularly important in service organisations where employees have close contact with customers and the general public. At this and subsequent levels of consciousness, organisations usually preserve their unique culture by promoting from within.

Collaborating

The focus of the sixth level of organisational consciousness is on deepening the level of internal connectedness in the organisation and expanding the sense of external connectedness with stakeholders in order to make the organisation more resilient.

Internally, the focus is on helping employees find personal fulfilment through their work. Externally, the focus is on building mutually beneficial partnerships and alliances with business partners, the local communities in which the organisation operates and in certain circumstances with non-governmental organisations. The critical issue at this level of consciousness is that employees and customers see that the organisation is making a difference in the world, either through its products and services, its involvement in the local community or its willingness to fight for causes that improve the well-being of humanity or the planet. Employees and customers must feel that the company cares about them, their futures and their needs.

Companies operating at this level of consciousness go the extra mile to make sure they are being responsible global citizens. They support and encourage employees' activities in the local community by providing time off to do volunteer work and making financial contributions to the charities in which employees are involved. At this level of consciousness, organisations create an environment where employees can find personal fulfilment. The organisation supports employees in becoming all they can become, both in terms of their professional and their personal growth.

A precondition for success at this level is developing leaders with a strong sense of empathy. Leaders must recognise that they must not only provide direction for the organisation, but they must also become the servants of those who work for them. They must create an environment that supports every employee in aligning their sense of purpose with the vision or mission of the company. At this level of consciousness leaders become mentors, thereby creating pools of talent that support succession planning. Leadership development is given significant emphasis at this level of consciousness.

Serving

The focus at the seventh level of organisational consciousness is a continuation of the previous level—a further deepening of internal connectedness, and a further expansion of external connectedness. Internally, the focus of the organisation is on building a climate of humility and compassion. Externally, the focus is on local, national or global activism in building a sustainable future for humanity and the planet. The critical issue at this level of consciousness is developing a deep sense of social responsibility throughout the organisation, by caring about social justice, human rights and the ecology of the global environment.

A precondition for success at this level of consciousness is selfless service, displayed through a profound commitment to the common good and to the well-being of future generations. To be successful at this level of consciousness, organisations must embrace the highest ethical standards in all their interactions with employees, suppliers, customers, partners, investors and the local community. They should always give full consideration to the long-term impacts of their decisions and actions on all stakeholders.

Using an IVA to measure the stage of development of an organisation

In order to illustrate how to evaluate whether the organisational culture your client is embedded in supports or hinders your client's psychological development, I am going to use two Individual Values Assessment (IVA) case studies.

The IVA requires your client to complete a survey which involves three questions. The first question involves picking ten values/behaviours that they believe represent who they are. The second question involves picking ten values/behaviours that they believe represent how the organisation they are embedded in operates. The third question involves picking ten values/ behaviours that they believe represents a high-performance organisation.

The lists of values/behaviours they pick from (templates) have between 80 and 100 words/phrases. Every value/behaviour on the template is classified in four different ways:

- Level of consciousness
- Positive or potentially limiting
- Individual, relationship, organisational, societal
- Six business categories

For a full description of all these classifications, with examples, please refer to Chapter 6 of *The Values-driven Organisation*.

Working in a toxic culture

My first example is an ambitious manager with a self-authoring mind who finds himself in a high-entropy, toxic organisation (see Figure 11.1).

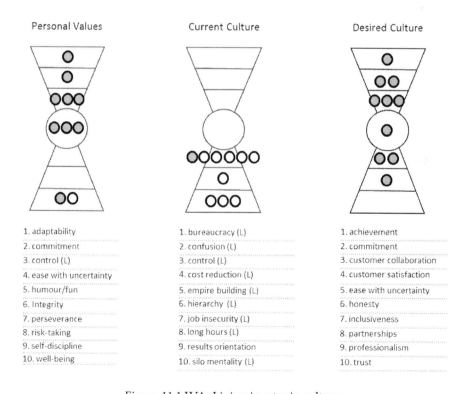

Personal Values	Current Culture	Desired Culture
1. adaptability	1. bureaucracy (L)	1. achievement
2. commitment	2. confusion (L)	2. commitment
3. control (L)	3. control (L)	3. customer collaboration
4. ease with uncertainty	4. cost reduction (L)	4. customer satisfaction
5. humour/fun	5. empire building (L)	5. ease with uncertainty
6. Integrity	6. hierarchy (L)	6. honesty
7. perseverance	7. job insecurity (L)	7. inclusiveness
8. risk-taking	8. long hours (L)	8. partnerships
9. self-discipline	9. results orientation	9. professionalism
10. well-being	10. silo mentality (L)	10. trust

Figure 11.1 IVA: Living in a toxic culture

On the left of this figure you see this person's top ten personal values distributed across the seven levels of consciousness. In the centre, you see his perspective on the current culture of his organisation. On the right you see his perspective on the desired culture.

At first glance, you can see this person is relatively ambitious because his personal values of risk-taking, self-discipline and perseverance, combined with his desired culture value of achievement, suggest that he really sets out to get what he wants. Significantly, also, 60 per cent of his personal values are located in Levels 4 and 5—the levels of the self-authoring mind. He is looking for challenges and opportunities to prove himself.

He wants to do well, and he probably will do well because he understands what it takes to create a successful business—his desired culture values are almost full spectrum—values at almost all levels, with more than 50 per cent of values at Levels 5 and 6, and well distributed across the value types—four individual values, two relationship values and four organisational values. He recognises the importance of customer satisfaction and collaboration and is aware of the need for partnerships.

He is also balanced in his personal life: The value of well-being suggests he is focused on balancing his physical, emotional, mental and spiritual needs.

He sees the current culture of his organisation as extremely toxic. Almost anyone would find this culture difficult to work in. The fact that he has self-discipline and control (a potentially limiting relationship value) in his personal values, and has no positive relationship values in his top ten personal values—all the rest are individual values—suggests that he might last longer in this culture than someone who is relationship oriented.

One of the key issues that the coach who is feeding back the results of this IVA needs to ask this individual is to what extent his value of control is linked to his value of self-discipline. It is highly likely that these two values work together to help this person to weather the toxic culture. In which case, the value of control is more likely to mean self-control to him, and would not therefore be a potentially limiting relationship value, but more of a positive individual value. What makes me suspect that this is the case is that we do not normally see control juxtaposed with ease with uncertainty and risk-taking in someone's personal values. Control and risk-taking are polarities that do not normally sit well together.

Based on the results of this IVA I suspect that this individual is shifting from the individuating stage of psychological development to the self-actualising stage—the fourth and fifth levels of consciousness. Meanwhile, his organisation is operating at the differentiation stage and has numerous secondary motivations at the first three levels of consciousness. This is not a good fit for this person. Staying in this organisation does not auger well for his future. He will not feel supported in his growth and development.

Getting grounded in the basics of business

My second example of an IVA, shown below in Figure 11.2, is typical of some of the individual consultants who are drawn to the work of cultural transformation and leadership coaching. They have values in the upper levels of consciousness; they have vision and wisdom and want to cooperate with others to make a difference in the world. What they are sometimes missing are the values associated with the first three levels of organisational consciousness.

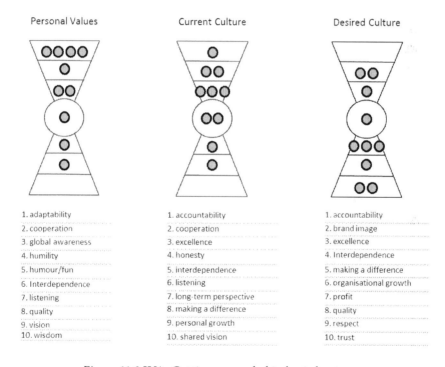

Personal Values	Current Culture	Desired Culture
1. adaptability	1. accountability	1. accountability
2. cooperation	2. cooperation	2. brand image
3. global awareness	3. excellence	3. excellence
4. humility	4. honesty	4. Interdependence
5. humour/fun	5. interdependence	5. making a difference
6. Interdependence	6. listening	6. organisational growth
7. listening	7. long-term perspective	7. profit
8. quality	8. making a difference	8. quality
9. vision	9. personal growth	9. respect
10. wisdom	10. shared vision	10. trust

Figure 11.2 IVA: Getting grounded in basic business

This particular individual who is in his mid-forties, has three matching personal and current culture values—cooperation, interdependence and listening; four matching current and desired culture values—accountability, excellence, interdependence and making a difference; and two matching personal and desired cultural values—quality and interdependence, one of which—interdependence—is common to all three lists.

The main difference between the current culture and desired culture are the four grounded organisational values that appear in the desired culture—brand image, organisational growth, profit and quality. There are only two organisational values in the current culture—long-term perspective and shared vision.

Intuitively, this person knows that in order to become a full spectrum leader of his own business, he needs to give much more focus to the first three levels of organisational consciousness. This will be difficult for him because it is not where he finds his passion. Taking care of business basics is not what gets his juices flowing.

Based on the results of this IVA, this individual appears to be operating at a high stage of psychological development, beyond what their age would suggest. In order to clarify what stage of psychological development this person is operating at you could either ask them to do some of the primary motivation exercises in Chapter 10 or carry out an LVA.

Based on age, I suspect that this person is probably operating at the self-actualising stage of development. The organisation also appears to be operating at this stage of development. This seems to be a reasonably good fit. This individual will feel supported in their growth and development in this organisation. The challenge for this person, which they clearly comprehend, is that in order to become more effective the organisation needs to take care of the blinds spots it has at the first three levels of consciousness.

This type of IVA is typical of people working in non-governmental organisations (NGOs). The people attracted to such organisations are so intent on living out their passion and making a difference, that they have little interest or energy for running an organisation. This can cause problems because it limits the ability of the organisation to be effective.

Private sector organisations tend to operate from the performing (differentiating) or empowering (individuating) stages of development and find it difficult to support people who are self-actualising or integrating. NGOs, on the other hand, tend to operate from the bonding (self-actualising) or collaborating (integrating) stages of development, and although they can support people who are self-actualising, their lack of skills (blind spots) at the surviving, harmonising (conforming) and performing (differentiating) stages of development, prevent them from being as successful as they could be. A high functioning, well-rounded professional, who is operating at the self-actualising stage of development or above, will find these blind spots frustrating to deal with, and could cause them to look for employment elsewhere.

Summary

Here are the main points of this chapter:

1. The third step in evolutionary coaching is to identify the stages of psychological development the cultures your client is embedded in are at to determine whether the cultures support or inhibit your client's psychological growth.
2. There are two ways you can evaluate these cultures: by determining the predominant world view of the culture or by carrying out a values assessment of the culture.
3. There are two types of values assessments you can carry out to measure the culture of your client's organisational culture: an Individual Values Assessment (IVA) or a Cultural Values Assessment (CVA).
3. Organisations grow and develop in the same way as individuals— by successfully mastering their needs.
4. There are seven stages in the development of organisational consciousness.
5. The most successful organisations are those that develop full spectrum consciousness—the ability to master the needs associated with every level of organisational consciousness.

In the next part of the book, I will discuss the practice of evolutionary coaching—what an evolutionary coach needs to know, in order to support their clients in mastering the needs of the individuating, self-actualising, integrating and serving stages of psychological development.

Note

1. See *http://valuescentre.com/products__services*

PART III

The Practice of Evolutionary Coaching—Mastery

The purpose of Part III of this book is to provide the reader with an overview of the key areas of expertise that coaches need to be familiar with in order to help their clients master the higher stages of their psychological development, namely, the individuating, self-actualising, integrating and serving stages.

Chapter 12 provides an introduction to the topic of mastery viewed from an evolutionary perspective. Chapter 13 discusses the key understandings required to support the mastery the individuating stage of psychological development. Chapter 14 discusses the key understandings required to support the mastery the self-actualising stage of psychological development. Chapter 15 discusses the key understandings required to support the mastery of the integrating stage of psychological development. Chapter 16 discusses the key understandings required to support the mastery of the serving stage of psychological development.

Chapter 12

Introduction to Mastery

The exercises and surveys presented in Part II of this book were designed to enable your clients to get a clear understanding of their primary and secondary motivations, and the personal issues and cultural obstacles that are hindering or preventing them moving ahead with their human emergence.

The third part of this book, explains how to use this information to support your client in their journey through the individuating, self-actualising, integrating and serving stages of their psychological development. You will also find additional exercises that are specifically tailored for achieving a deeper understanding of some of the growth stages of development.

I have entitled the third part of this book "mastery" because this concept lies at the core of human psychological development: you must be able to master the skills that are necessary to meet the needs of the stage of psychological evolution you are at, before you can successfully move to the next stage.

That does not mean you cannot begin to work on your self-actualisation before you have completed your individuation. You can! But your ability to successfully master the self-actualisation stage will be compromised to the extent that you have not fully mastered the individuation stage or any of the earlier stages of your development—surviving, conforming and differentiating. This is true for all stages. For example, your ability to master the integrating stage will be handicapped by your lack of mastery of any of the previous stages. I will explain why this is so later, after I have explained the two types of secondary motivations.

Two types of secondary motivations

Unless you are coaching young children, which I am assuming you are not, then every one of your clients (over the age of 20) will either be at the differentiating stage of development or higher. This means that your first task as an evolutionary coach, after you have identified your client's primary motivation is to help them identify and master their secondary motivations—the unmet needs they still have from the previous stages of their development.

As discussed in Chapter 10, we can divide people's secondary motivations into two types: the conscious and subconscious motivations associated with meeting their (ego) deficiency needs (from the surviving, conforming and differentiating stages of their development); and, the conscious and subconscious motivations associated with meeting their (soul) growth needs (from the individuating, self-actualising and integrating stage of development).

The difference between these two sets of needs—deficiency needs and growth needs, is that secondary motivations associated with your client's deficiency needs are sourced from their conscious and subconscious fear-based beliefs (also known as early maladaptive schema), whereas the secondary motivations associated with your client's growth needs are sourced from the lack of energetic alignment between their ego and their soul. It will be extremely expedient to your client's progress if you are able to help them master their unmet deficiency needs before they work on mastering their unmet growth needs.

In order to reflect this imperative, I have structured Part III of this book in the following way. Chapter 12 focuses on the general concept of mastery as it relates to all stages of psychological development. Each of the subsequent chapters focuses on the skills and expertise your clients must master to satisfy their growth needs. Chapter 13 focuses on what is required to master ego-soul alignment at the individuating stage of development. Chapter 14 focuses on what is required to master ego-soul alignment at the self-actualising stage of development. Chapter 15 focuses on what is required to master ego-soul alignment at the integrating stage of development, and Chapter 16 focuses on what is required to master ego-soul alignment at the serving stage of development.

Mastery

The most common definition of the concept of mastery I have come across is:

> Mastery is the ability to command the expertise necessary to manage a subject, an activity or a process with ease.

From the perspective of human emergence, mastery means something slightly different:

> Developing the skills and expertise required to attain and maintain your internal stability and external equilibrium at the stage of psychological development you have reached in the social and physical framework of your existence.

Viewed from the evolutionary perspective, we can say mastery is a life-long process of emergent learning. Every time you enter a new stage of psychological development your internal stability and external equilibrium will be disturbed. To meet the new needs, at the new stage of development, you will need to develop new skills and adopt new behaviours to enable you to re-establish your internal stability and external equilibrium.

Evolving from one stage of psychological development to the next is not the only way we disturb our internal stability and external equilibrium. We also disturb our internal stability and external equilibrium when we take on new challenges, are triggered by our subconscious fear-based beliefs, and allow our safety needs take priority over our growth needs.

Taking on a new challenge

No matter what stage of development you are at, when you take on a new challenge in your external world—shift from high school to university, from university to a paying job, when you get a significant promotion, or you take on an important new task or project you have never done before, you will automatically disturb your external equilibrium. This will, in turn, disturb your internal stability. You may worry about your ability to fulfil your expectations and the expectations of others or you may get anxious about your ability to cope with the demands placed on you by the new more complex framework of existence you are moving into. As you become proficient at satisfying your needs in the new framework of existence, your worries and anxieties will dissipate and you will be able to re-establish your internal stability and external equilibrium. When you do this often enough, you will overcome any fears you may have about taking on new challenges. You may even find them exciting.

Sub-conscious fear-based beliefs

Whatever stage of development you are at, if you have secondary motivations (unmet needs) associated with your deficiency needs, you will from time to time get triggered by your early maladaptive schema. The memories of the hurt associated with the unmet needs from your childhood will come crashing into your conscious awareness, causing you to experience some form of emotional reaction or emotional distress. You may become impatient, demanding or difficult to get along with, or you may get frustrated, angry or upset. During, or more usually, after one of these experiences, you may berate yourself for not having measured up to the situation, and you may feel guilty for the pain your words or actions have caused other people. When any of these things happen, you will experience a disturbance in your internal stability. Because of the adverse impact your reactions or outbursts may have on other people, you might also experience discord or disharmony and thereby experience a disturbance in your external disequilibrium.

Allowing safety needs to take precedence over growth needs

When you choose safety over growth—when the conscious or subconscious fear-based beliefs of your ego get in the way of meeting the needs of your soul—you will feel a disturbance in your internal stability. This ego-soul misalignment will show up as some form of unease—resistance, caution or feelings of sadness, shame or guilt. You may even feel depressed. All these feelings are an indication that your ego and soul are out of alignment and your internal stability has been disturbed. Only when the ego and soul are in energetic alignment do we experience internal stability.

You can also disturb your internal stability (ego-soul alignment) when you do something that is out of integrity; when you are less than honest with someone or you blame others for your mistakes in order to avoid punishment. At such times, it is important to recognise that your fears are preventing you from leading an authentic life. You cannot be authentic if you are economical or creative with the truth.

Perturbation in your energy field

No matter how the disturbance to your internal stability is caused, what you are actually experiencing is a perturbation in your energy field. The higher the stage you have reach in your psychological development, the more acutely you will feel the disturbances caused by the triggering of your subconscious fear-based beliefs or your ego-soul misalignments. Conversely, the lower you are in your psychological development the more acutely you will feel the disturbances caused by taking on new challenges.

In other words, taking on new challenges normally gets easier as you make progress in your psychological development (as you get older and more confident), and dealing with the impacts of your subconscious fear-based beliefs and your ego-soul misalignments normally gets harder unless you engage in some form of personal mastery. It gets harder, because each time you shift to a higher stage of development you increase the frequency of vibration of your energy field. Consequently, you feel the impact of your low vibrational frequency fears and ego-soul misalignments more acutely.

If you want to avoid or reduce the perturbations in your energy field, you will need to learn how to manage your secondary motivations by overcoming the fears associated with your unmet deficiency needs, and the reducing the misalignment of your ego with your soul.

The needs of the three minds

The definition of mastery we have used—*developing the skills and expertise required to attain and maintain your internal stability and external equilibrium at each stage of your psychological development in the social and physical framework of your existence*—is intended to not only acknowledge the embedded nature of our lives in our social and physical environment, but also the holistic nature of who we are—a body-mind, an ego-mind and a soul-mind associated with a physical human body.

Each of these minds has needs which must be satisfied before we can live in internal stability and external equilibrium. If you are unable to satisfy any one of these sets of needs, you will not be able to maintain the internal stability of your energy field for long. When your body needs food, you will get hungry. When you ego feels bruised, you will get angry. When your soul feels ignored, you will get depressed. Every one of these situations disturbs your energy field, resulting in sensations or feelings that command your conscious awareness and thereby prevent you from focusing on your primary motivation. When you are able to meet the needs of all of these minds you experience feelings of internal cohesion—ease, comfort, happiness, contentment and joy.

Of these three sets of needs—body-mind, ego-mind and soul-mind— two of them are fixed and constant and are exactly the same for every human being. These are the needs of the body-mind and the soul-mind. Every human body needs clean air, clean water, healthy wholesome food, exercise and shelter. Every human soul needs to have the freedom to live a values-driven and purpose-driven life.

Left to their own devices the body-mind and the soul-mind naturally live in harmony with each other because the conscious awareness of every atom, molecule, cell and organ in the human body is infused with the soul's will—to be present (survive) in our three-dimensional physical reality. Therefore, the only variable in the internal stability and external equilibrium equation, is the will of the ego-mind.

During the first four stages of psychological development the will of the ego-mind is directed towards the satisfaction of its surviving, conforming and differentiating needs. It is only when we reach the self-actualising stage of psychological development that the will of the ego-mind aligns with the will of the soul-mind. The individuating stage prepares us for this by causing us to question the values and beliefs we adopted or developed during the first three stages of our development.

Because the human energy field is comprised of the energy fields of the body-mind (etheric field), the ego-mind (emotional field), and the soul-mind (spiritual field), as well as the mental field, where all our conscious thinking takes place, the thoughts and feelings generated by the ego-mind have a significant effect on the functioning of the body-mind and soul-mind. Consequently, when the disturbances in the ego-mind are frequent, they can cause the body to get sick and compromise the functioning of the immune system, and when the will of the ego-mind is out of alignment with the soul-mind, the ego-mind causes the soul-mind to feel sad and depressed.

Ego-mind

The ego-mind is the aspect of your personality that identifies with your body: it is the interface between you and the rest of the physical world. The ego-mind is focused on one thing—maintaining its internal stability and external equilibrium (and the internal stability and external equilibrium of those it identifies with) at the stage of psychological development it has reached by getting its needs met.

The ego-mind has three basic needs which correspond to the tasks of the first three stages of psychological development—to survive and prosper (surviving), to love and be loved (conforming), and to be recognised and acknowledged (differentiating).

Whereas the primary purpose of your body-mind is to keep your body alive, the primary purpose of your ego-mind is to protect itself and everything it identifies with (the body and those it loves) from physical and emotional harm in its social and cultural framework of existence.

One of the ways the ego protects its internal stability is by projecting the feelings it finds difficult to accept, such as shame and guilt, onto others in its external world. In psychological literature this is called the shadow. In severe cases of trauma, the ego will disassociate itself from such feelings by creating a sub-personality. Another way of protecting itself, especially when it feels it has failed, is by adopting the role of the victim.

Whenever your ego-mind makes a decision that is sourced from fear, you lose your internal stability. Fear also affects your ability to use your mental field (neo-cortex) because our minds are programmed to give priority to processing fear. Consequently, whenever the ego feels fear or reacts to a situation with fear, the ability of the soul-mind or the ego-mind to use the mental field to get its needs met is adversely affected. When your ego harbours conscious or subconscious fears the whole of your energy field can become disturbed.

The body-mind

The body-mind is the interface between the atoms, molecules, cells and organs of the body and the body's external physical environment. It operates subconsciously, because our ego-mind is not aware of the millions of decisions that our atoms, molecules, cells and organs make every day of our lives. The body-mind is focused on one thing—maintaining the internal stability and external equilibrium of our physical being.

The body-mind is the natural (DNA encoded) response system that all *creatures* have for staying alive and assuring the continuation of their species. The body-mind regulates the internal functioning of the body and helps us deal with external threats, such as diseases and wounds that could harm or compromise the functioning of the body and life threatening encounters with other people or our environment.

Unlike the body-mind, which can only deal with threats to its external equilibrium through fight-or-flight, the ego-mind can protect itself by suppressing its needs and modifying its behaviours. The anxiety, frustration and stress this induces, causes the body-mind to produce chemical products which can, over the long-term, throw the body-mind into a state of internal instability. The roots of this chemical instability are the ego's anxieties which arise from your conscious and subconscious fears.

The needs of the body-mind generally take precedence over the needs of the ego-mind and the needs of the soul-mind. You cannot resist satisfying the body's need for water, food, defecating, urinating, and breathing for long periods, no matter what else is happening in your life. If you do, you will feel uncomfortable and eventually, if you ignore these needs, you will compromise the ability of your body to sustain your life, thus setting yourself in direct opposition to the needs of your soul.

Soul-mind

The soul-mind is the interface between your energy field and the energy fields of everything that exists in our three-dimensional physical world.

Your soul-mind is focused on living a value-driven and purpose driven-life in your physical body. The only thing preventing your soul from doing that is the focus of your ego-mind gives to meeting its needs at the stage of development it has reached and the stages of development it has passed through where it still has unmet needs.

Whilst your conscious awareness (mental field) is focused on your ego's needs it cannot focus on your soul's needs. Only when the ego: (a) aligns itself energetically with the soul by overcoming its fears; (b) chooses to live a values-driven life; and (c) aligns with the soul's purpose, is your conscious awareness fully and completely available to focus on satisfying your soul's needs. This begins to occur at the psychological stage of development known as self-actualisation.

If your ego-mind has not begun to align with the needs of your soul-mind by mid-life, your soul-mind will begin to prompt your ego-mind about getting its needs met. If you fail to recognise these prompts, you will feel some form of existential discomfort—a lack of alignment between the energy field of your ego-mind and your soul-mind. The most frequent form or existential discomfort people experience is a deep sense of emptiness or a lack meaning in their lives. I will explore this topic in more depth in Chapter 14.

Flow

Based on the above, we can clearly see that the core issues in maintaining internal stability and external equilibrium are: (a) the ego's ability to live in right relationship with the body; (b) the ego's ability to live in right relationship with the soul; and (c) the ego's ability to live in right relationship with its social and physical environment at the stage of psychological development it has reached. This is the key to human emergence. When you can fulfil these conditions you will experience your life as a state of flow.

Whilst you can experience a state of flow at any level of psychological development, the most potent and long lasting feelings of flow arise when you reach the self-actualisation stage and beyond—when you get into alignment with the will of your soul.

Whereas at the lower stages of development your experiences of flow may occur for a few minutes or hours at a time, at the higher stages of development you are can sometimes experience a state of flow for days, weeks or months. Whenever you experience flow, you are operating at peak performance: you are living in internal stability and external equilibrium.

What prevents flow, according to Milhaly Csikszentmihalyi author of the best-selling book *Flow,* is psychic entropy.[1] Psychic entropy arises from emotional upsets such as fear, rage, anxiety and jealousy. This is what I refer to in Chapter 10 as personal entropy.

One of the key signs that you are in a state of flow is the presence of synchronicity in your life. The psychologist Carl Jung described synchronicity as "unconnected events with a common meaning". The following words by William H. Murray, which appear in his book, The Scottish Himalayan Expedition (1951), succinctly capture the idea of synchronicity:

> *Concerning all acts of initiative (and creation), there is one elementary truth the ignorance of which kills countless ideas and splendid plans: that the moment one definitely commits oneself, then providence moves too. A whole stream of events issues from the decision, raising in one's favour all manner of unforeseen incidents, meetings and material assistance, which no man could have dreamt would have come his way.*

What I believe Murray is saying is, when you commit to a creative act which aligns with the desires of your soul, providence in the guise of synchronicity shows up in your life. You know you are receiving soul promptings when your attention is "accidentally" drawn to the same thought, the same book or the same person several times in the course of a few days. I used to notice these situations and wonder why they were happening. When I realised they were synchronistic happenings—soul promptings, I began to give them my full attention.

Another form of prompting that Murray points to are unforeseen incidents, meetings and material assistance. Over the years, I have noticed such experiences becoming more and more part of my everyday experience: So much so, that I don't think of them as unusual anymore. I am sure everyone reading this book has experienced synchronicity or promptings in their life. Ask yourself: "Did you recognise these as soul promptings?", "Did they occur when you were in a state of flow?"

Ten strategies for getting into flow

This raises an important question: How do you consciously get and stay in a state of flow? The answer is you don't. You cannot consciously move into flow, because flow is a gift from the soul that occurs when you surrender to your soul's desires. Although you can't switch flow on, you can encourage it by consciously committing yourself to your soul's purpose and then attempting to implement as many of the following strategies as you can.

- Become unbelievably adaptive.
- Surrender to the process.
- Never trick yourself into believing you have the best answer.
- Be at ease with what is.
- Focus on what is in front of you.
- Be at ease with uncertainty.
- Try to include everything.
- Consider the whole system.
- Stick to your values.
- Follow your passion.

Become unbelievably adaptive: Let go of any idea of the way things have to be. These are just your assumptions. Whatever wants to emerge and energetically feels right is the right thing to do. Focus on what you have energy for, and let go of anything that does not spark your juices. Go with your inspiration. The most successful people and companies are unbelievably adaptive. They are not attached to their idea of how things have to be. These people have self-transforming minds. They are constantly reinterpreting reality. The map of the world they use for meaning-making is always a work in progress.

Surrender to the process: This is hard at the beginning, especially when it means letting go of things that you identify with. I have let go of relationships, homes, and even being CEO of my own company. Letting go is a hard thing to do. In many situations it is only by letting go do that you find the freedom to do what you need to do. You have to surrender to your soul if you want to fulfil your destiny and experience fulfilment. In this situation, surrender does not represent defeat. It represents growth and most importantly, victory over fear.

Never trick yourself into believing you have the best answer: Forget everything you think you know. It just serves to block your intuition and inspiration. It stops the emergence of new ideas. Knowledge is a two-edged sword. It can be amazingly brilliant at helping you solve problems, and it can be amazingly obstructive in enabling you to think out of the box. What you think you know is a filter you apply to your experience. Always challenge your assumptions/beliefs. I frequently remind myself and even state it in front of others that I don't know anything. I do this so I can stay open. I know that only when the cup is empty can it be filled. Only when you become a void can you be a channel for things to flow through you.

Be at ease with what is: You always give everything that happens in your life all the meaning it has for you. I know it is hard to believe that everything that happens is neutral. It may feel right or wrong or good or bad, but, from the quantum perspective (a place without judgement), it is what it is. It is nothing other than an event or a situation. As long as you know this, and remind yourself of it, then you are free to examine your feelings and emotions from a place of neutrality. By not judging, you allow the meaning of the event to unfold. So often, I have found that what felt like something bad when it happened, turned out to be something really good. Holding off on your judgement allows you to see through the eyes of wisdom.

Focus on what is in front of you: Do not get distracted from your purpose. When you reach the higher stages of development, you will become recognised as an "influential" person. You will be "someone". People will want your attention: They will want to enlist your support in their endeavours. This can be a trap for your ego. If you become too distracted, you will lose your way. You must keep your energies focused on your soul purpose and your next immediate priority while allowing yourself quiet time for reflection or meditation so inspiration can flow. Don't seek the limelight. Choose your friends carefully. Don't get railroaded into projects that don't get your juices flowing. Learn to say no. You will know where to put your energies if you allow yourself to be guided by the inspiration of your soul.

Be at ease with uncertainty: Sometimes, the best answer to what seems like a problematic situation is to do nothing. Just standing back and letting the situation unfold with the energies that are driving it can be the perfect thing to do. Allowing things to fall apart can on some occasions be a positive strategy. At other times, intervening in a situation is totally the right thing to do. Knowing whether to intervene or not is a valuable skill that relies on intuition and inspiration. This means there will be times when you consciously decide to live with uncertainty. Being able to stay in a place of uncertainty is impossible if your ego is hanging on to fear. The urge to control what is happening is how the ego creates certainty. To live with uncertainty means detaching from your need to get to an outcome.

Try to include everything: Be incredibly curious. Never stop asking questions. Whenever you are considering ways to solve a problem, always bring into the picture everything that is related in some way, even if the relationship at first appears tenuous. Include the whole system in your inquiry. This is when patterns appear. Unseen patterns are behind everything. You will not be able to find them unless you engage in constant inquiry. Enlist your intuition and inspiration in your search for the truth.

Consider the whole system: Always stay in touch with the big picture. Whatever is going on and whatever issues present, ask yourself: "What are the needs of the whole system?" It is so easy to get stuck in trying to resolve a situation when the situation you are trying to resolve is a symptom of a larger problem. There is always a bigger picture to everything. Everything exists in a framework, and every framework exists inside another framework. There is nothing in our physical world that does not exist within multiple frameworks. What frameworks are you operating in?

Stick to your values: The only way you can maintain your authenticity is to use your values in decision-making. Let your values guide your decisions in everything you do. When you are faced with a choice, ask yourself: "What are the values I want to use to guide me in this situation?" Your values represent your needs, and your needs represent your motivations. Living your values is how you maintain authenticity; it is also how you live with integrity.

Follow your passion: Whatever shows up in your life as your soul's purpose, follow it until you die. This is your ticket to fulfilment and your passport to passion. Once you align your ego with your soul, you will begin to realise that living the life your soul intended for you is the only thing you have to do.

These ten strategies for getting into and staying in flow will seem like a step too far if you are living in a state of anxiety with unresolved conscious or subconscious fears. That's fine. Focus on the strategies you think you can live with. Remember the process of personal evolution is a life-time journey. Just because some of these strategies may seem a stretch too far to you now does not mean that they are wrong. It only means that they are not right for you yet.

Reducing entropy

When you are able to live in a state of flow, everything in your life improves. Let me explain why.

Human beings and human social structures (organisations, communities, and nations) use energy in three ways: (a) to maintain their internal stability; (b) to maintain their external equilibrium; and (c) to do useful work that enhances their ability to survive and prosper in their current framework of existence—to grow and develop by doing life-enhancing work.

Since the amount of energy available to us each day is relatively fixed, when the amount of energy we need to expend to maintain our internal stability and external equilibrium increases, the amount of energy we have available for doing life-enhancing work decreases; Mastery therefore enables us to maximise the amount of energy we have for growing, developing and doing value-added work.

We call the energy that is used for maintaining internal stability and external equilibrium, *entropy*. We experience low entropy when there is order, direction and harmony in our lives. Another way of saying order, direction and harmony is *internal cohesion*. We experience high entropy when there is disorder, confusion and emotional disturbance. Mastery enables us to reduce the entropy in our lives and increase internal cohesion.

The primary source of entropy in our lives is the fear-based beliefs we have about not being able to satisfy the unmet needs of the surviving, conforming and differentiating stages of our psychological development— the secondary motivations we have that are associated with our unmet deficiency needs. All the energy you expend on meeting your secondary motivations (the unmet needs of the stages of development you have passed through) is energy that is not available for working on your primary motivation (the value-added, life-enhancing work of the stage of psychological development you are at).

Your job as a coach is to help your clients master their fear-based secondary motivations so they can maximise the amount of energy they can devote to their primary motivation, and to help them to learn the skills required to master the stage of psychological development they have reached. The principal skills required at each of the higher stages of psychological development are as follows:

Individuating: Finding freedom to be yourself by mastering your fears.

Self-actualising: Learning to live a values-driven and purpose-driven life.

Integrating: Collaborating with others to make a difference in the world.

Serving: Leading a life of selfless service for the good of humanity and the planet.

Summary

Here are the main points of this chapter:

1. Mastery involves developing the skills and expertise required to attain and maintain internal stability and external equilibrium at the stage of psychological development you have reached in the social and physical framework of your existence.
2. There are four ways we can disturb our internal stability and external equilibrium—whenever we move from one stage of psychological development to the next; when we take on new challenges; when we are triggered by our subconscious fear-based beliefs; when we allow our safety needs to take priority over our growth needs.
3. The human energy field is comprised of the four energy fields: the energy field of the body-mind (etheric field); the energy field of

the ego-mind (emotional field); the energy field of the neo-cortex (mental field); the energy field of the soul-mind (spiritual field).

4. The thoughts and feelings generated by the ego-mind have a significant effect on the functioning of the body-mind and soul-mind.

5. To get into a state of flow the ego needs to: live in right relationship with the body; live in right relationship with the soul; and live in right relationship with its social and physical environment.

6. There are ten strategies you can adopt for getting into a state of flow.

In the next chapter of the book, I will discuss the key elements in mastering the individuating stage of psychological development.

Note

1. Milhaly Csikszentmihalyi, *Flow* (New York: Harperpereninial), 2008, p. 36.

CHAPTER 13

MASTERING THE INDIVIDUATING STAGE OF PSYCHOLOGICAL DEVELOPMENT

The individuating stage of psychological development usually begins in your 30s, although it could start earlier if you were brought up by self-actualised parents in a liberal democracy. If you were not brought up by self-actualised parents, or were brought up in an autocratic regime, you may experience difficulties or obstacles to moving through the individuating stage of development.

We should not forget that many people live in physical conditions[1] and cultural environments[2] that prevent, or actively suppress individuation. In some regimes, the path of individuation can be dangerous or potentially life-threatening, particularly for women.

The hallmark of the individuating stage of development is the will for autonomy, freedom and independence. It can also show up as the desire for adventure, involvement in extreme sports or activities that may be life-threatening or dangerous.

Individuation usually begins with a feeling of resistance that can eventually mature into rebellion. Resistance arises when you feel pressured to do things you do not want to do, because you cannot see how the things you are being asked to do meets any of your needs. Conversely, the things you may be asked not to do are things that you may want to do, because you believe they will help you to meet your needs. Resistance also arises when you are expected to obey rules, which viewed from your perspective, have no meaning or purpose.

At the conforming stage of development, your resistance to parental and cultural demands is usually low, because your overwhelming need at this stage of development is to keep yourself safe by belonging to a group. Resistance builds at the differentiating stage if you are pressured by your parents to follow a certain life-path or a line of studies that does not align with your interests.

By the time you reach your late 20s, if you are living in a culture that embraces the status, people or integrative world view (nations in the western world), you should have established yourself as a viable independent person, and you will feel free to respond to the pull you feel to individuating. You will be looking for opportunities to explore the world and take on new challenges that test your limits. You will be willing to challenge authority and go out on a limb to meet your needs because your desire for independence will be greater than your fear of not belonging or not being recognised in the cultural framework of your existence. Your growth needs will have become prepotent to your deficiency needs.

On the other hand, if you are living in a culture that embraces the survival, tribal, power or authoritarian world view, the pressures to conform may be so overwhelming that you dare not consider "following your dreams", especially if you are a woman or gay. You will need to suppress that part of you which is calling you to express more fully who you really are.

What you are feeling at this stage of development is the early pull/influence of your soul towards uncovering the attributes of your unique self. At this stage of development, you are looking for challenges that help you grow, develop and gain experiences that your soul can use when you reach the next stages of development.

Doing

Usually, the first pull of the soul during individuation is towards the *doing* part of your life rather than the *being* part. In other words, you are seeking to build your skills and experiences in domains that will be advantageous to your soul at later stages of your development. You are not usually aware of this. You are just following the path that seems right for you. You are making choices based on your conscious thoughts and subconscious feelings. You may not be aware that your thoughts and feelings may be coming directly from your soul.

Also be aware that the content of what you feel called to focus on may be less important to the soul than the context you will be working in. This is what happened to me. I spent the first twenty years of my life in a career that I later gave up completely. What was important about those years, I later found out, is what I learned about the context I was working in. I travelled the world, exposing myself to more than seventy different cultures, and learning how the international development banks and the United Nations worked. My soul was preparing me to work in a global context by giving me an in-depth understanding of the way in which politics, finance and economics influenced world events.

This is why, in the previous chapter I put stress on going with the flow. In particular, surrendering to the process, being at ease with what is, following your passion, and becoming unbelievably adaptive. When you can do all of those things you stay open to the influence of your soul. You may not know why you are doing what you are doing, but what you do know is that it feels right. That is the key.

Being

After you have engaged in the *doing* part of your life for several years, you will almost certainly feel the pull towards the *being* part of your life. You will realise that your way of *being* in the world can significantly affect your success in *doing*. In other words, you will begin to realise that *how* you interact with other people can have a positive or negative effect on your ability to meet your needs.

In his book, *How: Why How we do anything Means Everything … in Business (and in Life)* Dov Seidman states:

> *It is no longer what you do that sets you apart from others, but how you do what you do. Sustainable advantage and enduring success—both for companies and the people who work for them— now lie in the realm of how, the new frontier of conduct.*[3]

If your way of being is having a negative effect on your ability to meet your needs, then you will need to spend time understanding how you come across to others and what aspects of your behaviour are preventing you from getting what you want. The exercises in Chapter 10, particularly the Leadership Values Assessment, can help in this regard.

There are two things you need to focus on when you realise that your way of being may be hindering you from getting what you want—your world view and your level of personal entropy.

World view

My first point about being is, if you are a manager or leader over the age of 50 and living in a liberal democracy, you will need to recognise that the world view you grew up in, will not be the world view that the younger people in your organisation embrace. Conversely, if you are under the age of 30 and grew up in a liberal democracy, you need to recognise that the world view of the leaders of your organisation will be different from your own. One or two hundred years ago this would not have been case.

During the twentieth century, particularly the latter half, the rate of change in world views has accelerated to the extent that people from different generations living in the same country have different world views. This is why people in business are paying so much attention to the needs of generation X and generation Y. Leaders nowadays realise that people from these generations have grown up in a different framework of existence than they did, and therefore have different needs, which reflect their different world views.

If you belong to one of these more recent generations, you need to understand that you will still have to pass through the same stages of psychological development as your parents, but your approach to meeting your needs at each stage of development will be coloured by a different world view.

This means that you will be giving more focus to the needs of others (the people world view) and the needs of the system (the integrative world view) during your individuation stage of development than previous generations did. In other words, the values and the purpose of the cultures you work in will have more importance to you than they did to any previous generation. This focus on values and purpose will bring you into closer alignment with your soul and could result in an acceleration of your psychological development.

Personal entropy

My second point about being is, if you have conscious and subconscious secondary motivations associated with meeting your deficiency needs (surviving, conforming and differentiating), they may be causing you to behave in a manner that is not conducive to gaining the support you need from your colleagues and family. In other words, you may be operating with a high level of personal entropy.

If your personal entropy is preventing you from meeting your needs, you will need to reflect deeply on your values and uncover the subconscious fear-based beliefs that are affecting your behaviours: you will need to focus on leading yourself. If you cannot lead yourself, you will not be able to lead others. In the New Leadership Paradigm[4] you will find over one hundred pages and more than thirty exercises devoted to the process of learning how to lead yourself. The key aspect of leading yourself which relates to the individuating stage of psychological development is personal mastery.

Personal mastery

To become proficient in personal mastery, you have to realise that no one or no situation can upset you. You always upset yourself. Every bout of impatience, frustration, or anger is self-generated. The situation, actions, or words of the other person are simply the triggers that bring up the conscious or subconscious fears of your ego and cause you to either project the venom of your unresolved emotional scars out into the world or sit nursing your irritation and becoming increasingly grumpy and disconnected. If you want to stop behaving in these ways, you need to own your reactions and make yourself responsible and accountable for every emotion, feeling and thought you have. Please understand this. Nobody ever upsets you. You always upset yourself through your beliefs.

To be successful at personal mastery, you have to realise that the meaning you give to a situation creates your reality, and the reality you create is a function of your beliefs, particularly your subconscious fear-based beliefs.

Two people can experience exactly the same event and react or respond to it in completely different ways. Why? They have different beliefs.

A belief is an assumption we hold to be true. It may not be true, but it is what we believe to be true at the moment we create our reality. Thus, your beliefs control the meaning you give to a situation, and your beliefs are based on your past history. Your beliefs are the filters that give meaning to your world. If you have an air-conditioner and don't change your filters, you will always be breathing air that is conditioned by the dirt and dust accumulated from the past.

What you believe is happening may not be what is actually happening. It is the meaning that your mind has given to the situation based on your subconscious or conscious beliefs. We never get upset for the reasons we think. What upsets us is what is going on inside our heads or more precisely, in the energy field of our minds. Even if you feel like reacting, the best way to get your needs met is not to react, but to find a way to respond.

Mindfulness

To become proficient in personal mastery you must develop the practice of mindfulness. Mindfulness is the ability to focus one's attention on the present moment, calmly acknowledging and accepting one's feelings, thoughts, and bodily sensations without judgement.

The first component of mindfulness involves the regulation of your attention so you can focus on the experience of the present moment. The second component of mindfulness involves being curious, open and accepting of whatever thoughts or feelings you are experiencing.

Mindfulness enables you to shift from being the one who *experiences* your thoughts and feelings, which is our normal state of being, to being the one who *observes* your thoughts and feelings. You become the observer of the experiencer. This begs the question, who is the "you" that is experiencing and who is the "you" that is observing.

The proposal that I am putting forward in this book and my other books is, the part of you that is experiencing your emotional reactions is your ego, and the part of you that is observing your emotional reactions when you are in a state of mindfulness, is your soul. In order to experience mindfulness you have to shift the centre of your awareness from your ego-mind to your soul-mind.

Mindfulness is not the same as meditation, but it is relatively easy to move from a state of mindfulness into a state of meditation. Having regulated your attention to the present moment, and found your inner observer (self witness), turn the attention of your observer inwards: to the extent that you can, stop observing the thoughts and feelings of your ego and experience pure being—become one with your soul. If thoughts arise while you are in this state simply let them go without attaching any energy to them; don't be curious about them. If you do attach energy to them, you will find yourself spiralling out of meditation into ego awareness.

Mindfulness can be practiced at any moment of the day in any situation. You simply have to be calm enough to go within and shift your centre of awareness from your ego-mind to your soul-mind. This is not possible if you are in the middle of an emotional reaction because your mental field will be working overtime, processing negative thoughts and making judgements. You have to wait until you have calmed down before you can use the mindfulness technique. However, once you understand what is happening, with practice, and over time, you can learn to jump out of your ego-mind into your soul-mind relatively quickly.

When you have become proficient in practising mindfulness, you will come to the realisation that your reactions and upsets are sourced from your memories of unresolved past hurts about not getting your deficiency needs met.

Whatever emotions you are experiencing at a given moment in time are either driven by the survival instincts of your reptilian brain, or the fear-based beliefs of your limbic brain. Every bout of impatience, frustration, anger, rage or self-judgement is self-generated, usually subconsciously. The situations you are in and the actions or words of other people trigger your early maladaptive schemas. It is these schema (your subconscious fears) that cause you to project the unresolved hurts of your past emotional scars out into your immediate world. If you want to manage your frustration, anger or upsets, you need to make yourself accountable for every emotion, and thought you have. You must learn that your reactions to situations are the product of your unmet needs and limiting beliefs. They don't have to control you—you can control them.

Because many of your fear-based beliefs are subconscious, you may not be aware you have them. Your upsets are the only clue you have that they exist. An upset is any form of emotional reaction that disturbs your energetic balance—something that causes you to lose your composure by disturbing your internal stability.

Types of upset

The various types of upset you can experience range from resistance at one end of the scale to rage at the other end of the scale.

Resistance

You experience resistance when someone wants you to do something you don't want to do, or someone has an idea that affects you in some way that is not in alignment with your idea. As soon as you experience resistance, you feel out of alignment. Sometimes, it is difficult to understand why you are feeling resistance. The challenge you face after feeling resistance is to express what is on your mind without fear, without feeling you are compromising your relationship with the person who you are resisting. Say something along the lines of: "I need to tell you that for some reason I am feeling a certain level of resistance to this idea. I am not sure why." The truth of the matter is that you will be compromising your relationship if you do not express how you are feeling. If you don't say anything, it is almost certain that the other person will sense your resistance, so it is best to get it out into the open and be transparent.

Anxiety

Anxiety is a general, usually subconscious, feeling of fear, worry, and unease. You experience anxiety when you feel you cannot cope with the stresses involved in satisfying your deficiency needs. People with severe subconscious fear-based beliefs live in a constant state of anxiety. All other upsets (resistance, impatience, frustration, anger, and rage) occur in the moment and are situational, whereas anxiety is generalised and unfocused. Anxiety is not the same as fear. Fear occurs when you confront something that is intimidating or dangerous: something that can be directly recognised as a threat. If a situation you are experiencing brings on anxiety, it is best to declare how you are feeling; something along the lines of: "I am not sure why, but I am feeling a certain level of anxiety about this situation." Only then can you explore what is going on for you.

Impatience

You experience impatience when you are not able to get what you want when you want it, because you are unable to live without getting your needs met immediately. Impatience is a sign of your need to control what is happening in your world because you find it difficult to trust. People who suffer from severe impatience are often considered to be arrogant, insensitive and overbearing. Impatience can cause a person to cut others off mid-sentence and to make what appear to be uninformed, quick judgements. Impatience can lead people to snap at others in response to questions or requests. Impatience can have a negative impact on your career. One of the biggest causes of impatience is stress. The more stress a person feels, the more likely they will be to react impatiently to additional requests for time.

Frustration

If you can't resolve a situation—get what you need, when you want it— your impatience transforms into frustration. It is a common emotional response to opposition. It arises from the perceived resistance to your will. You experience frustration when, for whatever reason, you are finding it impossible to get your needs met. Frustration makes you even more fearful than impatience, because your belief that you cannot trust others to supply your needs appears to be confirmed. The causes of frustration can be internal or external. Internal frustration can arise from challenges in fulfilling personal goals or handling perceived deficiencies, such as a lack of confidence of speaking in public. Dealing with conflict can also be an internal source of frustration. External causes of frustration include things as traffic jams, being put on hold by an automatic telephone answering service, and incompetence on the part of someone who is trying to serve you. Too much frustration can lead you into anger and aggression.

Anger

You experience anger when you feel a sense of injustice or lack of fairness in the way you are being treated by others, or in a situation that thwarts you in some way—when you feel unable to satisfy your unmet needs. Whereas your fear-based emotions were bubbling up in frustration, now, with anger, they get unleashed. You begin to retaliate. When anger is ongoing, it leads to belligerence. When you hold back your anger over a long period, it may eventually surface as rage.

Rage

Rage is uncontrollable anger that has possessed your mind and your body. It can easily lead to violence or verbal abuse. When you are in rage, you are out of control: you experience a "fit of rage". Rage is always an immediate response to a situation. The situation can be hugely significant like the loss of a loved one or it can be a trigger that releases unexpressed emotions you have been storing in your mind for many years about not getting your needs met. Rage erupts when you tap into these unexpressed emotions.

All these different types of upsets have one thing in common: they all arise from your subconscious fear-based beliefs about either not being able to cope or not being able to get your needs met. In order to reduce these upsets you will need to learn how to become your own self-coach.

Self coaching

There are two things you have to do to become proficient in self-coaching: first, you must learn how to analyse your upsets so you can identify the subconscious fear-based beliefs that are the source of your unmet needs, and second, you must learn how to build new neural pathways to replace your fear-based beliefs with positive beliefs.

Identifying your fear-based beliefs

The self-coaching process shown in Table 13.1 and described in the subsequent paragraphs is designed to help you identify the subconscious fear-based beliefs that are causing your upsets. Whilst this process is similar to the series of exercises described in Chapter 10, the purpose is slightly different. Whereas the exercises described in Chapter 10 are designed to help you to identify your fear-based secondary motivations, the self-coaching process is designed to help you overcome the upsets caused by these secondary motivations. As soon as possible, after you have experienced an upset follow the process described in Table 13.1.

Table 13.1 The process of self-coaching

Step	Action	Explanation
Step 1	Release your emotions	If you are noticing any pent-up emotional energy or hurt, first allow it to dissipate.
Step 2	Engage your self-witness	Move into the balcony and observe what is happening to you on the dance floor of your life.
Step 3	Identify your feelings	Name your feelings, describe them to yourself in detail, and write them down.
Step 4	Identify your thoughts	Notice what you are thinking and the judgements you are making, and write down your thoughts.
Step 5	Identify your fears	What are the fears that lie behind your thoughts? What do you fear may happen? Write down your fears.
Step 6	Identify your needs	What needs do you have that are not being met? These unmet needs are the source of your fears. Write down your needs.
Step 7	Identify your beliefs	Develop belief statements about: (a) what you think you are lacking; and (b) what you think you need.
Step 8	Question your thoughts/ beliefs	Differentiate between your perception of what is happening and the true reality. Ask yourself, are these beliefs really true? You may want to get a reality check by asking your close friends for their opinions. After you have finished reflecting, reshape your thoughts and beliefs, and re-evaluate your needs.

Step 1: Release your emotions

The moment you recognise you are upset, say and do as little as possible. This is not the moment for action. It is the moment to stop, pause, and let the hurt or pain you are experiencing dissipate. It has taken possession of you. Your rational mind is no longer under your control. There is no way you can get your needs met while your fear-based emotions are driving your thinking.

For your own good, minimise the damage you can do by saying and doing nothing. Take a deep breath, excuse yourself, and find a way to release your emotions. Go for a long walk. Go for a workout. Talk to a friend. Shout out loud. Beat the hell out of a cushion. If you are driving, find a place where you can stop and take a break. Get the energy out and I repeat, don't do say or do anything while you are in a state of upset that you might later regret.

To help you get back your control, remember the following:[5]

Every event is neutral. Whatever happened that triggered your upset was a neutral event. You gave it all the meaning it had for you through your beliefs. You created the upset through the assumptions you hold to be true. Remember beliefs are assumptions. They may be true or they may not be true.

Everything is always perfect. Everything is always perfect because it either feels really good or it feels really painful. What you must realise is, pain is a gift. Pain and emotional discomfort are signals from your energy field that you are out of alignment. When you feel emotional pain you know you have work to do.

Problems are opportunities in disguise. Problems weigh you down and drain your energy because they cause you to shift into fear: You fear you will not be able to cope or you fear you will not be able to get your needs met. Once you identify the fear that the problem represents, you have an opportunity to overcome your fear.

Step 2: Engage your self-witness

As soon as you have calmed down, try to step into the space of the self-witness and remind yourself that whatever you just felt, you created subconsciously through your beliefs. The situation or other person did not create your feelings. You created them. Nobody has that power over you. The situation or the other person triggered your emotional upset, anger or resistance: they did not cause it.

The best time to develop your witness consciousness is when your life is going well. Practise asking yourself the following question: "What is alive within me today?" Observe what comes up for you. Stop reading, and ask yourself that question. What was the first thing that came to your mind? Was it a thought or a feeling? Was it something you are excited about that will happen soon? Was it something that has been worrying you for days? Whatever it was, that is where your consciousness is focused. Observe it for a few minutes. If you find the thought or feeling upsetting, find a way to soothe yourself. Think of a happy or pleasant situation or of a place where you feel safe.

Most people do not realise they can observe their feelings because the thoughts associated with their feelings totally mesmerise them. Whenever we get upset we immediately start judging others or ourselves. If we have a real or an imagined conflict with someone, our minds constantly rehearse what we are going to say to the person when we next meet or get in touch with them on the phone. We become righteous victims.

When you are operating in this way, you will use words and phrases that suggest to others that you are not responsible for the misfortunes in your life. You will probably be looking for someone or something to blame. This is a sure sign that you are not taking ownership of your thoughts, feelings and emotions. You are not being responsible for the reality you are creating. You are probably not even aware that you created your upset.

Step 3: Identify your feelings

To become adept at engaging your self-witness, you must learn how to become aware of the ebb and flow of the subtle and not-so subtle feelings (energies) associated with your emotions and the thoughts that go with them. To do this, you need to develop your feeling vocabulary. The following table provides a brief lexicon of the feelings that your body, ego, and soul experience. The feelings that create lightness are driven by alignment (love, connection or life-enhancing energy). The feelings that create heaviness are driven by misalignment (fear, separation or life-depleting energy).

Table 13.2 Examples of feelings generated by the body-mind, ego-mind and soul-mind

	Body-mind feelings	Ego-mind feelings	Soul-mind feelings
Lightness and alignment	Energetic	Eager	Bliss
	Enlivened	Friendly	Centred
	Rejuvenated	Happy	Compassionate
	Renewed	Proud	Fulfiled
	Rested	Satisfied	Joyful
	Revived	Secure	Trusting
Heaviness and misalignment	Exhausted	Afraid	Bereaved
	Lethargic	Anxious	Depressed
	Listless	Annoyed	Detached
	Sleepy	Impatient	Grief
	Tired	Jealous	Sadness
	Weary	Stressed	Withdrawn

Some of your feelings are driven by the disturbance in your ego-mind; some are driven by the lack of alignment of your ego-mind with your soul-mind; and some are driven by your soul-mind.

On the positive side, I have noticed that whenever I experience a deep sense of resonance with someone or a thought or idea, I feel a tingling sensation all down my spine. When this happens, I know my soul is in a state of resonance with the energy field of that person, or the thought or idea.

Step 4: Identify your thoughts

When you experience an upset, try to notice the thoughts that are going through your mind. They are usually thoughts of judgement, blame, shame or guilt. Write down your thoughts as soon as you can. Get them all down. You may not be proud of your thoughts. Do not judge them. Just get them out. Your ego creates these thoughts to justify and protect itself. They are the clues you need to identify your fears.

Step 5: Identify your fears

In order to work with your fears, you have to not only identify them, you also have to name them. You have to bring them from the darkness of your subconscious into the light of your consciousness. Only when they reach your conscious awareness are they malleable to reason and logic.

When you experience a negative thought, feeling or emotion, say to yourself: (Insert your name), I am noticing that you are angry/upset/ impatient/frustrated/sad/jealous. (Choose a negative feeling word that describes what is going on inside you.) Then say to yourself, (Insert your name), what is the fear you are holding on to that caused you to have this negative thought, feeling or emotion? Identify with your soul while you are asking this question. What you are attempting to do is identify the exact nature of your fears.

Step 6: Identify your needs

Ultimately, every energetic misalignment you experience can be traced back to either an unmet need, or a need you have satisfied by obtaining something which is then taken away from you. For example, you are likely to experience anger if someone burgles your house and you are likely to experience grief when a close family member dies. Ask yourself: "What needs do I have that are not being met that caused me to react in this way?"

Step 7: Identify your beliefs

Almost all your fears are based on your subconscious or conscious beliefs about not being able meet your deficiency needs. Consequently, there are three types of fear-based beliefs you may experience:

- I don't have enough … (fill in blank) to satisfy my need for survival and safety.
- I don't have enough … (fill in blank) to satisfy my need for love and belonging.
- I don't have enough … (fill in blank) to satisfy my need for recognition and self-esteem.

Now, take the list of your fears created in step 5 and the list of needs created in step 6, and put words around them to make them into a belief statement.

- I do not have enough *control* to satisfy my need for *safety.*
- I do not get enough *love* to satisfy my need for *belonging.*
- I do not get enough *recognition* to satisfy my need for *self-esteem.*

Fill in the words in italics that most represent your fears and needs. The belief statement you come up with should state what you are not getting enough of, and what need you have that is not being met. You can refer to the list of early maladaptive schema in Annex 3 to get an idea of what fear-based beliefs most affect you.

Let me give you some examples. If your fear-based thought is "Nobody likes me", turn it into a belief statement by saying: "I do not get enough *attention* to satisfy my need for *acceptance.*" The following table provides other examples of thoughts that have been turned into belief statements.

Table 13.3 Creating belief statements from your thoughts

Thought	Belief statement
Nobody loves me	I do not have enough *intimate connections* to satisfy my need for *love*.
I am not liked	I do not get enough *attention* to satisfy my need for *belonging*.
I am not good enough	I am not *recognised* enough by others to satisfy my need for *self-esteem*.
I am ignored	I am not *listened* too enough to satisfy my need for *respect*.
I am a failure	I do not get enough *recognition* to satisfy my need for *self-esteem*.
Nobody listens to me	I can't get enough *attention* to satisfy my need for *recognition*.

Step 8: Question your thoughts/beliefs

The next step is to question these beliefs to see if they are absolutely true, and see if there are other beliefs that might be truer. Remember, beliefs are simply assumptions we hold to be true. Early maladaptive schema are beliefs we learned in childhood that may have been true then, but are no longer true or do not apply to the situation that has triggered these beliefs. This technique for questioning the reality of your thoughts/beliefs has been promoted by many people including Byron Katie Reid.

Byron Katie, as she is known, discovered, after much personal suffering, that when she believed her thoughts, she suffered; when she didn't believe them, she didn't suffer. This is true for every human being. In other words, suffering is optional. By changing your attitude towards your beliefs, you can free yourself from them.

For example, take anyone of the belief statements in Table 13.3 and ask yourself a series of questions:

- Is this thought/belief true?
- Can I be absolutely sure this thought/belief is true?
- How do I react to situations when I believe this thought/belief?
- What would I be like if I didn't have this thought/belief?

- How does this thought/belief support me in getting my needs met?
- How does this thought/belief hinder me in getting my needs met?

So, if you have the thought/belief "I am a failure", ask yourself: "Is this thought true?", "Can I absolutely know this thought is true?", "How do I react to situations when I believe this thought?", "What would I be like if I didn't have this thought?", "How does this thought support me in getting my needs met?", "How does this thought hinder me in getting my needs met?"

When you realise that failure, like every other label you put on yourself, is an artificial construct of the mind with no other reality than the reality you give it, you are free to call it something else that is less emotive and judgemental. For example, you could replace the thought "I am a failure" with the thought: "I am someone who gladly accepts challenges and never gives up."

Another way of exploring the reality of your beliefs is to find a belief that rings more true. For example, if your thought is "My boss doesn't like me", turn it around so it becomes: "My boss does like me". Or make it into a statement about yourself, such as, "I don't like myself" or "I don't like my boss". The purpose of the turnaround is to see if any of these new thoughts are true. If they are, then you immediately have a perspective that you had not previously considered, that makes the original thought less believable.

When you explore "My boss does like me", think of all the times when your boss has connected with you or helped you. When you explore "I don't like myself", think of the ways that you criticise yourself or the ways in which you deny yourself. See if this relates in any way to the thought you are projecting on to your boss. When you explore "I don't like my boss", examine what you do not like about your boss. See if this relates in any way to what you believe your boss doesn't like about you.

The turnaround really helps you to identify your projections—the judgements your ego is unwilling to accept about itself, that are placed on another person so the ego can feel good. Whatever upsets you in your outer world is often related to what upsets you about yourself.

I am suggesting you use this methodology because it works. It is an excellent self-coaching tool. It works because you can use it to question your thoughts, assumptions and beliefs, and it helps you to realise that you may have an old belief that is no longer serving you, and you may find that it is no longer true.

As always, the purpose of this self-inquiry is to uncover your assumptions so they can be examined in broad daylight (conscious awareness). Your limiting beliefs or assumptions only have energy if they stay in the dark recesses of your mind. The constant exposure to daylight and rationality will make your limiting beliefs less believable. What is negative cannot survive in the light. Your limiting beliefs will gradually wither away, especially if you replace them with positive affirmations.

Ultimately, the place you want to get to is detachment from your internal judgements about what you assume is happening and your fixed ideas of how things have to be. These are the "shoulds" and "shouldn'ts" of life. When you believe things have to be a certain way, you block spontaneity, enthusiasm and innovation. The quickest way to get past this life-destroying attitude is to embrace "what is" without judgement and without fear.

Instead of assuming that your boss doesn't like you when he doesn't return your calls for a couple of days, just let any thoughts about the situation go, particularly the thought "He should call me" or any anxiety around "Why hasn't he called me?"

He didn't call you for a couple of days, so, get over it. Anything might have happened. He might be overwhelmed. He might have decided to take a break and forgotten to tell you. He might have had an accident. He might even be getting himself worked up about the fact that *his* boss hasn't called him in the last of couple of days. You have no idea what is happening. So don't make up a story. Whatever is happening is what it is. There is no point in worrying.

This is also the best way of dealing with your resistance to an idea or request for you to do something you think is a waste of time or something you don't want to do but are afraid to say so. When you are at ease with what is, instead of allowing your mind to see such situations as a conflict, first explore whether the request you are resisting might support you in meeting your needs, the needs of the other person, or the collective needs of the group you both belong to. If, from your perspective, it doesn't meet anyone's needs, or you have other needs that are more of a priority for you, then explain this to the person who is requesting your participation. When you can accept what is, without judgement, without thoughts of conflict, you remove anxiety and worry from your life and you are able to answer truthfully and honestly. The alternative is that you agree to do what is requested as a duty or obligation, resenting your involvement and not giving it your full attention. This is not good for anybody.

"Easier said than done", you might say. Yes, true. But you always have a choice of how you think about things. You can choose to see through the eyes of threat or conflict or the eyes of openness or neutrality. You can choose to worry about things or not. Do you want to be in control of your mind and emotions, or do you want them to be in control of you? That is the question you must ask yourself. Our fear-based thoughts and limiting beliefs are part of our personal programming and cultural conditioning. When your realise you no long have to be the prisoner of your beliefs you feel liberated. Doing this work is an important part of the individuation process.

You achieve personal mastery when you are: (a) able to successfully manage your emotions—remain in, or rapidly return to a state of internal stability and external equilibrium after you have been triggered by a subconscious fear-based belief; and (b) have become viable and independent in your framework of existence—not beholden or dependent on others for your survival, relationship and self-esteem needs.

Building new neural pathways

From the quantum energetic perspective, everything exists in all its possibilities until an observer is present. It is the observer that causes the wave of information to collapse into a specific outcome: In other words, we create our reality through our beliefs. Our beliefs are simply well engrained neural pathways.

My father, bless him, who died when I was seventeen, always used to say: "You can change your mind even when you cannot change your clothes." He had no understanding of quantum theory, but what he was tapping into was one of the most powerful ways we have of changing reality.

During the first three stages of your psychological development, you interpret the world through your ego's conscious and subconscious beliefs. If your ego has any fears (conscious or subconscious), these will be the first filters you use to interpret your reality. The information packages you receive from your senses will be filtered through your ego's fears before they are filtered through your ego' desires. In other words, your reality will be conditioned by your ego's fears—by the neural pathways you created during the formative years of your life.

There are three things you can do to build new neural pathways once you have understood what your fears are. You can weaken the hold your fears have over you by following the personal mastery process described above. You can then develop an affirmation which helps you to build a new neural pathway. In the example I gave above, I replaced the limiting belief "I am a failure" with a turnaround affirmation "I am someone who gladly accepts challenges and never gives up."

I have used affirmations frequently during my life. Some of the most effective affirmations have been: *I design my life the way I want it, I am fit and healthy in mind, body and spirit, and every day and in every way I am aligning my ego with my soul.* The most important property of an affirmation is that it is believable to you. You will not be able to create a new neural pathway if you cannot believe your affirmation. To help the affirmation take hold repeat it every day.

The third thing you can do is to use cognitive behavioural therapy (CBT) to help you to build new neural pathways. CBT is a psychotherapeutic approach to addressing early maladaptive schema (limiting beliefs) through goal-orientated behaviours. It helps individuals to challenge their beliefs and replace errors in thinking with more realistic and effective thoughts, thereby decreasing emotional distress and self-defeating behaviour. Step 8 in the personal mastery process is an example of this type of approach.

In *The Hidden History of Coaching*, Leni Wildflower describes CBT in the following way:

> *Therapist and client work together to uncover unproductive belief systems. They then view a client's belief as a hypothesis for [scientific] testing and develop experiments to test and challenge this hypothesis empirically. Once a test has been completed, therapist and client evaluate the results to determine whether the experiment has altered the client's original assumption.*[6]

Summary

Here are the main points of this chapter:

1. The individuating stage of psychological development usually begins in your 30s,

2. The first pull of the soul you feel is towards the *doing* part of your life: seeking to build your skills and experiences in domains that will be advantageous to your soul at later stages of your development.

3. The second pull of your soul will be towards the *being* part of your life: you will realise that your way of being in the world can significantly affect your success in doing.

4. There are two things you need to focus on when you realise that your way of being may be hindering you from getting what you want—your world view and your level of personal entropy.

5. We never get upset for the reasons we think. What upsets us is what is going on inside the energy field of our minds.

6. To become proficient in personal mastery, you have to realise that no one or no situation can upset you. You always upset yourself. You must also develop the practice of mindfulness. Mindfulness is the ability to focus one's attention on the present moment, calmly acknowledging and accepting one's feelings, thoughts, and bodily sensations without judgement.

7. In order to reduce the upsets in your life, you will need to learn how to become your own self-coach.

8. There are two things you have to do to become proficient in self-coaching: first, you must learn how to analyse your upsets so you can identify the subconscious fear-based beliefs that are the source of your unmet needs, and second, you must learn how to build new neural pathways to replace your fear-based beliefs with positive beliefs.

In the next chapter of the book, I will discuss the key elements in mastering the self-actualising stage of psychological development.

Notes

1. Poverty or harsh physical environments.
2. Cultures operating with survival, tribal, power and authoritarian world views.
3. Dov Seidman, *How: Why How we do anything Means Everything … in Business (and in Life)* (New York: John Wiley & Sons), 2007.
4. Richard Barrett, *The New Leadership Paradigm* (Bath: 2010), pp. 131–245.
5. For a fuller description of these different methodologies for getting back into control, see Chapter 10: Connecting with your soul, *What My Soul Told Me*, by Richard Barrett.
6. Leni Wildflower, *The Hidden History of Coaching* (McGraw Hill: London), 2013, p. 94.

CHAPTER 14

MASTERING THE SELF-ACTUALISING STAGE OF PSYCHOLOGICAL DEVELOPMENT

The self-actualising stage of psychological development usually begins in your 40s. Depending on the extent of the fear-based parental programming and cultural conditioning you received in your formative years, it could start slightly earlier or it could start slightly later.

The hallmark of the self-actualising stage of development is the search for existential meaning: the desire to have a purpose that is more than satisfying your deficiency needs, and more than satisfying your need for challenges and adventure. At the self-actualising stage of development you begin to feel your soul's desire to live a values-driven and purpose-driven life.

If you are lucky enough to have been raised by self-actualised parents in a liberal democracy and have had a higher education, followed by opportunities to build a career, by the time you reach your forties you will be well established in your life and your community. You will be completing the individuating stage of your development and, although you may not know it, you will be getting ready for self-actualisation.

If you are one of the large numbers of people who were not raised by self-actualised parents, who are living in a non-democratic regime, who have not had a higher education, and have had few career opportunities, by the time you reach your 40s you may still be battling to meet your survival, relationship and self-esteem needs. You may find these needs occupying your conscious and subconscious awareness almost all of the time and probably all of your life. They may be so predominant that you never get the opportunity to individuate or self-actualise. This was the situation of my parents and the majority of people living in Europe and North America during the first half of the twentieth century. This is also the situation of the majority of people currently living in middle- and low-income countries all over the world.

Search for meaning

For many people the self-actualisation stage of development has inauspicious beginnings; it starts with boredom or discontent—discontent that your life appears to have little meaning, or boredom with your job or career. What seemed like a great field to get into or terrific occupation when you were young, no longer gives you a feeling of excitement. You dread going into work each day. You feel your life is missing something. You may even feel a sense of emptiness.

To fill this existential void your ego-mind may begin to search for distraction or excitement—anything to avoid the feeling of emptiness. This may cause you to do things that you will later regret, such as having an affair or taking undue risks with your savings or your life. You may also try to overcome the numbness you feel inside by drinking alcohol or taking drugs.

At some point, hopefully not too late in your life, you will begin to realise that your search for meaning in the external world is futile. What you are searching for is not in your external world but in your internal world. If this is where your clients are, it is time for them to reflect and reassess their lives: a time to decide what they truly want.

This is the moment to ask the questions: "What am I passionate about?", "What is it that I love to do that brings me deep pleasure?", "What am I doing when I am feeling in the flow?" What you are searching for is an activity that gladdens your heart; something that you may always have been interested in that naturally calls you: something you may have overlooked.

The most frequent issue people have to deal with at the self-actualising stage of development, once they have discovered where their passion lies, is how to sustain their standard of living at the level they have become used to if they give up their successful career and decide to follow their calling. You may rest assured, if you have found your soul's calling you are on the right track. If you are truly aligned with your soul, you will not need to worry. All your needs will be provided for in a measure that is adequate to your situation.

Many people don't know their soul's purpose and never make any attempt to find it out. They assume that meeting their ego's needs is all there is to life—getting richer, so they can accumulate more possessions; seeking out new and more exciting sexual encounters, so they can reinforce their macho image; becoming experts in their fields, so they can get the recognition or adulation they are craving; accumulating more power, so they can influence people; and getting the largest and biggest of everything so they can feel a sense of their own self-worth. The problem with such pursuits is they do not bring you joy. They may bring you brief moments of happiness and a feeling of pride, but they don't bring any real meaning to your life. They do not feed your soul.

Find your calling

The best way to find out your purpose is to examine your life. You were born as a unique soul with a unique gift, something only you can contribute to the on-going dynamic of the evolution of human consciousness. You can be certain that your soul prints[1] will begin to manifest in the physical world from the moment you are born. If you want to find out what they are, ask yourself these questions: "What interests did you have as a child?", "What were you good at?", "What were you not so good at?", "What were you most afraid to do?" You will almost certainly find clues in the answers to these questions to clarify your purpose. When you have finished examining your childhood, repeat the exercise for your teenage years and then your adult years.

It is important to distinguish during this exercise between your ego's drive for achievement and your soul's drive for purpose. The difference is relatively simple: your ego focuses on goals. What you want to achieve has a concrete outcome or payback. Your soul, on the other hand, focuses on the joy of doing something or the satisfaction you get from making a difference in the world. When you are following your calling, you will frequently find yourself living in a state of flow. When you are driving for achievement, you will frequently find yourself struggling to overcome obstacles.

Your ability to follow your passion or live your calling becomes significantly easier when you begin to lead a values-driven life. Embracing your deeply held values enables you live with authenticity and integrity. The key values you need to embrace are freedom, equality, fairness, accountability, transparency, trust, empathy and compassion. When you allow your decisions to be driven by these values, people will not only be drawn to you, they will want to help you.

Some people find their calling early in life; others don't discover it until much later. If, after examining your life you are still not sure of your calling, do not worry. Do what is in front of you and what feels right. As long as you are living in alignment with your soul—not allowing your ego's motivations to take precedence over your soul's motivations—you will be on the right track.

Another exercise you can do to discover your sense of mission or purpose is called the "Four Why's" process. This is fully described in Annex 4. This exercise helps you to find your internal mission and vision—how you want to grow and develop, and your external mission and vision—what you want to do and the impact you want to have in your external world.

Live your values

The first step in living your values is to know what your values are. A good starting point is the free Personal Values Assessment described in Chapter 10 under *Exercises for identifying your secondary motivations*. You should complete the exercises that come with the results of your values assessment to discover why your values are important to you.

Working with your values is a life-long pursuit. Although some of your top ten values will change as you pass through the different stages of your psychological development, others value will remain in your top priorities. Knowing what your values are and using them to support your decision-making, will enable you to navigate through all the challenges that life puts in front of you.

Whereas beliefs are context-related, values are concepts that transcend contexts: they are the universal guidance system of the soul. I think it is important to repeat here what is written about values-based decision-making in Chapter 7.

> *Everyone on the planet shares the same deeply held human values, but not the same beliefs. Consequently, when people start to make decisions using their values they find themselves drawn together. When they make decisions based on their beliefs they find themselves separated. In other words, values unite and beliefs separate.*
>
> *When you shift to values-based decision-making, you can effectively throw away the rulebooks you learned when you were young. Every decision you make is sourced from what you consider to be "right action"—actions that are fully aligned with who you really are—your soul-self. You shift to values-based decision-making during the self-actualisation stage of psychological development.*
>
> *Values-based decision-making allows you to create an authentic way of operating in the world. That is not to say there is no place for conscious belief-based decision-making based or logic or rational thinking: there is. However, you will quickly realise as you proceed with your self-actualisation and get in touch with your deeply held values, that all the critical decisions you need to make in your life need to pass the values test. If a decision seems logical, but goes against your values you will feel uncomfortable. You need to give precedence to decisions that make you feel good, rather than decisions that focus on getting what your ego thinks it needs.*

Leading a values-driven life is an absolute prerequisite for living a purpose-driven life. Why do I say that? Because when you live by the universal values of the soul, you are instantly recognised as someone who can be trusted.

Trust

Trust is the key value in all personal interactions. It is the glue that holds people together and the lubricant that creates internal cohesion.[2] The components of trust are shown in Figure 14.1.

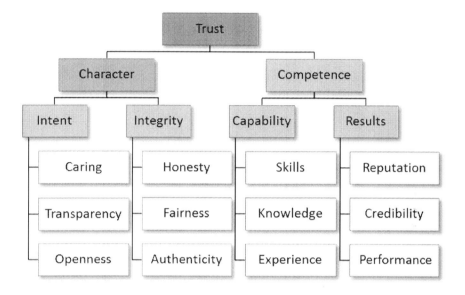

Figure 14.1 The trust matrix

The principal components of trust are character and competence. Character is a reflection of how you are on the inside, your intent, and the level of integrity you display in your relationship to others. These depend primarily on the level of development of your emotional intelligence and social intelligence. Intent is demonstrated by caring, transparency and openness; integrity by honesty, fairness and authenticity.

Competence is a reflection of how you are on the outside, your capability, and the results you achieve in your role. These depend primarily on the level of development of your mental intelligence, your education, and what you have learned during your professional career. Capability is demonstrated by skills, knowledge and experience. Results are demonstrated by reputation, credibility and performance.

Even though the focus on competence (capability and results) is important, these are skills that can be learned and accumulate over time. I believe the focus on character (intent and integrity) is more important, because these qualities are required for bonding and cooperation and are much more difficult to develop. Competence is about achieving results; character is about how you achieve them.

In *The Speed of Trust*, Stephen Covey states that trust means confidence and the opposite of trust (distrust) means suspicion. In other words, trust breeds connectedness. When we trust someone, we know they will have our interest at heart. Suspicion, on the other hand, breeds separation. When we are suspicious of someone, we will not disclose our innermost thoughts. We keep things back. We avoid connecting with someone we do not trust.

Trust reduces cultural entropy; a lack of trust increases cultural entropy. Covey puts it this way, "*Trust always affects outcomes—speed and cost. When trust goes up, speed will also go up, and costs will go down. When trust goes down, speed will also go down, and costs go up.*" Best-selling author Francis Fukuyama says, "*Widespread mistrust in a society … imposes a kind of tax on all forms of economic activity, a tax that high-trust societies do not have to pay.*"

This is why trust is important. You will not be able to move successfully from the self-actualisation stage of your development to the integrating stage if you have not learned how to trust.

Summary

Here are the main points of this chapter:

1. The self-actualising stage of psychological development usually begins in your forties.
2. At the self-actualising stage of development you begin to feel your soul's desire to live a values-driven and purpose-driven life.
3. For many people the self-actualisation stage of development has inauspicious beginnings; it starts with boredom or discontent—discontent that your life appears to have little meaning, or boredom with your job or career.
4. To fill this existential void your ego-mind may begin to search for distraction or excitement—anything to avoid the feeling of emptiness. This may cause you to do things that you will later regret.

5. When you are trying to find your calling, it is important to distinguish between your ego's drive for achievement and your soul's drive for purpose.

6. Many people don't know their soul's purpose and never make any attempt to find it out.

7. The best way to find out your purpose is to examine your life.

8. The first step in living your values is to know what your values are.

9. Trust is the key value in all personal interactions. It is the glue that holds people together and the lubricant that creates internal cohesion.

In the next chapter of the book, I will discuss the key elements in mastering the integrating stage of psychological development.

Notes

1. Your soul prints are like finger prints. They are a sign of your uniqueness, and they are always with you. For more information see Marc Gafni, *Soul Prints* (London: Penguin Books) 2001.

2. Steven M. R. Covey, *Speed of Trust: The One Thing That Changes Everything* (New York: Free Press), 2006.

Chapter 15

Mastering the Integrating Stage of Psychological Development

The integrating stage of psychological development usually begins in your 50s. If you have got this far with your psychological growth, you will have a clear understanding of your purpose, you will be attempting to live a values-driven life, and you will be feeling the need to use your gifts and talents to make a difference in the world.

The hallmark of the integrating stage of development is the pull you feel towards collaborating with others who share your sense of purpose and operate with similar values. You will want to collaborate with these people so you can make a bigger difference in the world than you could on your own. You will recognise who they are because you will resonate with them—you will feel an empathetic connection.

The challenge you have to face at the integrating stage of development is learning how to trust your soul. The voice of your soul comes through inspiration. Inspiration is always very personal and directive. You will recognise it as a persistent thought that will not go away. It delineates the next steps you have to take in your life journey. Inspiration keeps prompting you until you listen and follow through.

To make progress at the integrating stage of development you must learn how to trust your inspiration and listen to the voice of your soul.

There are consequences if you ignore the inspiration of your soul. You will disrupt the internal stability of your soul-mind, which will affect your whole energy field. You will begin to feel frustrated, sad and then depressed.

Trusting your soul

Trusting your soul requires immense courage when you are still in the ego stages of your development. That is because the ego takes its job seriously. It was given the task of keeping your body safe from harm, and it was never told that it was performing this service as the agent of your soul. It thought it was operating on behalf of itself and your body. It wasn't expecting the soul to show up and ask it to hand over the reins.

What you are attempting to learn by trusting your soul is that the best possible outcomes will always arise when you follow the inspiration of your soul. Even though the voice of inspiration can come through at any stage of your psychological development, you will not begin to recognise it as such until you reach the self-actualising stage, and you will not get fully tuned in until you reach the integrating stage.

In order to make progress at the integrating stage of development you must give yourself wholeheartedly to your soul's purpose and maintain your focus on leading a values-driven life. Your values will enable you to navigate your way through the three-dimensional physical world, so you can more easily facilitate the realisation of your soul's purpose.

Handing the control of your life over to your soul is not easy to do. If you still have any fears left after passing through the previous stages of your development, they will now emerge.

The following North American Hopi saying, entitled *The Wisdom of the Elders* captures the essence of the integrating stage of development well:

> *There is a river flowing now very fast.*
> *It is so great and swift that there are those who will be afraid.*
> *They will try to hold on to the shore.*
> *They will feel they are being torn apart and will suffer greatly.*
> *Know the river has its destination.*
> *We must let go of the shore, push off into the middle of the river,*
> *Keep our eyes open, and our heads above the water.*
> *See who is in there with you and celebrate.*
> *The time of the lone wolf is over.*

We are the ones we've been waiting for.

The time of the lone wolf is over because you have reached the point in your development when you are giving up your independence—you are handing over control to your soul. You are ready to jump into the river and see who is in there with you and celebrate, because you are now going to work with these people who have also committed to their souls' purposes. They are in the river with you for a reason. They are kindred spirits; together you are going to shift into a state of interdependence so you can leverage your efforts in making a difference in the world.

To operate in this way you have to get rid of any ego attachment you may have to things having to be the way your ego wants them. When your ego thinks it knows exactly what to do, beware! The ego is usually focused on satisfying one of its unmet needs. The mere thought of not being able to achieve your ego's needs generates anxiety and fear.

Whenever you allow fear to enter your mind, you are sending a message to your soul that you do not trust it to produce the outcome that is most beneficial to you.

Non-attachment to outcomes sends a different message to your soul. It says: "Soul, I trust you to organise the outcome so that it most perfectly fits with your needs. Even though I may find the situation painful, help me to recognise it as a learning experience."

I remember, about a year after my wife and I split up and sold our home, entering into a deep depression. I realised it was a healing experience. I did not seek medical advice. Every day during those first few weeks I said to my soul: "Bring it on. Let me feel all the pain. I knew the more pain that I felt the more healing I would be doing." I trusted in the outcome and I trusted my soul. It took me about nine months to get through that depression.

Trusting your soul is a big step because it may mean throwing caution to the wind, and it may mean stepping out into your life without a parachute. To do this, you must be able to trust that you will be able to survive, and whatever difficulties you are experiencing will pass.

If you have not tamed the unmet needs of your ego (your fear-based secondary motivations) you will find it difficult to progress with your integration. To successfully transition through the integrating stage of development you must not only be skilled at personal mastery, you must also be skilled in empathy.

Empathy

The reason you must be skilled in empathy is because the integrating stage of development requires you to cooperate with other people, so you can make a bigger difference in the world than you could on your own. Building connections is paramount to the integrating stage of development.

There are two components to empathy. First, the ability to imagine oneself in another's place: experience and understand their feelings and desires, and be able to communicate your understanding of their situation back to them. Second, the ability to see into the soul of the other person: understand what is important to them and what makes them tick. When you are able to do this, the other person automatically responds, because they have the feeling of being seen and understood.

If you are a man and you are operating in empathy mode, you have to fight your tendency to want to solve the problems of the other person. All you have to do is listen and communicate your understanding of the difficulties the other person is facing. Do not attempt to solve their problems, unless invited.

The ability to display deep levels of empathy requires you to make a soul-to-soul connection to other human beings, regardless of their ethnic origin. When this occurs, you experience a strong level of affinity and a deep energetic resonance with the person. The level of resonance you feel increases significantly when the person you are connecting with is operating from the same level of consciousness as you. You are literally on the same wavelength. The empathy connection arises from your ability to connect with another person at the energetic level.

True empathy transcends blood ties. In *The Empathic Civilization*, Jeremy Rifkin states:

> *Civilization is the detribalisation of blood ties and the resocialization of distinct individuals based on associational ties. Empathic extension is the psychological mechanism that makes this conversion and transition possible.*[1]

Summary

Here are the main points of this chapter:

1. The integrating stage of psychological development usually begins in your 50s.
2. The hallmark of the integrating stage of development is the pull you feel towards collaborating with others who share your sense of purpose and operate with similar values.
3. The biggest challenge you have to face at the integrating stage of development is learning how to trust your soul.
4. To successfully transition through the integrating stage of development you must not only be skilled at personal mastery, you must also be skilled in empathy.
5. There are two components to empathy: first, the ability to imagine oneself in another's place, experience and understand their feelings and desires, and be able to communicate your understanding to the other person; and second, the ability to see into the soul of the other person; understand what is important to them and what makes them tick.

In the next chapter of the book, I will discuss the key elements in mastering the serving stage of psychological development.

Note

1. Jeremy Rifkin, *The Empathic Civilization* (Cambridge: Polity), 2009, p. 24.

CHAPTER 16

MASTERING THE SERVING STAGE OF PSYCHOLOGICAL DEVELOPMENT

The serving stage of psychological development usually begins in your 60s. When you reach this stage of development you go where you are called to go, and you do what you are called to do. You are always listening to the promptings of your soul. Far from being a burden: it is a joy. You get to lead a life of selfless service on behalf of your soul. You live in a semi-permanent state of internal stability and external equilibrium because you are operating in a state of the flow. If you are lucky enough to be retired or have a level of income that meets your needs, you do whatever excites you, and you avoid or delegate the rest.

You observe your life rather than live it. You recognise whatever you are able to accomplish or create is what comes through you. Sometimes you are in awe of what your soul does and creates. Other people think it is you: but it is not you, and you know it is not you. It is your soul working through you.

Your job is to make sure your body stays healthy and your mind stays calm—that your ego, which has now aligned with your soul, remains in right relationship with your body and your soul. Of course, you will never be free of ego upsets, but you know how to deal with them when they arise.

You regard every upset you feel as an opportunity to deepen your personal mastery skills.

By this stage of development, you have truly become the servant of your soul. As you progress through this stage of development, you increasingly recognise that you lead a dual life. You are your soul *and* you are the servant of your soul. The more you are able to get out of your own way—the fewer needs or desires you have—the more you are able to live the life of your soul.

By this point in your development, synchronicity will be raining down on you. You will be able to rely on your intuition every moment of the day. You will know what is happening with other people as soon as you focus your attention on them. You will also catch glimpses of the future. Sometimes you know what will happen, but you do not always know when it will happen.

The mission and vision you established for yourself at the self-actualising stage of your development gets put aside, because you have become the instrument of your soul. You have your own personal guidance system. You no longer need your mission and vision to give your life direction. All you have to do is follow your intuition and just show up. There are no goals and no objectives to aim for. You just have to be, and let the voice of your soul direct you. This is the most comfortable and stress free existence you can imagine, because there is nothing you need and nothing you need to happen. You know that whatever emerges will be perfect because you are operating without judgement.

The hallmark of this stage of development is your desire to lead a life of selfless service for the good of humanity and the planet. To live such a life you need to move beyond empathy to compassion.

Compassion

Compassion is a more vigorous form of empathy that gives rise to an active desire to alleviate another's suffering. A compassionate person feels the pain of another and desires to alleviate that pain as if it were their own. This is the most important personal characteristic or soul quality for a leader to embody. It requires an even greater level of energetic fusion at the soul level than that required for empathy. When you operate with compassion, you viscerally feel the suffering of another. You are instantly connected to everyone with whom you interact.

206

In The Compassionate Mind, Dr. Paul Gilbert states:

> *When we fantasize and think about compassion, this does interesting things to our brains and bodies. ... In fact, focusing on kindness, both to ourselves and to other people, stimulates areas of the brain and body in ways that are very conducive to health and well-being. Researchers have found out that, from the day we are born to the day we die, the kindness, support, encouragement and compassion of others has a huge impact on how our brains, bodies, and general sense of well-being develop. Love and kindness, especially in early life, even affect how some of our genes are expressed![1]*

I have found the qualities of humility and wisdom are nearly always associated with compassion. Humility is a quality of unity that appears when the ego has become completely aligned with the soul: the ego loses all need for self-promotion. Wisdom is the quality of knowing that goes beyond normal intuition. Wisdom is intuition enhanced with personal experience. It provides us with a deep understanding of people, things, events or situations, empowering us to choose a response that consistently produces the optimum results with the minimum expenditure of time and energy. It gives us a comprehension of what is true or right (ethical) and allows us to see what wants to emerge in a situation.

This triumvirate of values (compassion, humility and wisdom) are the qualities of a soul that is deeply connected to and aligned with other souls. People who live at this level of personal consciousness live a life of selfless service that fulfils them and gives them a deep sense of joy.

Becoming one with your soul

There is a distinct difference between serving your soul and becoming one with your soul. When your ego serves your soul, it surrenders its freedom. When your ego becomes one with your soul, it surrenders its existence—a part of you, which has served you well, has to die. That's what it feels like viewed through the eyes of the ego. Viewed through the eyes of the soul, it looks different—while your ego is still serving your soul, the energy field of your ego and your soul are aligned but remain separate. When your ego becomes one with your soul, the energy field of your ego merges with the energy field of your soul. This merging occurs because the ego's frequency of vibration becomes the same as the frequency of vibration of your soul. It becomes the same because the ego is now living outside of fear.

For most of us, the shift from trusting your soul to becoming the servant of your soul is already a huge challenge. Going the next step—mastering the ability to live a fear-free existence, automatically satisfying your needs before you know you have them, and manifesting what your heart desires through thought—is beyond our wildest imaginings.

Everyone who has connected, befriended, trusted and become the servant of their soul has had the experience of doing all of these things during specific moments, hours or even days of their lives. Whenever, and in whatever manner you connected, befriended, trusted and served your soul, you were, during those moments, at one with your soul.

The reason you find this difficult to believe is because you have objectified your soul. You think you have a soul and your soul is separate from you. The truth is the opposite: your soul has you. Your soul (you) is attempting to master living in a three-dimensional physical reality in the same manner in which it lives in a four dimensional energetic reality—with love and a deep sense of connection to everything.

When you think you are reaching out to your soul, the aspect of your soul that is living in a three-dimensional world is reaching out to the aspect of your soul that is living in a four-dimensional world. There never was any separation. It was an illusion. There was never a separate self. You were always your soul living life in two dimensions of reality—one part in four-dimensional awareness, and one part in three-dimensional awareness.

Einstein was familiar with this concept. He once said:

> *The non-mathematician is seized by a mysterious shuddering when he hears of four-dimensional things, by a feeling that is not unlike the occult. But there is no more commonplace statement than the world in which we live is a four-dimensional continuum.*[2]

We live in a multi-dimensional world, but because of the limitations of our senses, we only perceive three of these dimensions. Thus we can state that three-dimensionality and physical form is not a property of the world but a property of our senses.

Consequently, the energetic, quantum reality of the fourth-dimension is difficult for us to experience and comprehend. A world where space and time become interwoven in a single continuum challenges our senses and our beliefs. Even though Einstein showed us that energy and mass are interchangeable ($E=mc^2$), a world that is totally made up of energy fields is almost impossible for us to imagine.

One of the ways we can begin to gain an understanding of the fourth dimension of awareness is by comparing the awareness that exists in a two-dimensional world with the awareness that exists in a three-dimensional world. Then, by extrapolating the difference between two and three-dimensional awareness, we can get a sense of how four-dimensional awareness compares to three-dimensional awareness. Let me explain how to do this.

The five-finger exercise

Take a sheet of paper and lay it down on a flat surface. Imagine that there is a very small person living on the surface of this paper in what is known as "Flatland". For this person, the world has length and breadth, but no height. In other words, this person operates in a world of two-dimensional awareness (she cannot perceive height). Along comes a human being with three-dimensional awareness (this person can perceive height) and places the ends of the fingers of one hand on the paper—on the surface of Flatland.

Imagine now, that the person living in Flatland is out for a morning stroll. When passing this place yesterday, she noticed nothing unusual. Suddenly, overnight five separate circles have appeared (the projection into two-dimensional consciousness of the five fingers). The two-dimensional being is mystified by the appearance of the five circles. She calls her friend, a two-dimensional scientist, and asks her to explain the nature of the five circles. The scientist explores the five circles using her two-dimensional logic.

Her experiments show that the circles can move independently within certain limits, but if she puts a force on one circle, eventually it will appear to drag the other circles with it (although the fingers of the hand are separate they are connected, but in a dimension of awareness (height) that the two-dimensional scientist cannot perceive). The two-dimensional scientist repeats her experiments. She builds equations to verify the relationship of the circles to each other and before too long she believes that she knows everything there is to know about the five separate circles.

She publishes a paper about the five separate circles and calls a meeting of the academy of two-dimensional scientists to show them her discovery. The two-dimensional scientists repeat the experiments and get very similar results. Everyone in the two-dimensional world believes they know all there is to know about the five separate circles.

Viewed from the perspective of three-dimensional awareness, we know that these are not five separate circles. They are five connected fingers, which form part of a living organism. The two-dimensional beings are completely unaware of this larger picture. They believed the five circles to be physically separate, but somehow linked, probably through some type of energetic force field. They have no sense of the connection that exists at a higher dimension of awareness.

This is exactly the situation we find ourselves in with regard to the fourth dimension of awareness. We have countless experiences that appear unconnected, but in reality are linked, and have their cause in the fourth or even higher dimensions of consciousness. Some we try to explain with our three-dimensional logic—this is the domain of science—and some are simply inexplicable—these we classify as paranormal, synchronistic, magical, religious or miraculous experiences. We use these classifications to cover up our ignorance because we do not have a full understanding of the linkages that exist at the higher dimension of consciousness where these experiences originated.

When we focus our awareness exclusively on the third-dimension, we are focusing on a world of symbols and effects, the origins of which can lie in higher dimensions of consciousness. The average person relying on his three-dimensional senses simply is unaware of the greater connectivity or unity that exists in the higher dimensions of consciousness.

Let us use another analogy. Take out a comb and cover up the top half. What you see are the unconnected teeth of the comb. You see separation. When you uncover the top half of the comb, you can see that the teeth are joined together at a higher level. You see connectedness; you see unity. Indeed, the teeth of the comb without the higher-level connection would fall apart and could not fulfil a useful purpose.

As human beings, this is how we are. What we perceive in our three-dimensional awareness are separate human beings (teeth of the comb). When we raise our awareness to a higher plane of consciousness, we can see the connection. Just as it is difficult to understand the meaning and purpose of the separate teeth, until we are aware that they belong to a comb, so too it is difficult for us to understand who we are and our purpose, until we become aware that we are all souls connected by energy fields in the fourth and higher dimensions of consciousness.

There is one more point we should consider about the five-finger exercise. Just as the two-dimensional beings experiencing the phenomena of "the five circles" did not suspect that the circles were controlled by the mind of a three-dimensional being, so we, in our three-dimensional world, are unaware of the control that our souls exercise in our lives from the fourth dimension of consciousness. When we come to understand this higher reality of our existence, we will see that certain events manifest in our lives because our souls have chosen them for us as opportunities to fulfil our soul's purposes.

What seem like random events or chance encounters may be due to purposeful connections occurring between souls at a higher dimension of consciousness, which we are simply unaware of. These are usually described as synchronistic events. In my experience, if you dig deep enough, you will always find that chance events and encounters almost always have a meaning that in some way furthers the soul's purposes. It is as if the synchronistic experiences are communications from our souls that are designed, not only get our attention, but to convey an important message.

Based on this understanding of the third and fourth dimensions of reality you can see that we do not have a clear idea about what is really going on in our physical world when we use three-dimensional logic. Just as the two-dimensional scientist believed she knew all there was to know about the five separate circles, so our three-dimensional scientists believe they fully understand the three-dimensional phenomena that occur in our world. What we are able to observe through our physical senses is only part of our reality. What we see is the projection of the higher dimensions of consciousness into our three-dimensional world, and we mistake it for the whole experience. Science and medicine are caught up in the illusion of explaining three-dimensional physical events that have their origins in the multi-dimensional energetic reality of our souls and the universal energy field.

Science would have us believe that nothing exists beyond the limits of our three-dimensional awareness, whereas much of what we are striving to comprehend is rooted in other levels of consciousness, of which we are only dimly aware. When you understand this, you begin to realise that our interpretation of events is at best fragmentary, and at worst a product of intense rationalisation from an incomplete base of knowledge. We are like the two-dimensional scientists trying to explain something that cannot be fully explained unless we lift our awareness to a higher dimension of consciousness.

You may ask: "Why are we not more aware of the fourth and higher dimensions of consciousness in our everyday living?" The answer is we learned to block out this perspective through three-dimensional conditioning. We were all born with soul consciousness, but we lost this awareness as we became involved in our three-dimensional physical reality and the need to keep our bodies alive. We developed our egos to support our survival and protect us from physical threats. As we became more engrossed in the three-dimensional world of form and mass, we gradually closed ourselves off from the energetic realm of the fourth dimension of consciousness.

Not everyone closes themselves off completely. Some people are able to hang on to certain aspects of their four-dimensional awareness. Others have discovered that they can reconnect with the fourth dimension of awareness through the conscious cultivation of the faculties of the soul. We call these faculties, psychic powers. They include telepathy, precognition, clairvoyance and clairaudience. What is common to all these experiences is they all involve tapping into information contained in the fourth and higher dimensions of consciousness.

Hundreds of thousands of people all over the world have developed these abilities. In the pre-modern era such people were called witches and wizards. In our modern era we call them psychics or shaman. For those who are strongly wedded to their three-dimensional reality, these abilities are considered abnormal and scary. For the rest—those who are open minded or are attempting to recover the faculties of their souls—they are affirmations of our larger multi-dimensional reality.

Summary

Here are the main points of this chapter:

1. The serving stage of psychological development usually begins in your 60s.

2. The hallmark of the serving stage of development is your desire to lead a life of selfless service for the good of humanity and the planet. To live such a life you need to move beyond empathy to compassion.

3. Compassion is a more vigorous form of empathy that gives rise to an active desire to alleviate another's suffering.

4. There is a distinct difference between serving your soul, and becoming one with your soul. When your ego serves your soul, it surrenders its freedom. When your ego becomes one with your soul, it surrenders its existence.

5. We live in a multi-dimensional world, but because of the limitations of our senses, we only perceive three of these dimensions. Thus we can state that three-dimensionality and physical form is not a property of the world but a property of our senses.

6. There is no more commonplace statement than the world in which we live is a four-dimensional continuum.

7. When you understand this, you begin to realise that our interpretation of events in our three-dimensional physical world is at best fragmentary, and at worst a product of intense rationalisation from an incomplete base of knowledge.

8. We are not who we think we are and we are not living the life we think we are living, we are living the life our soul intended for us.

Notes

1. Paul Gilbert, *The Compassionate Mind* (London: Constable), 2009, pp. 4–5.

2. R.W. Clarke, *Einstein the Life and Times* (New York: World Publishing), 1971, p. 159.

IDENTIFYING YOUR CLIENTS' PRIMARY MOTIVATION

The following exercises can be used to assess the stage of psychological development your client's have reached by identifying their primary motivation and their most important values.

My primary motivation exercises

Ask your client to study the list of descriptions of motivations and identify which one most aligns with where they are in their life at the current moment. Ask them to circle this motivation. Use the interpretation document to find what stage of development this is. Check this stage of development against their age using Figure 8.1. They should be approximately the same.

My primary motivation exercise
Circle the motivation that you most resonate with,
particularly with regard to your working life.

Motivation 1: I am primarily motivated by my need to achieve financial security, provide for myself, and my family and keep myself and them safe from harm.

Motivation 2: I am primarily motivated by my need to find a place in the world where I feel I belong and where I feel respected for who I am.

Motivation 3: I am primarily motivated by my need to feel recognised and acknowledged for my skills and talents and to have opportunities to excel at what I do best.

Motivation 4: I am primarily motivated by my need for autonomy and independence, to have challenges that test me and adventures that cause me to grow.

Motivation 5: I am primarily motivated by my need to find meaningful work or a meaningful occupation that aligns with my sense of purpose or the things I am passionate about.

Motivation 6: I am primarily motivated by my need to make a difference through my daily activities and collaborate with other people who share a similar sense of purpose.

Motivation 7: I am primarily motivated by my need to support and serve those around me in the pursuit of their purposes and help them find fulfilment in their lives.

My values/behaviours exercise

Another way of getting at your client's primary motivation is to find out their most important values. Ask you clients to study the list of values and pick ten that most reflect how they operate on a day-to-day basis. Ask them to circle the five they most resonate with. The motivation with the most circled values is likely to be their primary motivation.

My values/behaviours exercise
Circle the ten values/behaviours that you most resonate with,
particularly with regard to your working life.

Motivation 1: Survival, safety, control, wealth, financial stability, job security.

Motivation 2: Belonging, friendship, respect, loyalty, caring, harmony.

Motivation 3: Excellence, status, pride, achievement, recognition, continuous improvement.

Motivation 4: Autonomy, challenges, adaptability, accountability, continuous learning.

Motivation 5: Meaning, purpose, integrity, fairness, commitment, creativity, trust.

Motivation 6: Making a difference, coaching, mentoring, collaboration, sustainability.

Motivation 7: Compassion, humility, future generations, ecology, social justice, service.

If, when you have done these first two exercises, your client insists that they resonates with different motivations, check to see if they are adjacent to each other. If they are, this will indicate they are in the process of shifting from one stage of psychological development to the next, especially if the majority of the values they choose also align with the same two stages of development. If the stage of development with the most circled values is the lower of the two stages, they will be at the lower stage and beginning to think about transitioning to the upper stage. If the stage of development with the most circled values is the upper stage, they will be transitioning away from the lower stage to the upper stage.

If the stages of development associated with two motivations they choose are not next to each other (say motivation 3 and 6), you should help them to focus on the needs of lower motivation first because they will need to develop a solid foundation at that stage before they will be to master the needs of the higher motivation.

Interpretation document

Normally everyone over the age of 20 will be at the differentiating stage of development or above. If you have a client over the age of twenty who circles motivation 1 or 2 as their primary motivation, this will indicate they are either living in difficult circumstances or they have a strong secondary motivation at one or both of these levels which is preventing them from focusing on their primary motivation. The same is true of values/behaviours. If a half or more of the values/behaviours your client circles are at motivation 1 or 2, it will indicate they are living in difficult circumstances or they have strong secondary motivations at these levels. If they circle only two or three values/behaviours at motivation 1 or 2 this could simply represent a healthy expression of who they are.

Motivation 1	Focus on survival consciousness.
Motivation 2	Focus on relationship consciousness.
Motivation 3	Focus on differentiating stage of psychological development or self-esteem consciousness.
Motivation 4	Focus on individuating stage of psychological development or transformation consciousness.
Motivation 5	Focus on self-actualising stage of psychological development or internal cohesion level of consciousness.
Motivation 6	Focus on integrating stage of psychological development or making a difference level of consciousness.
Motivation 7	Focus on serving stage of psychological development or serving level of consciousness.

More exercises

If the primary motivation and values/behaviours exercises were not conclusive you can ask your clients to complete the following exercises. You may want to ask your clients to do these exercises in any case since they quite illuminating and provide your client with more self-understanding.

My in-flow days exercise

Ask your client to answer the following questions by writing down the answers or making drawings to illustrate the answers to questions (a) to (d). This is an exercise your clients should do on their own in a quiet space. They should allow 30–45 minutes.

(a) What is happening when you are having a really good day at work and at home? Describe where you are and what you are doing.
(b) What makes this a good day for you? Describe what you are feeling.
(c) Who are you with?

(d) What would need to change in your life to experience more in-flow days?

(e) What needs do you believe you are meeting when you are having an in-flow day. Circle 5–8 words in the following table that correspond to these needs. The motivation with the most circled words will be your primary motivation.

My in-flow days exercise

Circle five of the following words which reflect the needs you are meeting when you having an in-flow day, particularly with regard to your working life.

Motivation 1: Survival, safety, control, wealth, financial stability, job security.

Motivation 2: Belonging, friendship, respect, loyalty, caring, harmony.

Motivation 3: Excellence, status, pride, achievement, recognition, continuous improvement.

Motivation 4: Autonomy, challenges, adaptability, accountability, continuous learning.

Motivation 5: Meaning, purpose, integrity, fairness, commitment, creativity, trust.

Motivation 6: Making a difference, coaching, mentoring, collaboration, sustainability.

Motivation 7: Compassion, humility, future generations, ecology, social justice, service.

My levels of happiness exercise

Ask your client to study the list of descriptions of happiness/joy in the table provided and identify the one they most resonate with in their current life. They are allowed to circle two motivations as long as they prioritise them.

| **My level of happiness exercise** |
| Circle what makes you most happy, |
| particularly with regard to your working life. |

Motivation 1: Feeling safe and secure and being able to take care of comfort needs.

Motivation 2: Feeling accepted, cherished and nurtured by your family and friends.

Motivation 3: Feeling acknowledged and recognised by those who you respect.

Motivation 4: Experiencing adventure, autonomy and freedom and taking on challenges.

Motivation 5: Finding a sense of meaning in your life which gives you a sense of purpose.

Motivation 6: Actualising your sense of purpose so you can make a difference in the world.

Motivation 7: Leading a life of selfless service for the good of others and humanity in general.

It is important to recognise that whatever actions you undertake in your daily existence you are doing to satisfy a need. It may be an immediate need, a short-term need or a long-term need. When you are able to satisfy a need, you feel happy. Happiness is the feeling you get when you achieve internal stability and external equilibrium at the ego levels of consciousness—when you are able to satisfy your deficiency needs.

In *The Art of Happiness: A Handbook for Living*,[1] the Dalai Lama makes the following statement:

> *In identifying one's mental state as the prime factor in achieving happiness, of course that doesn't deny that our basic physical needs for food, clothing, and shelter must be met. But once these basic needs are met, the message is clear: we don't need more money, we don't need more success or fame, we don't need the perfect body or the perfect mate—right now, at this very moment, we have a mind, which is all the basic equipment we need for achieving complete happiness.*[2]

When asked to define the characteristics of a psychologically healthy or well-adjusted person, he gave the following response:

> *Well I would regard a compassionate, kind-hearted person as healthy. If you maintain a feeling of compassion, loving kindness, then something automatically opens your inner door. Through that [door] you can communicate more easily with other people. And that feeling of warmth creates a kind of openness. You'll find that all human beings are just like you, so you will be able to relate to them more easily.*[3]

Whether we are talking about happiness, contentment or joy, it is always an internal feeling. However, there is an important difference between happiness and joy. Happiness is usually sourced from the physical external world by getting what we think we need to relieve the fears or anxieties we may have about not being able to meet our deficiency needs. For this reason, happiness is usually short-lived. *Happiness is almost always associated with the emotion of relief.*

We feel happy when a loved one returns home safe and sound. We feel happy when we pass an important exam. We feel happy when we get what we need to feel good about ourselves. When these things happen we feel a sense of relief that everything is OK. The happiness you feel arises from letting go of the fear-based anxieties you were holding onto about not getting your needs met. Your energy field suddenly releases the low frequency vibrations associated with your anxieties and this energetic release is felt as happiness. Your happiness quickly disappears as the relief you feel dissipates and your energy field returns to its normal frequency of vibration.

Whenever you oscillate between happiness and sadness on a regular basis, you can be sure you are holding onto some subconscious fear-based beliefs that need to be released. When we are able to free ourselves of fear-based beliefs we feel a sense of equanimity; we are neither happy nor sad. We fall back into our normal way of being.

Joy is different from happiness. Joy is a deep sense of happiness that arises from within us when we experience internal alignment—the alignment of the ego with the soul, or a strong sense of connection with another person. In both situations, the source of our joy is a high level of energetic resonance.

The level of happiness/joy you experience depends on the stage of psychological development you have reached. The more you grow and evolve, the greater will be your potential for experiencing fulfilment. Fulfilment arises when you have been able to master the satisfaction of your basic needs *and* your growth needs—when your ego has aligned with your soul and your soul is living out its destiny by leading a values-driven and purpose-driven life.

The seven levels of happiness can be summarised in the following way:

Level 1: Survival

When you are operating from the survival level of consciousness, you will feel happy if you are able to satisfy the needs and cravings of the body—food, drink, sex, and being pain free, and the needs of the ego—to feel safe and secure by having enough money or protection.

Level 2: Relationship

When you are operating from the relationship level of consciousness, you will feel happy if you are able to satisfy your needs and cravings for love and belonging—when you have strong friendships, feel a sense of camaraderie at work or have loving family connections.

Level 3: Self-esteem

When you are operating from the self-esteem level of consciousness, you will feel happy if you are able to satisfy your needs and cravings for self-worth—when you feel recognised or acknowledged by those in authority or your peers.

Level 4: Transformation

When you are operating from the transformation level of consciousness, you may feel either happiness or joy if you are able to satisfy your need for freedom, autonomy or adventure, and have work-related experiences that challenge your mind, thereby enabling you to continuously grow and learn.

Level 5: Internal cohesion

When you are operating from the internal cohesion level of consciousness, you will feel joy if you are able to satisfy your need for meaning and purpose and find an avenue for your creativity and passion which enables you to spend significant amounts of time giving your unique gift to the world.

Level 6: Making a difference

When you are operating from the making a difference level of consciousness, you will feel joy if you are able to satisfy your soul's need to actualise your sense of purpose by making a positive contribution to the world around you, and engage in empathetic connections with others in a collaborative way.

Level 7: Service

When you are operating from the service level of consciousness, you will feel joy if you are able to satisfy your soul's need to live a life of service to others, and humanity in general on a daily basis.

My levels of identity exercise

Ask your client to study the list of descriptions of identity in the table provided and circle the one they most resonate with. They are allowed to circle two identities as long as they prioritise them.

Whatever you identify with you care for. For example, when you identify with your family, you care about the well-being of your family and your decisions are based on what is best for the family. When you identify with your organisation, you care about the well-being of your organisation and your decisions are based on what is best for the organisation. When you identify with your nation, you care about the well-being of your nation, and your decisions are based on what is best for the nation; when you identify with humanity, you care about the well-being of humanity, and your decisions are based on what is best for humanity.

My levels of identity exercise
Circle the description that most aligns with how you see yourself.

Motivation 1: Self as an individual seeking to meet your physiological and comfort needs.

Motivation 2: Self as member of a family or community with a shared heritage or ethnicity.

Motivation 3: Self as a member or supporter of a team or group that aligns with your work interests, religious faith, political or other interests.

Motivation 4: Self as a member of a team or group that shares the same goals and values and celebrates and encourages your unique abilities and talents.

Motivation 5: Self as a member of a group that shares the same values, mission or vision that aligns with your own sense of purpose and brings meaning to your life.

Motivation 6: Self as a member of an organisation, community or an affiliation of groups with shared values, a shared mission and a common overarching vision.

Motivation 7: Self as a member of the human race serving the needs of others and embracing full spectrum sustainability.

The seven levels of identity can be summarised in the following way:

Level 1: Survival

When you are operating from the survival level of consciousness you are concerned about satisfying the physiological needs of your body (food, drink, warmth, shelter, sex), and your security and comfort needs. You are focused on your survival and your ability to experience physical pleasure. This is the level of pure self-interest.[4] You care little for the needs of others. Your deeply felt need is to survive, keep safe and find pleasure where you can. You are focused only on yourself.

Level 2: Relationship

When you are operating from the relationship level of consciousness you are not only concerned about *your* safety needs, you are also concerned with the safety needs of those with whom you share a close relationship: your life partner, your family, your kin, your tribe or your co-workers. Generally, these are people who look like you, dress like you, and speak your language. In other words, they are people who share your ethnic identity. You are concerned with the well-being of those with whom you share a common heritage (ethnicity) or emotional bond of loyalty. Your safety and maybe even your survival will be dependent on your ability to conform to the mores of your group especially if you live in a poor multi-ethnic society.

Your sense of identity will deepen when your ethnic or cultural group is under threat from groups of a different ethnicity or a different culture. You will rally round each other to protect the group. Your deeply felt need is to feel safe by belonging to a group that cares for each other, not just in difficult times but in good times too.

The affiliations we choose at this level of consciousness keep us tied to our roots. I love football and am a supporter of the team of the city I was brought up in, but I haven't lived there for fifty years. I have no other ties to this city—no family or friends who are living there. At some deep level, the football team I support helps me maintain my "tribal" identity.

Level 3: Self-esteem

When you are operating from the self-esteem level of consciousness you are concerned about yourself and the groups with whom you share a common interest. These groups may be multiple, and may vary over time. They could include followers of the same religious faith, supporters of the same sports team, people who went to the same university or college, or the team you are a part of in your place of employment.

You may or may not share a common ethnic identity with the people that are members of these groups. What you do share is a commitment to winning. Often, the affiliations we choose when we are operating from this level of consciousness are subconsciously designed to increase our sense

225

of pride. We will support a sports team that is regarded as one of the best rather than the team of the city we grew up in which is not as well known.

Your ties to groups at the self-esteem level of consciousness are not usually as strong as the blood ties at relationship level, unless, for example, you are part of a religious group that has a shared ethnicity. Then the strength of the ties becomes additive. For example, Jews living in Israel and Catholics living in Northern Ireland are bonded at both levels of consciousness. The bonds are further strengthened in these groups because they are living along cultural fault lines, cheek by jowl with a group that has a different religion and a different national allegiance.

Level 4: Transformation

When you are operating from the transformation level of consciousness you are concerned about yourself and those individuals with whom you have a shared set of values, and with whom you interact to achieve a shared set of goals—a work team, a protest group, people with similar political ideologies—any group with a specific objective.

The people in these groups you associate with at this level of consciousness may not necessarily share your ethnicity or religion. The bonds you form with these people serve a different purpose than the bonds you form at the relationship and self-esteem level. It is not safety or success that you are seeking at this level of consciousness, but a deep-felt need for achievement, adventure or rebellion, which contributes to your feelings of autonomy and freedom. You want to find success on your own terms, not on the terms of your parents or the culture in which you were raised. You are attempting to embrace more fully who you really are.

Level 5: Internal cohesion

When you are operating from the internal cohesion level of consciousness you are concerned about yourself and those individuals with whom you share a set of values, a shared sense of mission (purpose), and a shared sense of the future you want to create together (vision)—a team, an organisation, a community or nation operating under a shared value system.

At this level of identity, you recognise that your future success is wrapped up in the success of the group, community, organisation or nation you identify with. Aligning with others that share the same values and purpose requires a high level of trust and strong sense of cohesion. Your deep felt need at this level of consciousness is to follow your passion, do what you love to do, and feel supported in this endeavour by bonding with others who share your values, purpose and passion. You are beginning to align with your soul.

Level 6: Making a difference

When you are operating from the making a difference level of consciousness you are concerned about yourself, your team, your group, your organisation, your community or your nation, and those groups that are external to your group that have similar values and a shared vision of the future.

You recognise the importance of collaborating with others and other groups, to form strategic alliances or partnerships, to gain leverage in furthering your collective purpose or vision, sharing in the benefits and also increasing your collective resilience. A high degree of mutual empathy is required for this to happen. Your deep felt need at this level of consciousness is to make a difference in the world. You are now responding to your soul purpose.

Level 7: Service

When you are operating from the service level of consciousness you are concerned about yourself, your group, the groups that your group is in partnership with, and everyone else on the planet—the whole of humanity: people from every race, religion, and creed.

At this level, your identity also expands to include Earth and all life forms that inhabit Earth. You recognise that your well-being and the well-being of everyone on the planet depend on a healthy global ecosystem. A high degree of compassion is required for this to happen.

You have reached the stage of your life where you recognise that everything is interconnected and that by serving others you are serving yourself. You are responding to the deep sense of oneness that is present in all souls.

Summary

During the first three stages of psychological development, you are seeking to establish identities that enable you to express who you are within the cultural framework of your existence. During the next two stages of psychological development, you are seeking to establish identities that take you beyond your parental programming and cultural conditioning and allow you to express your authentic self. During the last two stages of psychological development, you are seeking to establish identities that take you into the full expression of your soul self.

Notes

1. Dalai Lama, *The Art of Happiness: A Handbook for Living* (London: Hodder & Stoughton), 1998.
2. Ibid., p. 25.
3. Ibid., p. 27.
4. No matter what level of psychological development you have reached, you will always be operating from self-interest, but the self that has the interest will have an expanded sense of identity.

IDENTIFYING YOUR CLIENTS' SECONDARY MOTIVATIONS

The following exercises will help your clients to identify their secondary motivations. They include exercises and surveys for identifying both conscious and subconscious motivations.

My out-of-flow days exercise

Ask your client to answer the following questions by writing down the answers or making drawings to illustrate the answers to questions (a) to (d). This is an exercise your clients should do on their own in a quiet space. They should allow 30–45 minutes.

(a)   What is happening when you are having a bad day at work and at home? Describe where you are and what you are doing.
(b)   What makes this a bad day for you? Describe what you are feeling.
(c)   Who are you with?
(d)   What would need to change in your life to experience less out-of-flow days?
(e)   What needs do you believe you have that are not being met when you are having an out-of-flow day. Circle or underline the words listed in the following table that correspond to your unmet needs.

My out-of-flow days exercise

Circle five of the following words which reflect the needs you have that are not being met when you having an out-of-flow day, particularly with regard to your working life.

Motivation 1: Survival, safety, control, wealth, financial stability, job security.

Motivation 2: Belonging, friendship, respect, loyalty, caring, harmony.

Motivation 3: Excellence, status, pride, achievement, recognition, continuous improvement.

Motivation 4: Autonomy, challenges, adaptability, accountability, continuous learning.

Motivation 5: Meaning, purpose, integrity, fairness, commitment, creativity, trust.

Motivation 6: Making a difference, coaching, mentoring, collaboration, sustainability.

Motivation 7: Compassion, humility, future generations, ecology, social justice, service.

My anxieties exercise

Ask your client to answer the following questions by writing down the answers or making drawings to illustrate the answers to questions (a) to (e). This is an exercise your clients should do on their own in a quiet space. They should allow 30–45 minutes.

(a) What are the conditions that cause you to feel anxiety?
(b) What is happening?
(c) Describe your feelings?
(d) What thoughts are you having when you feel anxious?
(e) Identify the fears behind the thoughts you are having when you feel anxious.
(f) What needs do you have that are not being met when you are feeling anxious? Circle or underline the words listed in the following table that correspond to your unmet needs.

My anxiety exercise

Circle five of the following words which reflect your unmet needs when you are feeling anxious, particularly with regard to your working life.

Motivation 1: Survival, safety, control, wealth, financial stability, job security.

Motivation 2: Belonging, friendship, respect, loyalty, caring, harmony.

Motivation 3: Excellence, status, pride, achievement, recognition, continuous improvement.

Motivation 4: Autonomy, challenges, adaptability, accountability, continuous learning.

Motivation 5: Meaning, purpose, integrity, fairness, commitment, creativity, trust.

Motivation 6: Making a difference, coaching, mentoring, collaboration, sustainability.

Motivation 7: Compassion, humility, future generations, ecology, social justice, service.

My stressors exercise

Ask your client to answer the following questions by writing down the answers or making drawings to illustrate the answers to questions (a) to (e). This is an exercise your clients should do on their own in a quiet space. They should allow 30–45 minutes.

(a) What are the conditions that cause you to feel stress?
(b) What is happening?
(c) Describe your feelings?
(d) What thoughts are you having when you feel stressed?
(e) Identify the fears behind the thoughts you are having when you feel stressed.
(f) What needs do you have that are not being met? Circle or underline the words listed in the following table that correspond to your unmet needs.

My stressors exercise

Circle five of the following words which reflect your unmet needs when you are feeling stressed, particularly with regard to your working life.

Motivation 1: Survival, safety, control, wealth, financial stability, job security.

Motivation 2: Belonging, friendship, respect, loyalty, caring, harmony.

Motivation 3: Excellence, status, pride, achievement, recognition, continuous improvement.

Motivation 4: Autonomy, challenges, adaptability, accountability, continuous learning.

Motivation 5: Meaning, purpose, integrity, fairness, commitment, creativity, trust.

Motivation 6: Making a difference, coaching, mentoring, collaboration, sustainability.

Motivation 7: Compassion, humility, future generations, ecology, social justice, service.

My upsets exercise

Ask your client to answer the following questions by writing down the answers or making drawings to illustrate the answers to questions (a) to (e). This is an exercise your clients should do on their own in a quiet space. They should allow 30–45 minutes.

(a) Describe in your own words the situations that trigger your upsets.
(b) What is happening? Who are you with?
(c) Describe your feelings?
(d) What thoughts are you having when you feel upset?
(e) Identify the fears behind the thoughts you are having when you feel upset.
(f) What needs do you have that are not being met? Circle or underline the words listed in the following table that correspond to your unmet needs.

My upsets exercise

Circle five of the following words which reflect your unmet needs when you are feeling upset, particularly with regard to your working life.

Motivation 1: Survival, safety, control, wealth, financial stability, job security.

Motivation 2: Belonging, friendship, respect, loyalty, caring, harmony.

Motivation 3: Excellence, status, pride, achievement, recognition, continuous improvement.

Motivation 4: Autonomy, challenges, adaptability, accountability, continuous learning.

Motivation 5: Meaning, purpose, integrity, fairness, commitment, creativity, trust.

Motivation 6: Making a difference, coaching, mentoring, collaboration, sustainability.

Motivation 7: Compassion, humility, future generations, ecology, social justice, service.

My conflicts exercise

Ask your client to answer the following questions by writing down the answers or making drawings to illustrate the answers to questions (a) to (e). This is an exercise your clients should do on their own in a quiet space. They should allow 30–45 minutes.

(a) Describe in your own words the situations that cause you to feel conflict.

(b) What is happening? Who are you with?

(c) Describe your feelings?

(d) What thoughts are you having when you feel conflict?

(e) Identify the fears behind the thoughts you are having when you feel conflict.

(f) What needs do you have that are not being met? Circle or underline the words listed in the following table that correspond to your unmet needs.

My conflicts exercise

Circle five of the following words which reflect your unmet needs when you are feeling conflict, particularly with regard to your working life.

Motivation 1: Survival, safety, control, wealth, financial stability, job security.

Motivation 2: Belonging, friendship, respect, loyalty, caring, harmony.

Motivation 3: Excellence, status, pride, achievement, recognition, continuous improvement.

Motivation 4: Autonomy, challenges, adaptability, accountability, continuous learning.

Motivation 5: Meaning, purpose, integrity, fairness, commitment, creativity, trust.

Motivation 6: Making a difference, coaching, mentoring, collaboration, sustainability.

Motivation 7: Compassion, humility, future generations, ecology, social justice, service.

My fear/needs inventory

Ask your client to complete the table below for the previous four exercises. They should write down in each of the three columns the feelings, thoughts, fears and needs they identified as being associated with their anxieties, stressors, upsets and conflicts. This is something that they can do when you, the coach, are present with them.

	My anxieties	My stressors	My upsets	My conflicts
Feelings				
Thoughts				
Fears				
Needs				

Based on the above table, ask your clients to identify their most common feelings, thoughts, fears and needs. Then ask them to read the descriptions of the early maladaptive schema which are included in Annex

3 and indicate which of them they most closely align with their most common fears. Then ask them to complete the following sentences:

> When I am out of alignment my most common feelings are …
> When I am out of alignment my most common thoughts are …
> When I am out of alignment my most common fears are …
> When I am out of alignment my most common needs are …

When they have finished this last exercise they should have a very good understanding of their secondary motivations—the unmet needs they have.

Annex 3

Early Maladaptive Schema

Survival and safety needs

Abandonment/instability

Definition: The perceived instability or unreliability of those available for support and connection.

Involves the sense that significant others will not be able to continue providing emotional support, connection, strength, or practical protection because they are emotionally unstable and unpredictable (for example, angry outbursts), unreliable, or erratically present; because they will die imminently; or because they will abandon you in favour of someone better.

Mistrust/abuse

Definition: The expectations that others will hurt, abuse, humiliate, cheat, lie, manipulate, or take advantage.

Usually involves the perception that the harm is intentional or the result of unjustified and extreme negligence. This may include the sense that one always ends up being cheated relative to others "or "getting the short end of the stick".

Emotional deprivation

Definition: Expectation that one's desire for a normal degree of emotional support will not be adequately met by others.

The three major forms of deprivation are:

- Deprivation of Nurturance: Absence of attention, affection, warmth, or companionship.
- Deprivation of Empathy: Absence of understanding, listening, self-disclosure, or mutual sharing of feelings from others.
- Deprivation of Protection: Absence of strength, direction, or guidance from others.

Vulnerability to harm or illness

Definition: Exaggerated fear that imminent catastrophe will strike at any time and that one will be unable to prevent it.

Fears focus on one or more of the following:

- Medical Catastrophes: for example, heart attacks, AIDS.
- Emotional Catastrophes: for example, going crazy.
- External Catastrophes: for example, elevators collapsing, victimised by criminals, airplane crashes, earthquakes.

Relationship and belonging needs

Defectiveness/shame

Definition: The feeling that one is defective, bad, unwanted, inferior, or invalid in important respects, or that one would be unlovable to significant others if exposed.

May involve hypersensitivity to criticism, rejection and blame; self-consciousness, comparisons and insecurity around others; or a sense of shame regarding one's perceived flaws. These flaws may be private (for example, selfishness, angry impulses, unacceptable sexual desires) or public (for example, undesirable physical appearance, social awkwardness).

Social isolation/alienation

Definition: The feeling that one is isolated from the rest of the world, different from other people, and not part of any group or community.

Dependence/incompetence

Definition: Belief that one is unable to handle one's everyday responsibilities in a competent manner, without considerable help from others (for example, take care of oneself, solve daily problems, exercise good judgement, tackle new tasks, make good decisions). Often presents as helplessness.

Enmeshment/undeveloped self

Definition: Excessive emotional involvement and closeness with one or more significant others (often parents), at the expense of full individuation or normal social development.

Often involves the belief that at least one of the enmeshed individuals cannot survive or be happy without the constant support of the other. May also include feelings of being smothered by, or fused with, others or insufficient individual identity. Often experienced as a feeling of emptiness and floundering, having no direction, or in extreme cases questioning one's existence.

Emotional inhibition

Definition: The excessive inhibition of spontaneous action, feeling, or communication—usually to avoid disapproval by others, feelings of shame, or losing control of one's impulses.

The most common areas of inhibition involve:

- Inhibition of anger and aggression.
- Inhibition of positive impulses (for example, joy, affection, sexual excitement, play).
- Difficulty expressing vulnerability or communicating freely about one's feelings, needs, etc.
- Excessive emphasis on rationality while disregarding emotions.

Subjugation

Definition: Excessive surrendering of control to others because one feels coerced usually to avoid anger, retaliation, or abandonment.

The two major forms of subjugation are:

- Subjugation of needs: Suppression of one's preferences, decisions and desires.
- Subjugation of emotions: Suppression of emotional expression, especially anger.

Usually involves the perception that one's own desires, opinions and feelings are not valid or important to others. Frequently presents as excessive compliance, combined with hypersensitivity to feeling trapped. Generally leads to a build-up of anger, manifested in maladaptive symptoms (for example, passive-aggressive behaviour, uncontrolled outbursts of temper, psychosomatic symptoms, withdrawal of affection, "acting out", substance abuse).

Self-sacrifice

Definition: Excessive focus on voluntarily meeting the needs of others in daily situations, at the expense of one's own gratification.

The most common reasons are: to prevent causing pain to others; to avoid guilt from feeling selfish, or to maintain the connection with others perceived as needy. Often results from an acute sensitivity to the pain of others. Sometimes leads to a sense that one's own needs are not being adequately met and to resentment of those who are taken care of.

Self-esteem and recognition needs

Failure to achieve

Definition: The belief that one has failed, will inevitably fail, or is fundamentally inadequate relative to one's peers, in areas of achievement (school, career, sports, etc.).

Often involves beliefs that one is stupid, inept, untalented, ignorant, lower in status, less successful than others, etc.

Entitlement/grandiosity

Definition: The belief that one is superior to other people, entitled to special rights and privileges, or not bound by the rules of reciprocity that guide normal social interaction.

Often involves insistence that one should be able to do or have whatever one wants, regardless of what is realistic, what others consider reasonable, or the cost to others; an exaggerated focus on superiority in order to achieve power or control. Sometimes includes excessive competitiveness towards, or domination of, others: asserting one's power, forcing one's point of view, or controlling the behaviour of others in line with one's own desires—without empathy or concern for others' needs or feelings.

Insufficient self-control/self-discipline

Definition: Pervasive difficulty or refusal to exercise sufficient self-control and frustration tolerance to achieve one's personal goals, or to restrain the excessive expression of one's emotions and impulses.

In its milder form, there is an exaggerated emphasis on discomfort-avoidance: avoiding pain, conflict, confrontation, responsibility, or overexertion at the expense of personal fulfilment, commitment or integrity.

Approval-seeking/recognition-seeking

Definition: Excessive emphasis on gaining approval, recognition, or attention from other people, or fitting in, at the expense of developing a secure and true sense of self.

One's sense of esteem is dependent primarily on the reactions of others rather than on one's own natural inclinations. Sometimes includes an overemphasis on status, appearance, social acceptance, money, or achievement as means of gaining approval, admiration, or attention (not primarily for power or control). Frequently results in major life decisions that are inauthentic or unsatisfying; or in hypersensitivity to rejection.

Negativity/pessimism

Definition: A pervasive, lifelong focus on the negative aspects of life (pain, death, loss, disappointment, conflict, guilt, resentment, unsolved problems, potential mistakes, betrayal, things that could go wrong, etc.) while minimising or neglecting the positive or optimistic aspects.

Usually includes an exaggerated expectation—in a wide range of work, financial, or interpersonal situations—that things will eventually go seriously wrong, or that aspects of one's life that seem to be going well will ultimately fall apart. Usually involves an inordinate fear of making mistakes that might lead to financial collapse, loss, humiliation, or being trapped in a bad situation. Because potential negative outcomes are exaggerated, these patients are frequently characterised by chronic worry, vigilance, complaining, or indecision.

Unrelenting standards/hypercritical

Definition: The underlying belief that one must strive to meet very high internalised standards of behaviour and performance, usually to avoid criticism.

Typically results in feelings of pressure or difficulty slowing down, and in being hypercritical towards oneself and others. Often results in an impairment of: pleasure, relaxation, health, self-esteem, sense of accomplishment, or satisfying relationships. Unrelenting standards typically present as:

- Perfectionism, inordinate attention to detail, or an underestimate of how good one's own performance is relative to the norm.
- Rigid rules and "shoulds" in many areas of life, including unrealistically high moral, ethical, cultural or religious precepts.
- Preoccupation with time and efficiency, so that more can be accomplished.

Punitiveness

Definition: The belief that people should be harshly punished for making mistakes.

Involves the tendency to be angry, intolerant, punitive, and impatient with those people (including oneself) who do not meet one's expectations or standards. Usually includes difficulty forgiving mistakes in oneself or others, because of a reluctance to consider extenuating circumstances, allow for human imperfection, or empathise with feelings.

ANNEX 4

THE FOUR WHYS PROCESS

The Four Why's Process is a methodological construct for creating mission and vision statements for individuals and organisations. The process differs from other methods in that it differentiates between your internal and external motivations, and it addresses your needs and the needs of society.

The Four Why's Process presented here is designed for use with individuals. A description of the Four Why's Process for organisations can be found in Annex 8 of *The Values-Driven Organisation*.[1]

The objective of the process is to create four statements that represent your internal mission and vision, and your external mission and vision (see Table A4.1). The internal mission goes in Box 1, the internal vision goes in Box 2, the external mission goes in Box 3 and the external vision goes in Box 4.

Table A4.1 Four Why's overview

	Internal motivation	*External motivation*
Vision	**(2) Internal vision** Personal fulfilment	**(4) External vision** Impact on society
Mission	**(1) Internal mission** Personal development	**(3) External mission** Impact on others

The statement that goes in Box 1 describes the key ideas that will guide you in your own development. The statement that goes in Box 2 describes how you envision your future if you pursue the path described in Box 1. The statement that goes in Box 3 describes your key ideas about what you want to do in your external world. The statement that goes in Box 4 describes what the impact will be on society if you pursue the ideas contained in Box 3.

Mission statement

An internal mission statement keeps your energies focused on your evolution, and an external mission tells people what you want to do in the external world.

Vision statement

An internal vision statement gives direction to your evolution, and an external vision tells gives direction to your mission: it tells people the impact you want to have on society.

Table A4.2 provides an example of the four statements that I created for myself several years ago.

Table A4.2 My mission and vision statements

	Internal motivation	*External motivation*
Vision	**(2) Internal vision** To become all I can become	**(4) External vision** To create a values-driven society
Mission	**(1) Internal mission** To nurture and foster my creativity by becoming one with my soul	**(3) External mission** To develop models and tools that support personal and cultural evolution

The process usually begins by building a statement of internal mission. Two important questions must be asked to arrive at this first statement:

"What is your primary motivation?" and "What do you need to do to grow and develop?"

The answer to the first question tells you what you are about at the stage of development you have reached and the second question gives direction to your growth and development.

I want to nurture and foster my creativity by becoming one with my soul.

The next step is to build a statement of internal vision. You formulate this statement by asking "Why?" in front of your internal mission. The answer represents the vision—a deeper level of motivation. When you ask "Why do you want to nurture and foster your creativity by becoming all one with your soul?", I came up with the answer: "To become all I can become." That is the future I want to create for myself. If we now ask "How?" in front of the internal vision, we should be able to arrive back at the internal mission. "How am I going to become all I can become?" The answer is "by nurturing and fostering my creativity."

If these statements align and resonate with you, then you have completed the internal mission and vision.

Now we move to the external mission. This is a statement that describes the service you want to provide. If you ask "Why?" again in front of the internal mission, thinking in terms of the service you want to provide. "Why do you want to nurture and foster your creativity?" The answer we find is "To develop models and tools that support personal and cultural evolution." Again if we now ask "How?" in front of the external mission, "How are you going to develop models and tools that support personal and cultural evolution?" The answer is "by nurturing and fostering my creativity."

Finally, you tackle the external vision. This is a statement that describes the impact you want to have on society. If you ask "Why?" in front of the external mission, thinking in terms of the impact you want to have on society, "Why do you want to develop models and tools that support personal and cultural evolution?" we get the answer "To create a values-driven society." Again, if we now ask "How?" in front of the external vision, we should be able to arrive back at the statement of external mission, "How are you going to create a values-driven society?" The answer is "by developing models and tools that support personal and cultural evolution."

If these statements align and resonate with you, then you have completed the external mission and vision.

You can now do another check to see if the statements align by thinking about the external vision and asking "Why?" in front of the internal vision. You should be able to find an answer in the external vision. When you ask the question, "Why do you want to become all you can become?" we get the answer "to create a values-driven society." These statements align, and we can now be sure that the mission and vision statements have integrity.

You could also ask "How?" in front of the external vision. "How are you going to create a values-driven society?" The answer is by "by becoming all we can become."

Note

1. Richard Barrett, *The Values-Driven Organisation* (London: Routledge), 2013, pp. 202–206.

ANNEX 5

THE BOUNDARY WITH PSYCHOTHERAPY

It is quite possible to help most people to deal with their unmet needs using the techniques described in this book. However, in some cases, where the trauma associated with the unmet need has significantly destabilised your client, you may have to refer him or her to psychotherapist. Knowing where these boundaries lie is very important.

In *Coaching with the Brain in Mind*, David Rock and Linda J. Page provide some advice on this matter.[1] Here is a brief summary of this advice.

At any time before or during coaching, coaches should refer clients to psychotherapists when the following arise.

Persistent: When issues are persistent, having been around a long time or not responding to attempts to change. "How long as this being go on?"

Incongruent: When what they say does not match their non-verbal communication, as when clients smile and laugh when describing a very sad situation. "I hear that this a very sad situation, but I don't see sad in how you are acting. Am I missing something?"

Extensive: When something affects their ability to function in many areas of their lives, "Where else does this show up in your life?"

Strong: When something has an effect that is out of the ordinary, especially if the coach or client begins to worry someone might get hurt. "Are you thinking someone might get hurt? Is someone's well-being at stake?"

Note

1. David Rock and Linda J. Page, *Coaching with the Brain in Mind: Foundations for Practice* (Hoboken, New Jersey: John Wiley & Sons), 2009, pp. 316–320.

INDEX

Printed in Poland
by Amazon Fulfillment
Poland Sp. z o.o., Wrocław

50920307R00171